C000158066

The College of Law, London

S01877

INFLUENCING THE JUDICIAL MIND - EFFECTIVE WRITTEN ADVOCACY IN PRACTICE

THE UNIVERSITY OF LAW

WITHDRAWN

INFLUENCING THE JUDICIAL MIND - EFFECTIVE WRITTEN ADVOCACY IN PRACTICE

Andrew Goodman LL.B., MBA, FCI.Arb., FInstCPD

Of the Inner Temple, Barrister
Professor of Conflict Management and Dispute
Resolution Studies, Rushmore University

© A. Goodman 2006

Published by

xpl publishing
99 Hatfield Road
St Albans AL1 4JL
www.xplpublishing.com

ISBN 185811 360 1

All rights reserved. No part of this publication may be reproduced, stored in a retrieval system, or transmitted, in any form or by any means, electronic, mechanical, photocopying, recording or otherwise, without the prior permission of the publisher.

Typeset by DPSM

Printed in Great Britain by Lighting Source

Also available as an e-book with multiple user licences – see website for details.

To EF (Mr Smooth) JR (Mr Nice) JN (Mr Right) ZB (Mr Wise), and EB (Mr Cool). Observed at close quarters.

FOREWORD AND ACKNOWLEDGEMENTS

During the course of 2003 and 2004 I had the pleasure of interviewing a number of judges and practitioners in preparation for my book on deconstructing civil judgments. This was published under the modest but utilitarian title, *How Judges Decide Cases - Reading, Writing and Analysing Judgments.* I was persuaded by a reader that what actually influenced the judicial decision making process, effective advocacy, was worthy of greater attention. Many works have been written on advocacy, but despite the filing of skeleton submissions having been made a requirement some ten years ago, I had yet to see a work devoted entirely to written argument. We still fondly believe that our great oral tradition is what sways the court. Not a bit of it. Increasingly judges form pre-trial opinions of the likely outcome, and these they derive from written material. The application, or trial or appeal then becomes a process to measure the judge's pre-formed view, however strong that may be.

In order to find what makes a persuasive written argument I went in search of the best examples, composed by the most successful practitioners. I asked the judges exactly what they wanted from written advocacy, rather than what the Civil Procedure Rules formally require. And I wanted to consider the most common form of all written advocacy - the pre-action letter of claim and its reply, followed by Part 36 correspondence. The results of my quest are in these pages, together with an analysis of the best of advice from jurisdictions which have a much longer history of written argument by lawyers.

The advice given is entirely practical. And it works.

Any polemic which has strayed into these pages is entirely my own.

It goes without saying that I have a substantial number of people to thank for their kind assistance. For busy practitioners and judges to spare their time for my inane questions is most generous. And the willingness of senior and well known members of the Bar to give me permission not just to use their work, (anonymised where requested) but, in effect, to analyse their professional skills in writing, was a little overwhelming (not that I was prepared to take 'no' for an answer).

I also wish to thank a number of solicitors for permission to reproduce correspondence drawn from actual files, although edited to remove identification.

I would therefore like to express my warm gratitude to the following

David Anderson QC, Roger Bartlett, Her Honour Judge Bevington, David Bigmore, Edward Bishop, Zachary Bredemear, Charles Brown, Dr. Guiseppe Cala, Sue Carr QC, James Carter, Emma Chadwick, the Rt. Hon. Lord Justice Chadwick, Henry Charles, Spike Charlwood, Nicholas Davidson QC, Robin de Wilde QC, Edward Faulks QC, Robert Francis QC, Kate Gallavent, Toby Hooper QC, His Honour Judge Iain Hughes QC, The Hon. Mr Justice Jackson, Michel Kallipetis QC, Simeon Maskrey QC, Philip Naughton QC, The Rt. Hon.Lord Justice Neuberger, John Norman, Diana Oxford, Sarah Paneth, David Pannick QC, Guy Philipps QC, Michael Pooles QC, Simon Reedhead, Dinah Rose, John Ross QC, David Schmitz, Andrew Spencer, Roger Stewart QC, Jemima Stratford, Jonathan Sumption QC, Dr David Thomson, Andrew Warnock, His Honour Judge Welchman, Master Whittaker, John Zucker.

I also wish to pay tribute to Andrew Griffin and the staff of xpl publishing for turning this project into fruition so successfully.

Andrew Goodman
1 Serjeants Inn
October, 2005.

CONTENTS

TABLE OF CASES

INTRODUCTION

THE TREND TOWARDS WRITTEN ADVOCACY IN CIVIL PRACTICE

Many judges, whatever they may say for public consumption, read skeleton arguments or written submissions and make up their mind about who should win before hearing oral argument. The hearing then becomes a test of their first inclination. Even if they can resist that temptation, it is not possible to be immune to written legal argument which is concise, accessible in its language, well structured, persuasive, restrained and tactically astute.[1] Whether it stands alone or is a vehicle to introduce and then channel the strands of oral argument, the effective written submission is now a vital tool that attracts judicial favour to the advocate's claim. Yet written advocacy in England and Wales still seems to be in its infancy though the requirement to produce skeleton arguments has been with us for a decade or more. The hurried, ill thought-out and unstructured skeleton can do as much to damage the client's case as an unprepared oral presentation. Thus the advocate who pays lip service to the construction of a proper paper skeleton runs a considerable risk should his oral hearing not go well.

The truth is that skeleton arguments are now of essential importance in modern civil procedure. In his January 2004 lecture to the Chancery Bar Association Conference entitled 'Advocacy – A Dying Art?' Mr Justice Lightman described skeletons as "the first (and often enduring) opportunity to present the party's case without interruption in a clear and considered way. They may properly enable the judge to form a provisional view of the case as a whole and the merits of some or all of the issues, and it is perfectly legitimate for the judge to do so and so inform the parties, putting them on notice of the hurdles to be surmounted: see *Costello v Chief Constable of Derbyshire* [2001] 1 WLR 1437 @ 1440 para [9]. In a word cases can be won and lost on skeleton arguments."

This is an entirely modern practice. The development of required written argument in this jurisdiction is the product of our new obsession with case management, and the Treasury's bizarre idea that judges are "service

---

[1] *Inner Temple Advocacy Handbook* 7th edn 2004-5 ed. Toby Hooper QC p.55

providers" who should operate for the benefit of consumers on time/cost principles.

Less than forty years ago the Court of Appeal expressed strong disapproval at the presentation to it, by a litigant in person, of an American style written appellate brief.[2] Lord Justice Dankwerts described it as "wholly irregular and contrary to the practice of the court" and said, "in my opinion (it) should not be allowed as a precedent for future proceedings. It appears that counsel was in fact available to appear … without a fee, and the course mentioned …was deliberately adopted."[3]

Until the late 1970s the higher courts regarded the idea that a party could put before the court a written skeleton argument setting out his case with abhorrence. The suggestion that it should be mandatory in most cases would have been risible. Gradually through the 1980s the concept of the written submission became at first permissible and then an expected feature of any case of substance. From then on the primacy of oral advocacy in the traditional English adversarial system became substantially diluted.

A series of directions to regularise practice was given by the heads of division from 1982 onwards. In that year the Scarman Committee on the practice of civil appeals recommended that better use must be made of time: the Court's time, counsel's and solicitor's time and the parties' time. Amongst four main sources of wasted time, the committee identified the length of oral hearing as the most important because of the number of people involved. This led to the new RSC Order 59 and the creation of the office of Registrar of Civil Appeals. In trying to tackle the problem Lord Donaldson MR, in a Practice Note of 4th October 1982 on new practice and procedure in the Court of Appeal, Civil Division, said,[4]

> "This brings me to the question of whether it may not be possible to make more economical use of time spent in court. Such time, it must be remembered, is relatively very expensive because it involves the attendance not only of the judges but also of counsel, solicitors and often the parties. The Scarman Committee considered and rejected a change to the system of written briefs and limitations on the time allowed for argument which is the practice in some other jurisdictions. They did so on the ground that, although such an approach has advantages, it is alien to the British tradition of oral presentation and argument and is not necessarily less expensive because of the time which has to be devoted to preparing highly complex briefs.

---

[2] See *Rondel v Worsley* [1967] 1 QB 443. Admittedly the document was a typescript of 116 pages, closely argued, concerning the immunity of counsel from suit.

[3] @ p.509C

[4] [1982] 3 All ER 376 @ 377g *et seq.*

However, the Scarman Committee suggested that substantial savings in this expensive time could be achieved if, before the oral hearing began, the judges were able to inform themselves of the general background to the dispute, the decision of the court below and the effective grounds of appeal. With this in mind it recommended an adaptation of the system of perfected grounds of appeal which is in use in the Criminal Division. The judges would come to court having read the judgment under appeal together with the perfected grounds of appeal or some analogous guide to the issues in the appeal and counsel would be able to dispense with any lengthy opening as well as being able to display greater brevity in the argument itself.

We, for our part, fully accept the committee's approach. It is in everyone's interest that the cost of litigation should be reduced by a better use of time. Under the revised Ord 59 the registrar can give directions as to the documentation to be made available to the court before the hearing and appeals can be listed in such a way as to give the judge time to read appropriate parts of the documentation before the oral hearing begins. What can and cannot profitably be preread by the judges will vary from appeal to appeal, as will the best method of informing the judges of the issues in the appeal. In some cases it may well be that the original notice of appeal and the judgment appealed from may suffice. In others it may be desirable to ask for a perfected notice of appeal or even a skeleton of the argument for both parties. This is an area where there is really immense scope for innovation, experiment, trial and, let me stress quite inevitably also, error. But, with the assistance of counsel and solicitors engaged in particular appeals and that of both sides of the profession on a more general basis, there can be no doubt that very worthwhile improvements can be made."

In 1995 Lord Taylor CJ issued a Practice Note of 24th January[5] on Case Management in Civil Litigation for use in the Queen's Bench and Chancery Divisions of the High Court except where other directions specifically applied. For the first time this created an obligation for parties to provide a written skeleton argument prior to the hearing of every action, and provided for closing written submissions where necessary:

"8. Not less than three clear days before the hearing of an action or application each party should lodge with the court (with copies to other parties) a skeleton argument concisely summarising that party's submissions in relation to each of the issues, and citing the main authorities relied upon, which may be attached. Skeleton arguments should be as brief as the nature of the issues allows, and should not without leave of the court exceed 20 pages of double-spaced A4 paper.

9. The opening speech should be succinct. At its conclusion other parties may be invited briefly to amplify their skeleton arguments. In a heavy case the court may in conjunction with final speeches require written submissions, including the findings of fact for which each party contends."

---

[5] [1995] 1 All ER 385.

On 31 January 1995 Sir Stephen Brown P. issued a Practice Direction[6] for use in the Family Division which followed, in modified form, that for the other divisions. In paragraph 7 he added the qualification, 'It is important that skeleton arguments should be brief.' By 2000 in many cases skeleton arguments were to be included as part of the court bundle.[7]

With the coming into force of the Civil Procedure Rules 1998, and ever since, the obligatory contents and detail of written arguments were set out separately in the practice guides issued from time to time for the Queen's Bench and Chancery Divisions, the Commercial Court, the Technology and Construction Court, the Patent Court, arbitration proceedings within the CPR, the Court of Appeal, the Administrative Court and, in the Blue Book, the Judicial and Appeals Committees of the House of Lords and the Privy Council. These are dealt with in Part 1: 'What the Court Requires'.

We have now moved so far in the direction of core arguments always being in written form that in 2004 Mr Justice Lightman was able to say[8]

> "advocacy...today...transcends its traditional form of oral presentation in court and includes and finds critical expression in written forms in which expertise is called for of the advocate and which can have a decisive effect on the outcome of a case."

> "Skeletons can have a substantial if not decisive effect on the course and indeed the outcome of proceedings. Counsel now requires expertise at least as much in preparing skeletons as in making oral submissions...The judge generally comes to a case blind. On occasion he leaves the case in the same condition. He is in need of illumination of the task before him in concise form. The essential minimum requirements are: (1) a chronological account of relevant facts; (2) a statement of the issues of law and fact; and (3) a statement and evaluation of the rival answers to those issues. There is like importance to be attached to final written skeletons at the end of trials containing all relevant page and other references to the evidence adduced."

> "The advocate remembers that the judge is looking to counsel for assistance in reaching and reasoning his judgment. For many (if not most) judges the recourse to a written skeleton is the first resort in writing his judgment. The tedium in preparing a skeleton pays off."

For a long time experience in the American appellate courts has been that written arguments almost always decide the case. Here some Court

---

[6]   [1995] 1 FLR 456; [1995] 1 WLR 332; [1985] 1 All ER 586.
[7]   Practice Direction (Family Proceedings: Court Bundles) [2000] 1 WLR 737; [2000] 1 FLR 536; [2000] 2 All ER 287 per Dame Butler-Sloss P.
[8]   Address to the Chancery Bar Association Conference, 26th January 2004.

of Appeal judges will freely admit that cases are decided before oral argument on the strength of written skeleton arguments, and this must be so since, statistically, in about 40% of appeals heard since 2003, either one side or the other was not called upon to make an oral presentation. That figure is rising. Cases turn on the persuasiveness of skeleton arguments now more than ever before. Oral argument is much shorter than in the past.

Conversely, judges are now delivering more and more reserved judgments at every level. Whether for trial or on appeal, your written submissions are available for members of the court to use long after the oral hearing finishes. For that reason alone it is the written argument that must be the keystone of your advocacy. And if in a large number of cases judges reach a firm inclination in advance of the hearing just from reading a well prepared and argued skeleton, where oral argument fails to dissuade, the winning piece of advocacy is written, not oral. If the judge has formed a view on the merits, having read the skeleton at an early stage, the chances of persuading him to abandon an adverse inclination are not high.

What is also indicative of the overwhelming importance of written advocacy is the decline of skeleton arguments being, in fact, skeletal. The stated purpose of a skeleton argument 'is to identify and summarise in writing the relevant issues of fact and law. It is not to argue to them fully in writing'.[9] Received wisdom believes a skeleton is intended as a vehicle for putting your best points shortly and in the most attractive light – a clear, logical and precise exposition of your case, but most importantly, concise. Increasingly however, the courts are unconcerned with length where the material being provided is necessary, persuasive and assists the court to solve the problem before it. You will receive a written submission from your opponent running to 25, 30 or 40 pages, and wait in vain anticipation for the judge to tear into him for its size. If the arguments are sound, unambiguous and logical, and if the judge is enlightened by the proposed answer, he will not criticise a document unreasonably for being overlong.

In reality though, the written submissions of the finest advocates are, in fact, quite short. The worked examples in this book include cases in the House of Lords running to only six or eight pages. A particular skill of the really successful practitioner is to précis both the facts and the law, and to create a well-signposted, logical and irresistible path for the judge to follow to the desired conclusion over as few pages as are really necessary, whether they be 10, 20 or 30.

The winning advocate persuades the court to accept his skeleton as the most accurate and complete statement of the case; and this book is intended:

---

[9]   *Inner Temple Advocacy Handbook* 7th edn 2004-5 ed. Toby Hooper QC p.55

- to tell you how to do the same;
- to show you the means to create a written submission so powerful in its argument that you should not be called upon except to respond to your opponent;
- to persuade you that presentation matters enormously; and
- to make you understand that whatever attracts judicial favour to the advocate's claim is useful; whatever repels it is useless or worse.
- To have you take written advocacy seriously – it is an essential tool which enables you to damage your opponent without even opening your mouth, and a unique opportunity, not to be wasted.

PART 1
SKELETON ARGUMENTS AND WRITTEN SUBMISSIONS

CHAPTER 1
WHAT THE COURT REQUIRES

Advocates are now obliged to provide skeleton arguments to the court under the provisions of the Civil Procedure Rules 1998, the Queen's Bench and Chancery Guides, and the practice notes for the specialist jurisdictions of the civil court set out in volume 2 of the *Supreme Court Practice* (the "White Book"). Although separate directions are set out for the various divisions of the High Court, the Administrative Court and the Court of Appeal, the structure and contents of what is required for the different courts are broadly consistent with each other.

In practice the individual and personal style of advocates means that whatever the Rules Committee envisages as most helpful to the courts, judges are beginning to form strong views of what they want, and more particularly, what they do not want. By the same token successful advocates are discovering whether what they provide works or not.

In this section I set out the technical requirements of the CPR and other relevant directions, and compare them with what those members of the judiciary, who have been kind enough to assist me in this study, have indicated is most helpful to them. The Master dealing with a contested application, the first-instance Judge, and the Appellate Judge each have different concerns and different needs which are not always reflected in the rules of practice. You will want to address them. Equally those advocates who achieve great success, part of which they attribute to their written advocacy, are less concerned about complying with the strict requirements of the relevant directions than supplying the Court with a document which helps both their cause and eases the task of the Judge. In the third part I look at what it is that successful advocates provide built around the analysis of 15 examples drawn from actual contested cases.

Since it is fundamental that you, as an advocate, are familiar with the current Rules of the Court in which you practice in order to comply with them, let us start by considering what you are expected to provide to the court.

QUEEN'S BENCH DIVISION

Directions for Queen's Bench actions are contained in the *Queen's Bench Guide*.[1] The rationale for giving directions concerning preparation for hearings is to ensure that court time is used efficiently.[2] This includes the writing and exchange of skeleton arguments, the compilation of bundles of documents and giving realistic time estimates. Active case management means that the parties should use their best endeavours to agree beforehand the issues, or main issues between them, and must cooperate with the court and each other to enable the court to deal with claims justly; parties may expect to be penalised for failing to do so.[3]

In addition to lodging a bundle of documents in an approved form for use at the hearing, for trial and most appearances before a Judge, and substantial hearings before a Master, a chronology, a list of the persons involved and a list of the issues should be prepared and filed with the skeleton argument.[4] A chronology should be noncontentious and agreed with the other parties, if possible. If there is a material dispute about any event stated in the chronology, this should be stated.

Under paragraph 7.11.12 of the QB Guide a skeleton argument should:

- concisely summarise the party's submissions in relation to each of the issues;
- cite the main authorities relied on, which may be attached;
- contain a reading list and an estimate of the time it will take the Judge to read;
- be as brief as the issues allow and not normally be longer than 20 pages of double-spaced A4 paper;
- be divided into numbered paragraphs and paged consecutively;
- avoid formality and use understandable abbreviations; and
- identify any core documents which it would be helpful to read beforehand.

CHANCERY DIVISION

The general rule contained in the *Chancery Guide*[5] is that for the purpose of all hearings before a Judge skeleton arguments should be prepared. The

---

[1] *Civil Procedure 2005 Vol 2* QB Contents 1A-52 (7.11.12).
[2] 7.11.5.
[3] 7.11.6.
[4] 7.11.10.
[5] *Chancery Guide* Civil Practice 2005 Vol.1 1-62, 1-65, 1-71 (7.43); 1-197; Vol. 2 7.20.

exceptions to this are where the application does not warrant one, for example because it is likely to be short, or where the application is so urgent
that preparation of a skeleton argument is impracticable or where an application is ineffective and the order is agreed by all parties. Skeleton arguments
should be prepared in respect of any application before the Master of one or
more hour's duration and certainly for any trial or similar hearing.[6] In most
cases before a Judge, a list of the persons involved in the facts of the case, a
chronology and a list of issues will also be required. The chronology and list
of issues should be agreed where possible.[7] They are to be lodged by the same
time as applies to the lodging of bundles. Where a skeleton argument is required, photocopies of any authorities to be relied upon should be attached
to the skeleton argument.[8]

The Court suggests that advocates should consider preparing their skeleton
arguments as soon as the case is placed in the Warned List, so that they are
ready to be delivered to the court on time. Preparation of skeleton arguments
should not be left until notice is given that the case is to be heard since it is
possible that a notice may be given that the case is to be heard the next
day.[9]

In the more substantial matters (e.g. trials and applications by order) skeleton arguments must be delivered not less than two clear days before the date
or first date on which the application or trial is due to come on for hearing.[10] On applications without notice to a Judge the skeleton may be placed
with the papers which the Judge is asked to read on the application.[11] On all
other applications to a Judge, including interim applications, the skeleton
should be filed as soon as possible and not later than 10 a.m. on the day
preceding the hearing. If the name of the Judge (other than a Deputy Judge)
is known, skeleton arguments should be delivered to the Judge's Clerk, otherwise where the name of the Judge is not known, or the Judge is a Deputy
Judge, skeleton arguments should be delivered to the Listing Office.[12]

Unless the court gives any other direction, the parties arrange between themselves for the delivery, exchange, or sequential service of skeleton arguments
and any accompanying documents or authorities. Such an exchange should
be made in sufficient time before the hearing to enable them to be properly
considered.[13]

---

[6] 7.43.
[7] 7.28.
[8] 7.44.
[9] 7.24.
[10] 7.21.
[11] 7.22.
[12] 7.25, 7.26.
[13] 7.41, 7.43.

Appendix 3 to the *Chancery Guide*[14] sets out specific guidelines on the contents of skeleton arguments, chronologies, indices and reading lists. The contents of skeletons should be as follows:

"Skeleton arguments

1. A skeleton argument is intended to identify both for the parties and the court those points which are, and those that are not, in issue, and the nature of the argument in relation to those points which are in issue. It is not a substitute for oral argument.
2. Every skeleton argument should therefore:

   (1) identify concisely:

      (a) the nature of the case generally, and the background facts insofar as they are relevant to the matter before the court;
      (b) the propositions of law relied on with references to the relevant authorities;
      (c) the submissions of fact to be made with reference to the evidence;

   (2) be as brief as the nature of the issues allows - it should not normally exceed 20 pages of double-spaced A4 paper and in many cases it should be much shorter than this;
   (3) be in numbered paragraphs and state the name (and contact details) of the advocate(s) who prepared it;
   (4) avoid arguing the case at length;
   (5) avoid formality and make use of abbreviations, e.g. C for Claimant, A/345 for bundle A page 345, 1.1.95 for 1st January 1995 etc."

The Judge may also direct that the parties submit written summaries of their final speeches before they begin to set out the principal findings of fact for which the party contends and grant an adjournment for this purpose. The guidelines in Appendix 3 are intended to apply to written summaries of opening and final speeches. Even though in a large case these may necessarily be longer, they should still be as brief as the case allows.[15]

---

[14] Vol. 2 *White Book* 1-197.
[15] 1.2(2) Appendix 3 to the *Chancery Guide*.

ADMIRALTY, COMMERCIAL AND MERCANTILE COURTS

The practice directions for the Admiralty Court and Commercial Court are set out in section 2 of the Specialist Proceedings under Part 49 of the Civil Procedure Rules and Part 58 dealing with the Commercial Court. Guidelines on the preparation of skeleton arguments are set out in Part 1 of Appendix 9.[16]

Unlike the other guides the Commercial Court provides for the sequential service of pre-trial skeletons. Each party should prepare written arguments and unless otherwise ordered, these should be served on all other parties and lodged with the court as follows:

(i) by the claimant, not later than 1 p.m. two days (i.e. two clear days) before the start of the trial;

(ii) by each of the defendants, not later than 1 p.m. one day (i.e. one clear day) before the start of the trial.[17]

In heavier cases it will often be appropriate for skeleton arguments to be served and lodged earlier, in which case the timetable should be discussed between the advocates and may be the subject of a direction in the pre-trial timetable or at any pre-trial review. The claimant should provide a chronology with his skeleton argument. Indices (i.e. documents that collate key references on particular points, or a substantive list of the contents of a particular bundle or bundles) and *dramatis personae* should also be provided where these are likely to be useful. Guidelines on the preparation of chronologies and indices are set out in Part 2 of Appendix 9.

Appendix 9[18] of the Admiralty Court and Commercial Court direction follows almost exactly the wording of Appendix 3 of the Chancery Guide with regard to the nature and contents of skeleton arguments. Although it contains the stricture that parties should avoid arguing the case at length, it does not state that the written summation be as brief as the nature of the issues allows, or that it should not normally exceed 20 pages of double-spaced A4 paper.

As far as possible chronologies and indices should not be prepared in a tendentious form.[19] The ideal is that the court and the parties should have a single point of reference that all find useful and are happy to work with. Where there is disagreement about a particular event or description, it is useful if that fact is indicated in neutral terms and the competing versions

---

[16] Vol.2 *White Book* 2A-165.

[17] J6.2 *Admiralty and Commercial Courts Guide.*

[18] Vol.2 *White Book* 2A-165.

[19] Appendix 9 Part 2.3 - 2A-166.

shortly stated. If time and circumstances allow its preparation, a chronology or index to which all parties have contributed and agreed can be invaluable. Chronologies and indices once prepared can be easily updated and are of continuing usefulness throughout the life of the case.

The directions of the Admiralty and Commercial Courts are not confined to pre-trial skeletons. Unless the judge directs otherwise the parties should prepare skeleton arguments for the hearing of applications in the course of trial;[20] and in a more substantial trial, the court will normally also require closing submissions in writing before oral closing submissions.[21] In such a case the court will normally allow an appropriate period of time after the conclusion of the evidence to allow the preparation of these submissions. Even in a less substantial trial the court will normally require a written skeleton argument on matters of law. Express provision is made that if the authenticity of any document or entry in any document is challenged, such challenge must be contained in the skeleton argument.[22] In collision claims the skeleton argument of each party must be accompanied by a plot or plots of that party's case or alternative cases as to the navigation of vessels during and leading to the collision. All plots must contain a sufficient indication of the assumptions used in the preparation of the plot.[23]

As with the Commercial Court, Mercantile Courts function as specialist lists within the Queen's Bench Division of the High Court. Since 25 March 2002, the functions and procedures of the Mercantile Courts have been governed by CPR Part 59 and its accompanying Practice Direction, with most Mercantile Courts using the Commercial Court Guide to regulate their practice.

THE TECHNOLOGY AND CONSTRUCTION COURT

In the case of all but the simplest applications, the Court[24] expects both parties to lodge with the judge's clerk skeleton arguments and a list of any authorities to be relied on no later than 4 p.m. on the day before the date fixed for the hearing.[25] Directions concerning the exchange and filing of trial skeletons or opening written submissions will be given at the pre-trial review.

---

[20] J9.2.
[21] J.11.1.
[22] 2A-136 N9.2.
[23] N9.3.
[24] Vol 2 *White Book* 2C-1 *et seq.*
[25] 7.5 PD to Part 60.

ARBITRATION

Where arbitrations are governed by section 2E of the Specialist Proceedings under Part 49 of the Civil Procedure Rules standard directions are provided for the filing and contents of skeleton arguments[26] to be used at the hearing:

"Not later than 2 days before the hearing date the claimant must file and serve—

(1) a chronology of the relevant events cross-referenced to the bundle of documents;
(2) (where necessary) a list of the persons involved; and
(3) a skeleton argument which lists succinctly—

(a) the issues which arise for decision;
(b) the grounds of relief (or opposing relief) to be relied upon;
(c) the submissions of fact to be made with the references to the evidence;
(d) the submissions of law with references to the relevant authorities.

Not later than the day before the hearing date the defendant must file and serve a skeleton argument which lists succinctly—

(1) the issues which arise for decision;
(2) the grounds of relief (or opposing relief) to be relied upon;
(3) the submissions of fact to be made with the references to the evidence; and
(4) the submissions of law with references to the relevant authorities."

THE PATENT COURT

In the Patent Court,[27] in addition to the Reading Guide parties should lodge skeleton arguments in time for the Judge to read them before trial. That should normally be at least two days before its commencement, but in substantial cases a longer period may be needed (to be discussed with the clerk to the Judge concerned). It is desirable that each party should summarise what it contends to be the common general knowledge of the man skilled in the art. Following the evidence in a substantial trial a short adjournment may be granted to enable the parties to summarise their arguments in writing before oral argument.

---

[26] 2E-44 (6.5-6.7).
[27] Section 2F-124 of the Specialist Proceedings under Part 49 of the Civil Procedure Rules.

THE ADMINISTRATIVE COURT

In bringing claims for judicial review and other relief provided by the Administrative Court[28] issues concerned with application bundles and skeletons arguments are set out under CPR Part 54.16 and the Practice Direction at 54 PD 15. The claimant must file and serve a skeleton argument not less than 21 working days before the date of hearing. The defendant and any other party wishing to make representations at the hearing must file and serve skeletons not less than 14 working days before the hearing. The claimant must also file a paginated, indexed bundle of all relevant documents. It must include those documents required by the claimant, the defendant and any other party wishing to make representations.

Skeleton arguments must contain:

(1) a time estimate for the complete hearing, including delivery of judgment;
(2) a list of issues;
(3) a list of the legal points to be taken (together with any relevant authorities with page references to the passages relied on);
(4) a chronology of events (with page references to the bundle of documents;
(5) a list of essential documents for the advance reading of the court (with page references to the passages relied on) (if different from that filed with the claim form) and a time estimate for that reading; and
(6) a list of persons referred to.

THE COURT OF APPEAL

Skeleton arguments for and written submissions to the Court of Appeal are governed by CPR 52.4.4, 52.12.4, 52.5.6 and the associated Practice Direction at 52 PD 5.9 – 5.11, 7.6 – 7.8, 11A – 12.4, 19, 20, 36, 37 and 64. Every appellant who is represented is required (and appellants in person are encouraged) to prepare a skeleton argument, which, if short can be inserted into part 8 of the appellant's notice, or otherwise can be contained in an accompanying separate document. Alternatively the skeleton argument must be lodged and served within 14 days after filing the appellant's notice.[29]

The Court of Appeal now regards the appellant's skeleton argument as a vital document: together with that of the respondent it assists in case management, allows the court to focus its attention on the true issues and proposed solution of the parties, and enables the members of the court to

---

[28] CPR 54.16.4; 54 PD 15.
[29] See 52 PD 5.9.

form a preliminary view, which is more often than not reflected in the Judges' approach to counsel at the outset of the hearing. For the designated lead judgment writer, written submissions are a critical aid in the consideration and preparation of reserved judgments.

The content of skeleton arguments is dealt with in 52 PD 20 at paragraph 5.10 which states

"(1) A skeleton argument must contain a numbered list of the points which the party wishes to make. These should both define and confine the areas of controversy. Each point should be stated as concisely as the nature of the case allows.

(2) A numbered point must be followed by a reference to any document on which the party wishes to rely.

(3) A skeleton argument must state, in respect of each authority cited—

(a) the proposition of law that the authority demonstrates; and

(b) the parts of the authority (identified by page or paragraph references) that support the proposition.

(4) If more than one authority is cited in support of a given proposition, the skeleton argument must briefly state the reason for taking that course.

(5) The statement referred to in sub-paragraph (4) should not materially add to the length of the skeleton argument but should be sufficient to demonstrate, in the context of the argument—

(a) the relevance of the authority or authorities to that argument; and

(b) that the citation is necessary for a proper presentation of that argument[30].

(6) The cost of preparing a skeleton argument which—

(a) does not comply with the requirements set out in this paragraph; or

(b) was not filed within the time limits provided by this Practice Direction (or any further time granted by the court),will not be allowed on assessment except to the extent that the court otherwise directs.[31]"

By paragraph 5.11 the appellant should also consider what other information the appeal court will need. This may include a list of persons who feature

---

[30] This paragraph incorporates the relevant requirements of the *Practice Direction (Citation of Authorities)* [2001] 1 W.L.R. 1001.

[31] Paragraph 5.10 is specific in its requirements and these are the costs consequences for noncompliance.

in the case or glossaries of technical terms. A chronology of relevant events will be necessary in most appeals.

Paragraph 7.6 of the Practice Direction obliges the respondent to provide a skeleton argument "in all cases where he proposes to address arguments to the court" and must either accompany the respondent's notice or else be lodged and served within 14 days after filing the notice. The content of a respondent's skeleton must conform to the directions at paragraphs 5.10 and 5.11 with any necessary modifications. It should, where appropriate, answer the arguments set out in the appellant's skeleton argument.

Where the appeal relates to a claim on the small claims track or the respondent is not represented, the respondent is not obliged to provide a skeleton argument, but he is entitled to do so. In cases where there is no respondent's notice, the respondent need not serve his skeleton argument until 7 days before the appeal hearing.[32] However, if an appeal to the Court of Appeal is allocated to the short warned list, the respondent's skeleton argument may be required at short notice.[33]

Paragraph 15.11A of the practice direction permits the filing of supplementary skeleton arguments. The appellant's supplementary argument must be filed at least 14 days before the hearing and that of the respondent at least 7 days before. Any argument which is not contained in the original or supplementary skeleton arguments (timeously served) may be shut out by the court.[34]

Skeleton arguments and written submissions are not the only pieces of written advocacy which are received by the Court of Appeal. Where a refusal to give permission to appeal has been made on consideration of the papers alone, an appellant, who is represented, may make a request for a decision to be reconsidered at an oral permission hearing. By 52PD.9 paragraph 4.14A(2):

> "The appellant's advocate must, at least 4 days before the hearing, in a brief written statement—
>
> (a) inform the court and the respondent of the points which he proposes to raise at the hearing;
> (b) set out his reasons why permission should be granted notwithstanding the reasons given for the refusal of permission; and
> (c) confirm, where applicable, that the requirements of paragraph 4.17 have been complied with (appellant in receipt of services funded by the Legal Services Commission).

[32] See 52 PD 20 para. 7.7 (2).
[33] *Scribes West Ltd v. Anstalt (No. 1)* [2004] EWCA Civ 835 at [24].
[34] 52 PD 20 para. 15.11A(4) and *Scribes West Ltd v. Anstalt (No. 1) op.cit.* at [25]–[27].

CASES FOR THE HOUSE OF LORDS

The Practice Directions and Standing Orders Applicable to Civil Appeals and Criminal Appeals, November 2003 govern the presentation of written material for consideration by the Appellate Committee of the House of Lords. The document which contains a party's written argument in the Appellate Committee, and also the Judicial Committee of the Privy Council, is known as a 'case'. This is separate from any statement of facts and issues.

By paragraph 15.9 of the Standing Order all the appellants must join in one case, and all the respondents must similarly join in one case unless it can be shown that the interests of one or more are distinct from those of the remainder. If that is the position the respondents' agents first lodging their case must certify by letter that an opportunity has been offered for joining in one respondent's case but that the interests represented in the case lodged are, in their opinion, distinct from those of the remaining respondent(s). All remaining respondents wishing to lodge a case must respectively petition to do so in respect of each of their separate cases. Such petitions must be consented to by the appellants, and must set out the reasons for separate lodgment. Parties whose interests in the appeal are passive (e.g. stake-holders, trustees, executors, etc.) are not required to lodge a separate case but need to ensure that their position is explained in one of the cases lodged.

The preparation and lodgment of cases is sequential, not an exchange. The appellants must lodge eight copies of their case in the Judicial Office and serve it on the respondents no later than five weeks before the proposed date of the hearing. The respondents must lodge their case in response, as must any other party lodging a case no later than three weeks before the proposed date. Where there is a cross-appeal the cross-appellants' case for the cross-appeal is to be lodged three weeks before the hearing as part of their reply to the original appellants' case. Permission can be granted for the lodging of supplemental cases.

The Directions[35] applicable to Appellants' and Respondents' Cases are both detailed and specific:

"1. A Case must start by setting out the correct title and address of the party on behalf of whom it is lodged.
2. Where the House has granted leave to appeal, it should not be assumed that those who will hear the appeal will be familiar with the arguments set out in the petition for leave to appeal.
3. A Case should be a succinct statement of a party's argument in the appeal. It should omit the material contained in the statement of facts

---

[35] Part 15 Practice Directions and Standing Orders Applicable to Civil Appeals. Vol. 2 *White Book* 4A-49.

and issues and should be confined to the heads of argument which counsel propose to submit at the hearing.

4. If either party is abandoning any point taken in the courts below, this should be made plain in the Case. Equally if they intend to apply in the course of the hearing for leave to introduce a new point not taken below, this should be indicated in their Case and the Judicial Office should be informed. If such a point involves the introduction of fresh evidence, application for leave must be made either in the Case or by lodging a petition for leave to adduce the fresh evidence.

5. If the parties intend to invite the House to depart from one of its own decisions, this intention must be clearly stated in a separate paragraph of the Case, to which special attention must be drawn. A respondent who wishes to contend that a decision of the Court below should be affirmed on grounds other than those relied on by that Court must set out the grounds for that contention in the Case.

6. All Cases must conclude with a numbered summary of the reasons upon which the argument is founded, and must bear the signature of at least one counsel who has appeared in the court below or who will be briefed for the hearing before the House.

7. Transcripts of unreported judgments should only be cited when they contain an authoritative statement of a relevant principle of law not to be found in a reported case or are necessary for the understanding of some other authority."

The appellants must prepare a Statement of Facts and Issues involved in the appeal, which they initially draw up and submit to the respondents for discussion. The Statement as lodged must be a single document agreed between the parties. It should not contain material more appropriately included in a Case and should there be any disagreement, the disputed material will be included in each party's Case. It need not set out or summarise the judgments of the lower courts, nor set out statutory provisions, nor contain an account of the proceedings below since the Statement will be read in conjunction with the Appendix which the appellants must also prepare and lodge. This contains such documents used in evidence or recording proceedings in the courts below as are clearly necessary for the support and understanding of the argument of the appeal. This should again be prepared in consultation with the respondents, and the contents of the Appendix must be agreed between the parties before lodgment in the Judicial Office.

Direction 30 deals with the requirements of the Statement of Facts and Issues.

"1. The Statement and Case should be produced with letters down the inside margin. The outside margin should carry references to the relevant pages of the Appendix.

2. The front page of the Statement should carry the references of every law report of the cause in the courts below. A head-note summary should be given, whether or not the cause has been reported.

3. The front page of the Statement should carry an indication of the time occupied by the cause in each court below.

4. The Statement should be signed by counsel on both sides above their printed names.

5. Each party's Case should be signed by counsel on both sides above their printed names."

CHAPTER 2
WHAT JUDGES WANT

Although the Civil Procedure Rules and practice guides set out what is required when providing the courts with skeleton arguments, and this is enforced by the penalty costs regime, in practice many of the successful advocates who have contributed to my research pay only lip service to such technicalities as maximum length, form and subject matter. Curiously so do many Judges. There are those of an older disposition who disapprove of any form of written advocacy and will not even consider written submissions; conversely some members of the judiciary want as much assistance in writing as possible, believing that it will shorten the hearing. By far the majority appreciate and are genuinely assisted by written arguments which are clear, concise, coherent, structured intelligently, and formulated with a view to assisting the Judge to solve the problem immediately to hand.

IMMEDIATE AND FUTURE USE

Judges rely on skeleton arguments and written submissions to find the quickest way into the case. The pressure of business and the distribution of work, particularly in the superior courts, are such that applications and even trials will come before tribunals who do not have the time to absorb the papers. There are, of course, exceptions, such as the Technology and Construction Court where active case management, in most cases by the eventual trial Judge, means that he will know the case quite well. But where it happens that the Judge comes to a contested matter entirely afresh, it is the well-presented and coherent skeleton that will be read before the statements of case and, if reliable, in place of them. In the Court of Appeal a dependable skeleton will subsume and deal with all of the live grounds of appeal: in an average appeal contesting the legal basis for the decision of the court below, unless skeleton submissions are unclear or extremely short, the Lords Justices of Appeal need read only the two sides' skeleton arguments and the relevant part of the first instance judgment.

For a Judge, the skeleton should tell him whether it is necessary to read anything else, and if so what, and in what order. This is particularly true for applications before the Master and District Judge. For these the case summary and skeleton are required to deal only with what arises at the instant hearing. That is not to say that Judges do not differentiate between different forms of written advocacy. They do. The skeleton prepared for a two hour application before a Master or a contested issue of case management will have a different structure and dissimilar contents from opening notes or closing submissions at trial; and between the style of written advocacy prepared for trial and that for appeal.

The impact of a well thought out and carefully crafted skeleton argument should not be underestimated. Written submissions do not cease to be useful to the court merely because the trial or appeal has commenced. In the Court of Appeal upwards of 60% of appeals now have reserved judgments: the written argument is not only used before the hearing to enable the Judge to formulate a preliminary view, but also *afterwards* as an aide memoir to write his judgment. Much the same can be said of trial Judges, and increasingly it is common for advocates to be asked to prepare closing submissions in writing, usually in lieu of closing argument, and to furnish the Judge with a copy in electronic format.

WHAT DO JUDGES WANT?

Judges want to get on with the job. They first want to be told what the case is about, succinctly and in the first two or three paragraphs of the skeleton. Then they want to know what is the problem, and what answer is proposed. Masters and Judges dealing with applications need to know what you want them to do as quickly as possible, and will then test what is wanted against the submissions made.

In all but written advocacy prepared for trial, the salient facts, dates, features, issues and relevant law should be reduced to a pithy synopsis: the tribunal does not want to be overburdened, just receive well-focussed information. Most Judges wish to be guided into the case in a neutral way: they appreciate that the argument will, of course, be loaded, but the introduction which gives the reader the geography of the case is expected to be neutral.

The Judges to whom I have spoken ask that advocates always bear in mind the following:

- If the Judge or Master has had no prior contact with the case the skeleton must tell him what, if anything, he needs to read next.
- In order for the Judge to grasp points quickly, clarity of presentation is essential. For some this means that complex issues of fact or law should be broken down into small portions - the issues being identified, but not

necessarily simplified. For all, this means well reasoned argument which, though skeletal, is thorough, internally coherent, has a logical progression and leads to clear conclusions.

- In form the skeleton will be more akin to the outline of a judgment, particularly where the document is a written closing submission at trial, or a written submission for the Court of Appeal. Coherence in any written document intended to assist the court is very important.

- If the Judge has difficulty with a skeleton argument, because it is not easy to read, has no coherent structure, or is unreliable as to its contents, he is likely to abandon it and go to the statements of case. Should he do so there is a real risk for the advocate that he will not return to it.

THE TRIAL AND APPELLATE JUDGE

There is a dichotomy between Judges at first instance and those sitting on appeal, or hearing applications, as to what they want from a claimant's or appellant's skeleton argument. The trial Judge wants the skeleton or opening note to set the scene, to enable him to Master the facts and the law, and to understand the arguments. He does not want to form a view from one side's argument only. Experienced trial Judges are progressively less willing to come to an early conclusion as provisional views are often wrong, and cases come alive when they are argued. They wish to see what the facts and arguments are and to go into the hearing with an open mind. That is what the parties expect.

Appellate Judges view the skeleton submissions for an appellant slightly differently from those in a claimant's opening note for trial. Because of the pressure of time, the parties written submissions and the judgment given below are about as much as can be read in advance. The Judge will want to begin the appellant's submissions before reading the judgment since it may well be unnecessary to read the whole judgment. The appellant should tell him what the case is about and what points he wants to argue - in effect, 'why he is where he is'. This skeleton will not set out the facts in any detail but show the court where the detail is to be found in the judgment if it is wanted. Generally the only facts that are wanted are those needed to address the points in the appeal since invariably many points will not be in issue. The appellate Judge wishes to receive substantive points of law not points of procedure, and expects the submissions to build upon the grounds of appeal. Again, clarity and coherence are the watchwords, with perhaps each part of the written argument dealing with one ground of appeal.

DIRECTIONS

It is rare for Masters and Judges to provide express directions as to the style, form and content of skeleton arguments since these are to be found in the

Civil Procedure Rules and specialist practice guides. In some jurisdictions, slightly specialised directions may be given, for example that a case summary be directed at certain issues, that partnership accounts be drawn in a way that invites comment or argument, or that Scott Schedules in the Technology and Construction Court be expanded to enable parties to provide support or argument for any particular contention.

More usually there will be a direction that the issues between the parties be agreed, and perhaps formulated in a particular way. In asking for written closing submissions a trial Judge may well invite the parties to frame agreed questions for him to decide.

Occasionally Queen's Bench Masters will issue a personal direction which modifies the operation of the relevant Civil Procedure Rules Practice Direction, and this is something you will have to watch out for and learn by experience. For example Master Eyre issues a direction dealing with the names of parties that:

> "The parties must in any statement of case or other document prepared for use by the Master, and notwithstanding anything in the Rules, be referred to as parties - "the Second Claimant", "the Fourth Defendant", "the First Third Party", &c. as the case may be - and not by names or initials, &c., save in those rare cases in which some other approach is required if the meaning is to be made clear."

To cater for the fact that a statement of claim and probably a defence will already have been filed before the parties receive notice of this direction, it goes on to say

> "Original documents that have been filed must not be altered. Instead, copies cleanly-corrected using 'Find-and-replace' must be provided for use at any hearing."

You may find these quirky local directions at county court level as well.

LENGTH

There is no consensus among Judges as to the optimum length of a skeleton argument. It is broadly accepted that the length of opening and closing notes must be appropriate to the case and a distinction is drawn between these and skeleton arguments in interim applications.

Two schools of thought seem to have developed. There are many Judges, including members of the Court of Appeal, who are unconcerned about length and like argument being developed. By contrast there are those who find excessive length irritating, and who feel that, while the element of spoon-feeding is sometimes an aid, it can be too long, except where unavoidable technicalities in the law require explanation. Only by discovering or gaining experience of any particular Judge's views on this subject will you discover which your particular tribunal prefers.

An extreme view, taken in some parts of the Queen's Bench Masters' corridor, is that where a written argument is considered too long, the advocate should be put to an election whether the Master should receive that document only and not hear oral argument, or whether the document be not read. I don't know how that squares with Article 6 European Convention on Human Rights. The Masters with whom I have spoken were inclined to think that a document of between 2 and 3 pages in length was the maximum they required on most occasions.

Judges tend to advise that being succinct is far more convincing than being verbose – all they need is a sufficient understanding of what will lead to oral submissions.

OVERALL VISUAL IMPRESSION

Many of my interviewees instinctively said they were not concerned with the visual impression of the written submissions presented, as long as these skeletons were generally in accordance with the rules. However, when pressed, they agreed that readability, the setting out of the page, and ease on the eye did have an impact on them. Many made jottings in the margin or otherwise liked to write on the white space available. They do not, though, like line spacing set too wide: it is unnecessary and renders the document less succinct.

Comfortable readability for most Judges means a decent sized margin, 12-point type using a font such as Times New Roman or Arial typefaces, and a line spacing of 1.5. Two other matters were frequently mentioned: that skeleton arguments be page numbered; and that the title should always say on whose behalf the document was being filed, particularly with supplemental skeletons and on any appendices.

CITATION

Broadly speaking, the Judges interviewed wished for a sparing use of authorities in skeleton arguments. The citation of obvious cases was unnecessary, as were authorities concerning procedure or first or general principles. Members of the court do not react well to the tendency of those advocates who put in authority for every proposition, whether it is contentious or not: the less contentious the proposition, the less authority is required.

Having said that, and subject to the Practice Direction on the citation of authorities,[1] most Judges will accept patiently as many authorities as are felt necessary, particularly where the case is comparatively unusual. Advocates should not get carried away. If there is a recent House of Lords decision on the point, or a case that reviews all predecessors in an area, it should be sufficient to refer only to that.

No universal rule is offered on the length or frequency of the quotation of judgments from authorities within written submissions; these must be appropriate to each case. However most Judges want citation references only, since quotations merely extend the skeleton. Experienced counsel are expected to make sensible decisions about what and how much to cite. Judges prefer pithy, accurate quotes limited to a paragraph or two, which are very much on point. If anything longer is necessary the judge will go and read it himself.

It is sometimes helpful to provide a separate appendix dealing with the pertinent and recent law[2] that is the subject of the proceedings where the judge is, or is likely to be unfamiliar with it. It is useful to have key cases attached to the skeleton, especially Lawtel reports or short transcripts if the authority is new and not reported elsewhere.

FOOTNOTES

It may come as a surprise but the use of footnotes in written submissions is still regarded by many Judges as both a modern and unorthodox phenomenon. On balance the Judges who have assisted with this project were marginally against their use, seeing them at best as a repository for citation references and at worst as a distraction, forcing the eyes of the reader to drop to the foot of the page. The only discussion by Judges was whether or not the names and references to authority should be kept in the main body of text or removed to a footnote, but all agreed that substantive argument should not appear there.

HEADINGS

Judges find that topical headings provide useful guidance in breaking up issues. Most prefer a heading to be neutral rather than argumentative, that is, an assertive, contentious statement of the party's position on the next issue being advanced. Nonetheless it is accepted that argumentative headings are useful in summarising passages of argument if used well and imaginatively.[3]

---

[1] *Practice Direction (Citation of Authorities)* [2001] 1 W.L.R. 1001.
[2] See the examples in Part 3 at C *Martindale* and J *Phelps*.
[3] See p. 50.

Judges tend to prefer the use of sub-headings to numbered sub-paragraphs; this helps a Judge find his way around the skeleton more easily. All Judges are keen on marked signposts.

SUMMARIES

Summaries are generally thought to be useful, particularly at the beginning of the skeleton, and condensed into the first three paragraphs which tell the Judge: what is the claim for; what is the central feature of the claimant's case; and what is the central feature of the defendant's case.

In skeletons produced for applications the court should be told immediately what it is being asked to decide. For closing submissions at trial or as appropriate in opening notes, the relief sought and the basis for granting it should be summarised.

REPETITION

Almost all Judges questioned do not like repetition in written submissions and find it irritating. They do not want any skeleton argument to be longer than is necessary. A short introduction or summary is acceptable. Tribunals wish to make sure they have every point, but the idea of repetition for emphasis is for juries not the Judge. One circuit judge informed me that he would skip over anything he had read before, except material in a general introduction.

ABBREVIATIONS

Of all the various matters of style it is the use of abbreviations that gives rise to the most intense debate. You would imagine that Judges find abbreviations quite helpful to keep things short, as specifically encouraged by paragraph 5 of the Appendix to the Chancery Guide dealing with skeleton arguments.[4] Most prefer the use of C for Claimant, D for Defendant, A for Applicant, P for Petitioner and R for Respondent except where it is not practical, either because it is easier to use the actual names of parties who are, say, companies, or where there are multiple parties, or where parties either change or have different status during different parts of the claim (e.g. in a counterclaim, Part 20 Claim, or by reference to parallel proceedings, such as an arbitration). I denote a tension, however, between Judges and the advocates who appear before them about the use of names that manifests itself in the argument concerning abbreviations. Judges want to know *what* people are, not *who* they are. In most cases it is better, not only for

---

[4] See p. 6.

them but also for observers or readers of law reports, that abbreviations denote status rather than *persona*. Advocates, on the other hand, often want to *personalise* the case, hoping for example that a Judge will be more reluctant to find Mr Bloggs or Mr Jones liable than Big Conglomerate Plc, perhaps referred to as BC Plc. They therefore want to avoid abbreviations and use real names. Even if the Judge favours the use of status, abbreviations can be avoided by the use of 'the architect' or 'the surveyor.' In certain cases it will be better for all to depersonalise.

Beyond the use of initials to abbreviate the names of parties or to denote their status, most Judges dislike abbreviations. They do not help clarity. Judges dislike having to keep referring back to the beginning of the document or to the *dramatis personae* or other key to find out about whom the writer is talking. Judges much prefer descriptive names to initials, and are usually only comfortable with abbreviated names where the name is obvious from its shortened form.

Old-fashioned courtesies should be observed. If you chose to abbreviate the parties to Smith and Jones, the Judge will expect it to be Mr Smith and Mrs Jones. Personal titles are to be respected and are seen as important.

Statutes and authorities should be referred to in full when first cited, and afterwards may be abbreviated, for example, from the Inheritance (Provision for Family and Dependants) Act 1975 to "the 1975 Act", and say, *Metalloy Supplies Ltd (In Liquidation) v MA (UK) Ltd* to 'Metalloy'.

TEXTUAL ENHANCEMENT

The over liberal use of italics and bold type face can often be seen as a challenge to the Judge's intellect. Therefore use textual enhancement sparingly. Italics should always be confined to the name of a case and those important few words that are cited as the key to or turning point in the argument. The use of bold should be even more restricted, and confined to the emphasis of small key parts of a document.

As with all kinds of enhancement, it is the sparing use of augmentation that makes it more effective and of greater worth as a visual aid.

STRUCTURE OF THE ARGUMENT

Most tribunals say they want the skeleton argument to be just that – skeletal. The oral tradition forces them to maintain the view that the court operates most effectively with short introductory statements in writing that indicate each party's position, with oral argument used to develop, amplify and explain points, and to be a dialogue between the advocate and whatever the court is interested in or troubled by.

However short the skeleton, the argument must raise all live issues. The court and your opposing number should be aware of all points being taken, since Judges strongly disapprove of surprises which arise because an advocate has either withheld a matter or has not dealt with his own client's position adequately. Apart from anything else, such a defect is likely to attract adverse costs consequences as being incompatible with the overriding objective under the Civil Procedure Rules.

Well-structured arguments are appreciated. They help the Judge to focus, to concentrate and to reach a conclusion quickly. Muddle and ill thought out propositions irritate Judges. They like a progression - logical consecutive arguments, broken down into a series of questions or stages. They welcome familiar signposts in the law, and, if by chance you come before the right Judge, the development of the law on a point previously decided by him. But to score really well, find a hook to interest your tribunal – the great appellate advocates of our age, like Jonathan Sumption QC and David Pannick QC – succeed because they find something to say which the court has not thought of.

PART 2
DEVELOPING WRITTEN ADVOCACY SKILLS

CHAPTER 3
INTRODUCTION

The tradition of written argument is central to European systems of civil litigation, exemplified by those of France and Italy. There, as proceedings develop, advocates submit for filing on the court roll lengthy formal and technical documents which combine statements of case, argument, evidence and the procedural history of the claim. The court requires little oral argument. However for linguistic and cultural reasons, there is not much from these jurisdictions to assist us in developing a written style and design for our own. Rather let us turn for know-how to that common-law jurisdiction which has a mature and sophisticated procedure for drawing up formatted written argument in Federal and Supreme Court appeals, the United States.

The process of settling 'briefs' or written argument for the use of the American appellate courts is not only well developed, it has for decades attracted both judicial commentary and academic guidance. In 1961 Col. Frederick Bernays Wiener wrote his classic *Briefing and Arguing Federal Appeals*[1] and prior to this John W. Davis was producing material giving direction on drafting written argument to the New York Bar.[2] From then on American attorneys were given the benefit of regular advice on how to argue effectively in writing and how to write persuasively, a tradition which remains vital,[3] and which should be of practical help to us all.

Persuasive writing by lawyers is founded on the use of good and effective English. A body of literature has developed in this area as well, with two American practitioners being particularly prominent. Bryan A. Garner, who is to this generation of lawyers what Weiner was to his, has written *The Winning Brief: 100 Tips for Persuasive Briefing in Trial and Appellate*

---

[1] Reprinted in 2001 by Lawbook Exchange, N.Jersey.

[2] See *The Argument of an Appeal* (address to Association of the Bar of the City of New York 22.10.1940) 26 ABAJ 895.

[3] See *Appellate Advocacy: Some Reflections from the Bench* (1993) 61 Ford L. Rev 829; *Writing to the Ear* James W. McElhaney Dec 1995 *ABAJ* 71; *Effective Appellate Advocacy* Hon. Paul R. Michel *Litigation* Summer 1998 19; *Winning on Appeal: Better Briefs and Oral Argument* Judge Ruggero J. Aldisert (1999); *Effective Appellate Brief Writing* Hon. Clyde H. Hamilton (1999) 50 SCL Review 581; *Appeals: The Classic Guide* William Pannill *Litigation* (Winter 1999) vol 25. no 2 p6; *The Art of Appellate Brief Writing* Brian L. Porto 2003 29 Vermont Bar Journal and Law Digest 30.

Courts[4] and *Legal Writing in Plain English: A Text With Exercises*[5] and Richard C. Wydick *Plain English For Lawyers.*[6] Although these texts are for American consumption, they travel across the Atlantic reasonably well and should be read by anyone who is serious about wishing to develop their skills in written argument.

As I noted in the introduction to this book, even after a decade of being a requirement in all civil actions, in terms of development and sophistication, written advocacy in England and Wales remains in its infancy. Only in recent years have the judicial proponents of good written argument been offering advice to practitioners. Among the forefront of these are Mr Justice Lightman,[7] Mr Justice James Hunt,[8] and Lord Justice Mummery.[9] Toby Hooper QC and Michel Kallipetis QC who organise respectively the Inner Temple and Gray's Inn advocacy training schemes ensure that modules are available for training in writing skeleton argument; and the Bar vocational courses now provide for some, albeit cursory, introduction to the subject. The Council of the Inns of Court's Advocacy Training Council now regulates training in advocacy.

Distilling the experience of sixty years of American brief writing, and fusing it with judicial commentary from our own jurisdiction, let us consider how to develop a style of written advocacy, what literary techniques are available for the advocate to use, how to write persuasively, how to apply the lost art of précis, and what tasks you have to remember before lodging your finished document.

---

[4]   2nd edn. OUP 2004.
[5]   Chicago 2001.
[6]   4th edn 1998.
[7]   See 'Advocacy – A Dying Art?' Lecture to the Chancery Bar Association Conference, January 2004.
[8]   The Anatomy Lesson *Counsel Magazine* Feb 2002 18.
[9]   Lecture to the Gray's Inn Advocacy Training Course for pupils 2004.

CHAPTER 4
CREATING A STYLE FOR WRITTEN ADVOCACY

Let us start with the premise that, if nothing else, Judges read skeleton arguments in advance of the hearing. It is worth ensuring at the commencement that they have done so, on pain of a short adjournment. In tribunals with more than one Judge, the members of the court will confer with each other not solely after argument but also having at least made a cursory examination of the skeleton submissions beforehand. So, just as you would consider with care how to approach your audience – the hearer of your oral argument – so should you approach your reader. Your Judge is intelligent and eager to get on with his job but knows nothing about your case or what you want the court to do. If you focus on telling him swiftly and precisely what he needs to know, in the order he needs to know it, pre-empting and anticipating questions where possible, you will assist both him and your client, and in the process you will develop a personal style of written advocacy.

ORGANISING YOUR THOUGHTS

The impression received by the Judge is of the utmost importance, and not merely the first reaction to the appearance of the document he is encouraged to read. The impression derived from a skeleton argument carries over into examination of the statements of case and trial documents. If you can arouse the interest of the Judge and create a good impression at the outset of the hearing, that is something which is not easy for your opponent to dispel. Conversely, a poor impression can lead to a case being lost which should be won; or at the very least you will give yourself an unnecessarily hard time.

Without considerable planning you cannot hope to develop a successful technique that you can then replicate whenever you need it. You must learn to write with clarity, precision, confidence, forthrightness and lack of verbosity. This is the key to the rapid communication of ideas. But if you don't organise your thoughts before writing you are being inefficient with and wasteful of your time, and your document will ramble. A lack of organisation will give the impression that your writing has been dictated off the cuff and makes your argument difficult to follow, frequently repetitious, often internally inconsistent, and always unpersuasive.[1]

Begin planning by considering the live issues - how many and what they are - and completing your basic research. Weiner suggested[2] things that most lawyers already do: "concentrate on your problem, turn it over in your mind, think about it in the bath or shower, try out your hypotheses on your associates, live with the case in every spare waking moment - but don't start to write until the sequence and direction of your points have fallen clearly into place in your mind." And before doing so ask yourself, 'do I understand this? Can I explain it to my reader?' Don't begin to write until you are satisfied the answer to both is 'yes'.

There are two principal techniques for preparing a working draft, the first of which lends itself to the lawyer who has a fixed idea of where he wants to take the court, and how he is going to get it there. This is to write a draft argument straight through without stopping to edit, using a form and language as near as possible to the way it would be expressed in speech. Revise it afterwards, in whatever detail is necessary, but only after letting it settle, or breath for a while.

The second technique is for the more meticulous practitioner, the more conservative, the more pedestrian if you like, and I suspect it suits most of us better. This is for the note sifter, and follows this pattern of activity: make accurate notes prior to writing; set out every good point to be made; sift through, disgarding some ideas.

What's left is the heart of your argument: sort out the order; prepare it as an outline and develop the argument from the outline.

THE PRACTICAL PROCESS

Write or type out your skeleton yourself. Do not dictate. That only produces wordy writing, and worse, the formal legal vernacular which can be so oblique in its meaning. If you cannot resist the temptation to dictate, because it is your standard working practice, at least never dictate an argument or any other kind of argumentative writing. As a process it undermines logical thought and the progression of ideas.

SUGGESTIONS FOR WRITING

Catch and seize the court's interest in the opening three paragraphs of your skeleton. The easiest way to do so is to provide a statement of purpose, one

---

[1] See *Weiner* op. cit. at 136-137 (Note, all references are to the 2001 reprint edition).
[2] *Ibid.*

that controls the form, content, style and length of the rest of the document and gives by way of introduction a brief overview of your position. Within the space of a few lines tell the Judge what the hearing is for; who you represent; what you want; something of the parties; the subject matter of the case; the pertinent facts; as briefly as possible the recent procedural history, and if necessary describe previous argument accurately. If you state the nature of the case and outline its prior history it brings what is to follow into immediate focus for the Judge. Carefully drafted headings and subheadings provide a good road map of the argument and in most cases make a summary unnecessary.

These suggestions work:

• Deal with the facts before you write the argument

You should never forget the primacy of the facts – *ex facto jus oritur* – or that legal argument flows from the facts, and not *vice versa*. An analysis of the facts will receive and deserve primary attention because that is how the Judge, more often than not, arrives at his decision on the merits of the case. Therefore, once you have compiled a summary of the facts it is easier to structure legal argument, and new arguments may suggest themselves.

• State the facts chronologically

Do not analyse facts on a witness-by-witness basis.

• Use relative time to add interest to the reader

In a narrative of chronological events, you can use time relatively but only after starting with a date (e.g. "On 12 April 2003 Mr Smith hired a car; he returned it two days later.") This enables you to avoid having a string of dates outside a formal chronology.

• Write your argument consecutively

It is easier to write, read and, importantly, persuade if there is a natural progression to your argument. It does not matter whether you are following chronological steps, the elements of a cause of action, or a logical sequence. The pattern of development must be easy to follow. For the basic argument start with the opening point and follow through to the conclusion. Embellishment can come later. If you are able to do this you will avoid the strong temptation to deal with the easy points first and then tackle the difficult ones once your writing flows. To do this makes both the substance and form look lopsided.

- Make the most of your affirmative case

Write in such a way as to accentuate the affirmative features of your own case. In sequential skeletons do not content yourself with a point-by-point reply to the other side, even if that is necessary, because to do so is to let the other side both put you on the defensive and shape your own document. Even if you must reply to all of them, do not follow the other side's outline of points. Put your own strongest point first. Never let the other side write or even shape your skeleton.

- Write the summary last

If you are going to provide a summary of your argument, whether as a concluding or introductory paragraph, compose it only after all else is finished. You will thereby distil the virtue of what has been written, and not create some new tangent. It is difficult to summarise an argument that is incomplete and not fully understood and it may be dangerous to do so. Certainly you should never address in the summary subjects the argument does not address.

THE WEINER ESSENTIALS

In 1961 Col. Weiner suggested[3] there were nine really essential features necessary for effective written advocacy in U.S. federal court appeals. These can be viewed both generically and applied regardless of jurisdiction. I have modified them for our purposes and put them in the form of those questions you should ask yourself of your draft written submissions:

1. *Have I complied with the relevant rules of Court?*
   You must be familiar with the current rules and practice directions. Obsolescence is dangerous. Check the relevant specialist court guide,[4] on line if possible, with regard to the layout and presentation, contents and length of what you are about to provide to the Court. Discover whether the inclusion of irrelevant or immaterial matter might actually offend the rule or direction and cause the document to be rejected. Remember that all rules are subject to change and to interpretation. If you are not a specialist in the particular area check with a colleague more familiar with the practice of that court. This goes back to the same adage, know your audience – the Master or Judge whom you are trying to persuade. Be aware of the jurisdiction and powers of the tribunal before which you are appearing.

---

[3] *Op cit.* pp.37-127.
[4] See chapter 1.

2. *Have I provided an effective summary of the facts?*
Judges are sensitive to the facts because they want to do substantive justice between the parties. The Court is concerned with the merits of a case at every level of jurisdiction, not merely at trial. You must therefore bring the facts to the Judge's attention in such a way as to shape his decision. Write your summary in such a way that the Court will want to find in your favour before it even gets started on the legal argument.

3. *Do I use good, clear, forceful English?*
Write your skeleton in such a way as you yourself would want to read it. Provide a clear, consecutive understandable picture of what the case is really about.

4. *Do my headings assist the Court?*
Orient the reader from the outset. Tell him where you are going. If you provide signposts for the Judge you relieve him of the need to engage in either physical or mental work. This can be in the form of headings, or within argument, argumentative propositions e.g. this appeal is without merit for the following three reasons...

5. *Have I presented the questions for the Court in an appealing way?*
Do not present the Judge with a problem unless there is a solution to go with it. Provide a question that will make the Judge think the answer, which favours your case, is self-evident.

6. *Is my legal analysis of the problem sound?*
Try to make the solution appear straightforward – the answer to the question posed by you together with what you want the court to do

7. *Is my presentation of the evidence in arguing the facts convincing?*
Properly written your analysis of the facts should be a complete story of vital events and, where relevant, the procedural history of your case. As you compile this you should identify to yourself the evidence available to prove all of those facts that you require in order for your argument to succeed. If you can do this you will be ready to cross-refer your argument to the evidence as you come to write it.

8. *Have I paid careful attention to all parts?*
It is essential to cover all live issues in adequate detail. If they are no longer live, an explanation of this must be given consistent with protecting your client's position on costs.

9. *Have I allayed the reader's doubts and satisfied his curiosity?*
Does the document do the job? If there are obvious deficiencies be candid. But above all 'be clear, concise, honest, balanced, buttressed, convincing and interesting'[5] Associate Justice Minton of the United States Supreme Court said,[6] 'Be concise, while at the same time elaborate in written form all the propositions laid out in your pleading.' If

---

[5]   Wiley B. Rutledge The Appellate Brief (1942) in *Advocacy and the King's English*.
[6]   Foreword 1961 edn. Weiner.

you can do this let the bench call upon your opponent with the awkward questions.

AND SOME NEGATIVE SUGGESTIONS:

- Never distort either the fact or the law: the discovery of this by the judge or the other side will be extremely painful.
- Avoid hyperbole – overstatement leads to misrepresentation.
- Avoid personality attacks; the Court will discern how bad your opponent is without you having to say so.
- Avoid slang. Advocates are expected to have an adequate vocabulary without recourse to this.
- Avoid sarcasm. It demeans your profession.
- Do not repeat the adage for oral presentation – say what you're going to say, say it, then say what you've said – show some recognition of the Court's intelligence.
- Do not forget the Court's valuable time: don't waste it.
- Never be shy about seeking the criticism of a colleague.

In Part 3 we look at the techniques of some of today's most successful advocates. However you do not need to follow models slavishly. Use other people's work intelligently and eclectically and so develop what works for you.

CHAPTER 5
LITERARY TECHNIQUES FOR THE ADVOCATE

ENGLISH USAGE

Legal writing is stuffy, pompous, wordy, artificial, often ungrammatical, jargon-filled, and pretentious.[1] And bad writing makes the reader's job harder. So, since you are trying to get the Judge to accept your client's case, why make your task more difficult by failing to use plain language? Avoid any word that does not command instant understanding - you need to let the reader see your ideas without struggling to grasp your meaning. Sentences should be constructed so the reader may read with understanding effort-lessly. You are aiming to persuade the Judge with good, lucid, forceful English that is grammatical, clearly written and reads naturally.

The writers to whom I have referred agree that the use of language is em-bedded in the way we perceive the world and that it is impossible for the lawyer or judge to focus exclusively on the merits of a case without being affected by the language used to express those merits. It follows that it is not enough to have a strong case. You must be able to convey that to the Judge.

Poor English is not tolerated by Judges, and when written down becomes an unnecessary distraction on the page. Advocates should know how to use English properly.

The creation of written submissions is as much a process of creative writing as any work of non-fiction. The purpose, however, is to persuade and not merely to inform or entertain. The best way to do so in literary form is to make your points as simply as possible. Master your thoughts so you can communicate them clearly. Simple arguments are winning arguments. Con-voluted arguments will not persuade.[2]

---

[1] *Legal Writing in Plain English: A Text With Exercises* Bryan A. Garner (Chicago 2001) Pt 1.
[2] *The Winning Brief: 100 Tips for Persuasive Briefing in Trial and Appellate Courts* Bryan A. Garner (2nd edn. OUP 2004) Ch.15.

Therefore:

- Use the active voice wherever possible to keep writing vivid: the passive voice leads to additional words and unnatural inflexion. We do not speak in the passive voice without seeming pompous and indirect – passivity fails to say who has done what and subverts the normal word order of English, making it harder for the reader to process and digest information. It should be used only sparingly, for example when the focus is the thing being acted upon and not the doer; when you wish to hide the doer; to avoid sexist language; or to generalise without using 'one' as the subject.

- Use short sentences, averaging no more than 20 words, with occasional variations up to 25 words. It is very effective, as any reader of Lord Denning's judgments will discover.[3] Reduce sentence lengths by stripping out the unnecessary and the verbose. This gives momentum to the material. It makes things seem simpler for the reader. It makes the argument appear more focussed, more confident and sharper. If you are not disciplined in this try the process mechanically – write and count – until it comes naturally.

- Break up the text with headings. Subject to the overall effect on the length of the document, show the Judge often where you are going. Let him know what's coming next. Surprise him only with your efficiency, clarity, the extent of your knowledge, and the assurance shown in your problem solving.

- Use non-lawyerly language where possible: this demonstrates confidence in the simplicity of your argument. It follows the philosophy (unknown to most lawyers) that less is more and small is beautiful: small words; economical sentences; short documents; the exception being only the conclusion, where lawyers' custom is to write less than they should.[4]

- Use short paragraphs, on average less than 100 words or five sentences. If you vary the length while keeping them short you will have two or more paragraphs on the page. Visual variety is appealing to the reader. If you can begin each paragraph with an express or implied reference to the previous one you build a 'word bridge' to ensure that the narrative flows easily from one paragraph to the next.

- Do not 'argue by adverb':[5] 'clearly', 'obviously', 'undeniably', 'patently', 'undoubtedly' or use them in a different form e.g. 'it is plain that.' Let the Judge formulate his own view based on substantive argument and reference to the evidence.

---

[3] See for example *Hinz v Berry* [1970] 2 QB 40 @ 42; *Lloyds Bank Plc v Bundy*[1975] QB 326 @ 334.
[4] Pannill. *op.cit.*
[5] Garner *The Winning Brief op.cit.* Ch.79.

- De-clutter the text by moving citations into footnotes. Write in such a way that the reader will never have to look mid-sentence at what authorities you are relying upon.[6] He can focus on what you are saying, and then look for support for your propositions as a matter of choice after he has considered the argument.
- Use questions. They tend to arouse the curiosity of the Judge and therefore command his attention more than, say, an incomplete sentence used as a heading.
- End sentences with an assertion. To write forcefully do not end a sentence with a name, a date, citation or a qualifying phrase.

Since you are writing creatively it wouldn't go amiss to adopt the advice of professional writers. For example, George Orwell promoted five basic rules for the use of language in his essay writing:[7]

1. Never use a metaphor, simile or other figure of speech which you are used to seeing in print.
2. Never use a long word where a short one will do.
3. If it is possible to cut out a word, always cut it out.
4. Never use the passive voice where you can use the active. It makes the writing easier to read and feel more vivid and lively.
5. Never use a foreign phrase, a scientific word, or a jargon word where there is an everyday English equivalent. Translate them into everyday English words or leave them out.

And if you want to develop a literary style that uses English at its best, even when idiomatic, study Francis Bacon, Winston Churchill and Ernest Hemingway or writers known to you for good English usage. For excellence in judicial writing look at the speeches of Lord Devlin in *McCutcheon v David McBrayne Ltd.*,[8] Lord Wilberforce in *Anns v Merton L.B.C.*[9] and in *Ansiminic v Foreign Compensation Commission*,[10] Lord Lloyd of Berwick in *Marc Rich & Co v Bishop Rock Ltd*[11] (dissenting), and compare the speech of Lord Goff in the House of Lords in *White v Jones*[12] with the judgment of Sir Donald Nicholls V-C in the Court of Appeal.[13]

Good legal writing, as exemplified here, actually reduces the number of legalisms. Such Judges simplify jargon without affecting its meaning and it does not take many words to do so. They use verbs that are strong and

---

6   *Ibid.* Ch.22.
7   *Politics and the English Language* George Orwell 4 Collected Essays, Journalism, Letters of George Orwell (New York 1968).
8   [1964] 1 WLR 125@132.
9   [1978] AC 728 @ 749.
10   [1969] 2 AC 147 @ 206.
11   [1996] AC 211 @ 218.
12   [1995] 2 AC 207 @ 252.
13   [1995] 2 AC 207 @ 216.

precise. They avoid double and multiple negatives, unnecessary Latin, legal formalisms (such as 'the said' 'hereinbefore' 'thereinafter'), and keep facts straightforward, unembellished and minimise the use of adjectives and adverbs.

Through vast experience in writing the Judges point the way with certain other literary tips which they have recognised when honing careful reserved judgments: they tend to avoid tiresome repetitions including a party's status and name, authorities which have to be cited extensively and references to Judges and jurisdiction. They are careful with acronyms. They use shorthand terms that assist understanding. Often they refer to people and companies by name rather than status to aid clarity and avoid confusion in a multi-party or secondary level matter. They avoid clichés, slang and contemporary idiom, which may pass out of everyday speech more quickly than we would imagine.

You can improve the clarity of your own writing with some basic guidance in English usage, and you may find much assistance in standard books on the subject.[14] From among many rules of style the following are particularly useful:

- Don't use *however* to start a sentence, use *but* instead. It quickens the prose and strengthens contrast.
- Change *'pursuant to'* to *'under'* or *'according to'*.
- Remove ambiguity in sentence structure by ensuring the words *'that'* or *'which'* immediately follow the noun they refer to. Use *'that'* to identify the object about which you are speaking. The word *'which'* provides further information about the object.
- Restrict the use of *'such' 'said'* and *'same'* as pronouns or as demonstrative adjectives.
- Use dashes to highlight interruptive phrases – not parentheses - as they are far more useful for rhythm and emphasis.
- Avoid gratuitous quotation marks and typographical oddities.
- Don't irritate the judge with the incorrect use of apostrophes.
- The lead sentence of any block of writing is immensely important. Begin each paragraph with a topic sentence (but do not repeat the title, heading or subheading). This lets the reader know the focus of the paragraph. Do not end the preceding paragraph with what should be the first sentence of the next paragraph

---

[14] See e.g. Garner *op.cit.*; *The Chicago Manual of Style* (Chicago 1982); *The Economist Pocket Style Book* 1986.

A LITERARY STYLE FOR LAWYERS

Having mastered a basic approach which suits your use of language, look for opportunities to grab the court's interest by using an engaging turn of phrase or unusual word to make a point, perhaps from outside the law but one that is not clichéic or slang.[15]

It is important to remember that argumentative writing is not too concerned with beautiful English and does not have to be overly lyrical or discursive. Passages of argument should be forceful since advocates are not and should not be impartial. Look in particular at dissenting judgments as a source of good and forceful legal writing. Here the Judge is justifying his opinion to his brethren who disagree, and as a minority he is doing so knowing he will not influence the immediate result. He hopes that his view may be accepted on appeal, or by specialist practitioners in the area under consideration, or at some point in the future, and his writing has to be all the better to give force to his argument. In doing so he must reign in any emotion both about the case, and about being put in the minority and therefore seeing the wrong side win. Emotive language is unnecessary. The facts and law should speak for themselves.

Davis recommended[16] that a safe stylistic structure is "chronology, candour and clarity". Chronology, because that is the natural way in which to tell a story; candour – telling the worst as well as the best, because the court has a right to hear it and any lack of candour, whether real or apparent, will destroy the most carefully laid argument. And clarity, because the heart of advocacy is persuasion, which cannot be accomplished without clear thought and argument. So make one point at a time. Edit systematically. Cut out and replace words as necessary. Polish the language. Check for misused words. And cut down sentence lengths wherever possible.

DOCUMENT DESIGN

It is apparent from the comments of Judges and practitioners in chapters 2 and 9 that you must use a legible typeface and ample white space. But you can modify the text to make it more visually attractive. For example,

- highlight ideas with attention-getters such as indented bullets, which are particular useful for presenting important ideas in lists.

Use charts, diagrams and visual aids when you can. Graphics break up text, add interest, and can be used to present information that is difficult or

---

[15] Pannill. *op.cit.*
[16] Davis *The Argument of an Appeal op.cit.*

lengthy to describe in words. Use a table of contents for longer documents. This can itself be a persuasive document (see p. 51).

In terms of visual effect, where you are using white space put more above a heading than below it. According to research by Garner[17] white space above a heading informs readers to expect a change of subject; below suggests that the next writing functions as a unit.

HEADINGS

For the design of a descending sequence of headings, the various manuals of style suggest: Roman boldface large; boldface; boldface italic; italic. These may be underlined as you consider appropriate. Headings should not be divided into two sentences. This weakens their assertiveness when introducing passages of argument. You should ensure that they are both consistent and will not generate judicial disbelief or resistance on a first reading.[18]

CROSS-REFERENCES

Your page design must accommodate cross-references to pagination in exhibits, the appropriate bundles and other documentary evidence. It is imperative for you to support all assertions of fact by reference to their appearance in the evidence. In appellate skeletons particular reference will be made to the judgment and findings of fact of the Judge below. When arguing law in an appeal, it is effective and convenient to state "for the purposes of this appeal we accept the facts found by the trial judge at ..."

FOOTNOTES

Do not use footnotes in skeletons merely as a show of erudition. Use them for citation references and qualifications to statements or secondary points that would otherwise interrupt thought if they remained in the text. Minimise the interruptions to the Judge's progress through your submissions. Let him concentrate on the primary information. Never use them for substantive argument, e.g. parallel lines of argument – to do so detracts appreciably from force of your contentions.[19] If a point is important it belongs in the text; if not, it does not belong in the skeleton.[20]

---

[17] Garner *The Winning Brief op.cit.* Ch.65.
[18] Weiner *op.cit.* p.71.
[19] *Ibid.* p.245.
[20] *Ibid.* p.246.

TEXTUAL ENHANCEMENT

Try not to insult to the judicial reader's intelligence. To that end only use italics sparingly and preferably to cite names of authorities and for headings. It is perfectly possible to write a forceful skeleton without using a single word italicised for emphasis. Do not use capitals for emphasis. Resist the temptation to use bold in the text.

CITATION

Put all citations in footnotes. Otherwise you hamper the coherency of your substantive argument and break the narrative flow. Taking citations out of the text increases readability and understanding dramatically. As it is, citations should be unobtrusive and used sparingly. Unless absolutely necessary you should refer only to leading and recent cases. Remember, when quoting passages of *dicta*, absolute and unswerving accuracy must be the goal. Inaccuracies of substance are particularly unforgivable and always dangerous. A court particularly dislikes a citation to fact A when all that citation establishes is fact B from which you proceed to draw an inference that fact A exists.[21] This must stem from a linguistic as much as a legal error.

---

[21] ibid. p.222

CHAPTER 6
THE TECHNIQUE OF PERSUASION IN WRITING

ORGANISATION

The mechanics of presenting your client's case in the most effective and cogent manner should be little different whether your argument is oral or written, but the written argument provides you with a significant benefit. The distinction to the recipient is that the *listener* hears, notes what he wants from the presentation, listens to something else and then returns later to consider what impression you made; the *reader* has something complete in tangible form to keep and scrutinise at length. If your work passes muster with the Judge, and impresses him by the persuasiveness of your argument, he will carry it away as a reader to make use of, to your client's advantage. If it does not, he will discard it, and you will have failed your client.

In theory the task of writing persuasively should be straight forward: identify the points you wish to convey; state them cogently with adequate reasoning and support, and offer a workable solution to the Judge which enables him to do substantive justice. The reality is that many lawyers fail through lack of organisation. There is an inadequate architectural structure to their writing. Lawyers act too quickly and think too little.[1] Writing involves thinking too, and revising, cutting back and simplifying the argument to perfect its flow.

You will have observed in chapter 5 not to commence writing your argument until you have carried out a sound analysis of the legal problem, researched your authorities, and you fully understand what you are to write about. Then try the following method:

- Start with a working statement of the issues.

- Draft these before writing anything else in order to keep your attention focussed.

- Break down each legal problem into its component parts.

---

[1] Garner *The Winning Brief op.cit.*Ch.2.

- Determine which are principal and which subsidiary issues.
- Decide in what order to present the points, and how many you wish to advance without overwhelming the reader.

You may consider there should be one principal point of attack or defence only, together with two or three material subordinate points.

Remember that an argument is written to persuade. It should pull no punches, but it must be honest, and it must be accurate.[2]

Ensure that all matters required by the respective jurisdictional rules are there, whether the Civil Procedure Rules, Blue Book or particular tribunal practice notes or directions. Compliance with basic requirements is an imperative.

USING THE FACTS TO PERSUADE

The facts are always the most important part of the skeleton. I shall say that again. *The facts are always the most important part of the skeleton.* If you can explain the facts clearly and completely, you will take a giant step towards persuading the court since generally there is no trouble over the law, not only because the law flows from the facts but so also does the equity of the case. If the equity of the case is with you, even if it takes a trip to the House of Lords, you should win.

Tell a complete story arranging the facts in a logical, usually chronological order. Recite the facts fairly. Never misstate them. Highlight what is crucial. Let them be sufficient to enable the court to receive your narrative without having to supplement it by its own independent efforts,[3] but not in stultifying detail. Marshal the topics according to the development of the argument, dealing with evidence relating to each logical progression. Make sure the Judge's interest does not flag and is carried forward in the direction you wish to take him.

Writing out the facts forces you to understand and organise the evidence in your own mind in a way that reading alone will not. It enables you to see logical connections, and to focus on using the facts alone to persuade without argument.[4]

Do not argue or editorialise, since it is better always to be straightforward. You want the court to feel it is getting the facts, not your opinion, comments or contentions. Indicate conflict where it exists. Strive to make the most

---

[2] Weiner *op.cit.* 274.
[3] *Ibid.* 45.
[4] *Ibid.* 44.

favourable impression with the facts without actually arguing, by being honest, candid and accurate. And try to progress in a way that makes your conclusion irresistible – you want to analyse the facts so that they alone will make the court want to decide in your favour.[5]

CHOOSING THE BATTLE GROUND

Justice Frankfurter of the United States Supreme Court said 'In law the right answer usually depends on putting the right question.'[6] This is as true of our own courts and in particular the Court of Appeal. The phrasing of the question or issue to be decided is therefore of the utmost importance. If you can pose the question in a way which most effectively impels the reader to answer it as you want, you are choosing the battleground on which your litigation or application will be contested, with all the advantages of that choice.

Most courts expect the question or issue for decision to be formulated in a neutral way and agreed by the parties, invariably following a case management direction to that effect. Within such constraints you must select your own battleground wherever possible – do not permit opposing counsel to choose it for you. Never accept issues as framed by the other side. Wherever possible you should always re-work them to favour yourself. The aim is to frame issues as questions, to which the only reasonable response is, 'yes, of course'.[7] If you can do so, apply the technique of constructing the question or issue from salient facts or relevant citations which, *while fairly stated*, is strongly suggestive of an answer in your client's favour. The facts must be fairly stated – your opponent can have no objection to their inclusion as facts – and accurate, or this approach will backfire and prejudice you in the eyes of the court.

Not all situations are suitable for formulating the question presented by loading it with facts favourable to you. In particular where the factual merits are not with you it is not desirable to remind the court of this at the outset of the hearing. But *even where the merits are not with you* it should be possible for you to construct your case in the form of a question, usually using the word *'whether'*, in a way that is clearly and appealingly stated.

The position is even better defined on appeal. When seeking permission for an appellant to bring an appeal you must dress up questions invitingly in order to ensure the higher court will want to take the case. If acting for a respondent you want to preserve the *status quo ante* by adopting any premise in your client's favour found by the judge – you must minimise the effect of questions raised by your adversary and make them appear unimportant or

---

[5] Pannill *op.cit.*

[6] *Estate of Rogers v. Comm'r* (1943) 320 US 410 @ 413.

[7] Ursula Bentele & Eve Cary *Appellate Advocacy: Principles and Practice* 3rd edn 1998 333.

uninteresting to anyone other than parties involved or as turning on mere questions of fact.[8] Do so without belittling your opponent, and if the question is obviously of importance do not urge that it is unimportant: rather say the decision does not require further review.[9]

CONVEYING THE ISSUES

Since the court does not have luxury of time for detached contemplation never force the court to guess, even for a moment, the issues it will have to decide. They should be stated so simply and so clearly that the Judge will grasp them at once. Give a sense of introduction to generate interest - do not miss the opportunity of capturing the Judge's interest at the outset. It is part of your task to make a favourable first impression that will last.

To frame a good persuasive issue:

- Put it up front.

- Break it into separate sentences using a format based on asserting a fact, stating a premise that flows from the fact, then raising the legal issue to be decided by the court.

- Weave in enough facts so that the reader can truly understand the problem, but summarise – don't over particularise.

- Present each issue in a way that suggests that there is only one possible answer: the one you want.

- Phrase the issues in separate sentences.

- Use a maximum sentence length of no more than 15 – 20 words.

- Do not start with 'Whether'[10] or any other interrogative word ('why', 'where', 'how', or 'what'.

- Wherever possible use 'Can', 'Is', 'Should', 'Must', and 'Was' since these tend to push the reader towards the desired answer.

- Limit the total of the issues to a maximum of about 75 words, or five sentences. If you cannot do so you do not have a sufficient understanding to be able to convey the issues clearly to the reader.

The consistent theme of these suggestions is that issues raised before the court should not be merely informative, they should be influential too. You are writing them fairly but persuasively. The way issues are written will govern the court's first impression of the merits. Put each matter simply, concisely and accurately, without overstatement or being strident.[11]

---

[8] Weiner *op.cit.*80.
[9] *Ibid.*
[10] See Garner *Legal Writing in Plain English* op. cit. 58. *Quaere* unless you know the factual merits are not with you: contrast with p. 47.
[11] Garner *The Winning Brief op.cit.* Ch. 11.

If you provide the question, the Judge will not have to; if you don't, the Judge may formulate a question you do not want. It is therefore vital to give the Judge the issue, to pose the question he must answer, and to pose the answer. Your skeleton will thus provide him with the justification for finding in your favour.

ADVANCING YOUR ARGUMENT

So we come to the nub of the matter – constructing your winning argument on paper. There seem to be two typical approaches, which I will call the logical development and the early knockout blow. Either way your goal is to write an argument your opponent cannot answer. For both if anything, err on the side of understatement. This forces you to build up your case by citing successive references to the evidence.

Whether logical development or knockout blow, find the strongest point in your case and lead with it. Be brief and to the point. Demonstrate fairness, justice, practicality and principle, but grab your opponent by the throat with the very first sentence of your argument and say something positive. Where you can, seize upon the central feature of the case and drive it home, shutting out anything for your adversary.

If you are creating an argument based on logical progression elaborate the legal premises and show how the facts fit. Imagine you are creating a flow chart. You proceed in a logical step-by-step progression where you must prevail on every point in order to win. If you come to a juncture in the argument where alternatives present themselves, place the most appealing one first, i.e. that which will meet the least judicial resistance to accepting the fact or the premise or the legal principle being advanced.

Where one alternative involves requesting the court to overturn an unfavourable recently considered decision and the other has a clear path not so obstructed, always argue the latter first due to the effect on the court on the former. Occasionally a situation will call for grasping the nettle firmly and dealing with a really difficult point at the outset. Do not go back and forth. Stick to one course.[12]

If there is no logical sequence to adopt, you require the knockout blow strategy. Advance first the point that goes to the very heart of the matter. Build your argument around the court doing substantive justice by accepting your submissions on that point. If you have sufficient evidence to support your proposition, your opponent will have nowhere to go.

---

[12] Weiner *op.cit.* 96.

- Always remember that you are performing an exercise in persuasion.
- Do not fight the court on unessential propositions, either general or specific.
- Do not make your argument a crusade – it will diminish its effectiveness
- Keep your emotions to yourself

USING ARGUMENTATIVE HEADINGS

This is a technique recommended by both Weiner[13] and Pannill[14] which is generally unfamiliar in this jurisdiction where Judges have indicated that generally they prefer neutral headings. It is this: in passages of argument the headings and sub-headings should not be merely topical or even assertive, but must be argumentative. For example an argument concerning limitation gives you these options:

Topical heading (the label):

'Limitation'

Assertive heading (the statement):

'The Claim Is Barred By Limitation'

Argumentative heading (incorporating the contention):

'The claim is time barred having been issued after six years from the date of accrual of the cause of action pleaded.'

The argumentative heading is more wordy but effective. It tells the Judge immediately and in a nutshell what your case is on the point. It goes straight to the heart of the issue. If used for each separate contentious matter, the court will see instantly the progression and substance of your argument. If you learn to use this technique with flair, you should be able to create memorable headings that are single sentence summaries of your case which will become fixed in the mind of the Judge. In that sense this is an opportunity that an advocate should not waste.

If you do adopt this style there are some basic rules to remember:

- Always set out your contentions affirmatively not negatively.
- The 'argumentative' element requires you to say *why* you make an assertion.

---

[13] Weiner *op.cit*. 67,68.
[14] Pannill *op.cit*.

- The heading must be sufficiently detailed and specific so your reader knows the precise substance and scope of your argument, but at the same time, succinct.
- Never follow a main heading immediately with a single sub-heading. If you are unable to follow the argument without more than one sub-heading the main heading has not been correctly formulated and needs re-writing.
- If you are using an argumentative heading, the sub-headings should be argumentative as well.

Weiner suggested[15] that the absence of full and detailed argumentative headings detracts materially from the effectiveness of a skeleton argument, albeit that the text of the argument must be complete without the need for the court to refer back to the heading or to read footnotes. There are two other advantages. First, by carefully reviewing your headings and sub-headings you will see the progression of your argument and can ensure completeness. This will also help strengthen any necessary revisions. Second, if you have a long document that warrants a list of contents, the court will glean the whole flow of the argument merely by looking at the contents page.

If you are uncomfortable with this idea and find it too alien, at least make the headings you use within your argument assertive. Avoid verbless headings e.g. 'Introduction', 'The Limitation Point', 'Damages' which are merely labels. Do not use blind sub-headings, i.e. those that give the reader no clue as to what the substance of the following argument will be. Do not use argumentative sub-headings when introducing the facts at the outset of the document. And do not repeat headings in the substantive text, particularly in the opening words of the next paragraph.

MARSHALLING FACTS IN ARGUMENT

All cases turn on their facts. However frequently they turn not on the facts *simpliciter*, but on how they are arranged, and therefore how the Judge views the factual matrix. Or, for your purpose, how the Judge is guided to that matrix. Do not just line them up repeating, as it were, the introduction to your skeleton. Use facts as part of the argument by stating what you intend to show in three steps:

1 make an assertion;
2 present the facts to support that assertion;
3 submit what conclusion is to be derived from your presentation.

---

[15] *Op.cit.* 69,70.

Marshal the evidence to make it thoroughly convincing to the judicial reader. Lay it out using quotations from documents stressing any inconsistencies in the case against you. Make sure the extracts you cite are accurate, being taken *verbatim* from the evidence. Highlight, in particular, any discrepancies or contradictions between your opponent's documents and his witness statements, or any damaging passages from contemporaneously made letters or notes. Whatever you can find, you must make the facts work for you. In an argument you will either rely upon such inferences as are to be drawn from undisputed facts or you will have to argue frankly a conclusion from disputed facts.[16]

ARGUMENT AND REASONING

The supporting reasons for the conclusion you are urging are the key to success.[17] Do not fall into the trap of merely repeating your own opinion on the matter using different words, since that will not be enough. You have to make the Judge agree with you, either by allowing him to form his own conclusions from the way the facts are presented[18] or by constructing some attractive reasoning that will connect with him. Merely asserting the rightness of your client's position is not a convincing argument: you have to establish in the Judge's mind why your position is correct and what the implications of a decision in your client's favour will be.

More often than not it will be easier to negate the value of your opponent's position. To that end your reasoning can be wide enough to focus on whether what you want the court to do is both fair according to the merits, and right under the circumstances and, where necessary, that it is good public policy.

SUPPORTING YOUR ARGUMENT

It is clear from what Judges want[19] that you should not crowd your argument with long quotations from the reports and offer multiple citations. It is better to cite a few leading and controlling decisions than assemble an encyclopaedic collection, although keeping them proportionate (I knew that wretched word would get in somewhere) to the case in hand.

A citation on all fours is likely to be weakened if accompanied by others only having a tangential bearing on the issue. You should go for the most recent decisions covering broad principle in the highest jurisdiction available, and avoid valueless authority i.e. cases that do not bind the court in question, or where the key question is evidential, or where the question is secondary or

---

[16] *Ibid.* 115
[17] Garner *The Winning Brief* op. cit. Ch.13.
[18] *Ibid.*
[19] See chapter 2.

essentially illustrative.[20] You should keep the support for your argument vital.

You may have a strong temptation to show off your learning with what writers have called ornamental citation.[21] Occasionally this bit of vanity may give your submission an appealing overtone of erudition that a court may respect, if it does not interfere with or detract from the main stream of argument. Every once in a while the search for an ornamental citation pays off and compensates for what may also be seen as a vulgarly ostentatious display of learning.

There is a fairly basic approach you can use to support your argument:

- Get the citation right i.e. the approved designated reference: do not irritate the judge with mistaken citation references or misspelt names of well-known cases.
- Use accepted typographical conventions i.e. do not use personal abbreviations.
- Know and follow the Practice Directions on the citation of authorities and the order of citation.[22]
- Say something critical about the cases you cite – how and why they apply. Put them in context.
- Never quote elementary propositions.
- Never quote sentences out of context, unless you want to gift ammunition to the other side.
- Quote only when the quotation adds something to the proposition being asserted. This does not preclude you from using the language of a Judge who has expressed something far better than you can.
- Use a quotation where:

    (i)   the statement for which you seek support is insufficient to satisfy the curiosity of the reader;
    (ii) you are relying on unfamiliar decisions – areas of the law untouched for some time;
    (iii) your materials are obscure and not readily accessible to the court;
    (iv) where the support for your point cannot fairly be summarised;
    (v)   where it is necessary to go back to fundamentals in a situation where later authorities have developed and altered the original proposition of law to be advanced;[23]

---

[20] Weiner *op.cit.* 206, 208-9.
[21] *Ibid.* 212
[22] *Practice Direction (Citation of Authorities)* [2001] 1 W.L.R. 1001.
[23] Weiner *op.cit.* 211.

(vi)   where there is a clear diversity of opinion, or where the court below has apparently disregarded settled law.

- When abbreviating your repeat citation references use *supras* and *infras* sparingly. Judges do not like to have to go back and forth to find references.[24] Repeat the reference at least to the name of the case.
- Never cite an overruled case.

Irrespective of their source, the accuracy of your quotations is imperative. You must check carefully against the original to prevent significant words or even whole lines dropping out or becoming distorted. This is particularly the case where lawyers use dictation to prepare. Errors in transcription can be a significant problem for the Judge, and the impact of a Judge discovering that he cannot rely upon you may be disastrous.

Persuasive argument is the product of careful research, of unearthing authority, of dealing with trends – especially at appellate level – and of identifying whether the Judge will extend an existing trend in a particular direction and, if so, by how much, and whether he is likely to want to do so. Confine your law to the vital statute, or the strongest cases at the highest level. Identify the essential passages – as few as possible – and then apply the law to the facts, point by point. Where there is no obvious authority use analysis, reason, logic, credible analogy, legislative history, social history and invite the court to consider what the practical solution should be.

Remember that citing authority is not an end in itself. It is only the means by which your argument gains legal weight. Therefore ensure that your legal argument contains appropriate references to the facts as agreed or in contention or on appeal to the facts as found, the evidence paginated according to the trial bundles, and where appropriate the procedural history of the claim or appeal.

THE VALUE OF CANDOUR

You must be candid with the Court to preserve its goodwill. Never intentionally misstate a position, either affirmatively or by omission. There is no such thing as a white lie. You must be fair, honest and accurate. This does not preclude you from using emphasis or nuance to advance facts in their most favourable light, as long as you don't exceed the limits of accuracy. Consider this - if you lose the trust of the Court on the facts it may not take the law from you: *falsus in uno, falsus in omnibus*.[25] The misstatement of facts by you will impeach your argument as much as a bad witness.

---

[24] *Ibid.* 222.
[25] Weiner *op.cit.* 49.

In spite of some of the survey results that I have referred to from experienced practitioners[26] the advice of Weiner,[27] Pannill[28] and Garner[29] is sound - grasp your nettles firmly: tell the Court about facts that hurt you, or your opponent will, and no matter how unfavourable they are, they will hurt you more if the Court finds out about the from your opponent or worse, by itself. Draw the sting and deal with all pertinent facts. Do not gloss over them but present them as best you can indicating how you will deal with them.

ARGUMENTS IN REPLY

You must deal with the counter-arguments and do so firmly, in keeping with the credo of dealing with your weaknesses and grasping nettles firmly. But do not reiterate them. The purpose of your argument is to persuade the court that your position is the correct one: restating the other side's contentions will not help you do that. There is also a real danger that you may re-state the other side's argument better than they have said it. If your opponent establishes that a point you have made is bad, concede it where it is possible to do so without fundamentally undermining your case.

If you are responding to an appeal always support the merits of the decision appealed against before dealing with any jurisdictional or legal argument. If an altogether new point is taken, reply to it directly. If the other side confuses an issue, make a short reply re-clarifying the situation. But if matters are accepted or issues are clear do not burden the court with more reading matter. To draw to the attention of the court a misstatement by the other side – not a minor error – it must be both material and significant since the Court dislikes point scoring. Do not give in to the impulse to get in the last word by putting in additional skeletons unless it is vital and you have the Court's permission to do so. You are justified only where you are meeting a request by the Court to deal with something missing.

Work out how to handle the authorities which are being used against you. Ignore precedent only when you can afford to, either because it is off the point or you can properly argue that the law, or indeed society, has moved on. Distinguish boldly, using broad grounds rather than finicky analysis.[30] Use dissenting opinion, particularly where it is expressed in strong terms. Avoid stirring up opposition on non-essential or collateral matters. Sometimes the answer is in a painstaking analysis of the controlling statute. Where that might be so, consider the setting and social context of the particular provision then check its legislative history and, where you have time, the parliamentary papers.

---

[26] See Chapter 3.
[27] *Op.cit.*104
[28] *Op.cit..*
[30] *Legal Writing in Plain English op.cit.* 85.
[30] Weiner *op.cit.* 152-3.

MATTERS TO AVOID

There are a number of common faults[31] that are bound to backfire in a costly way if you commit them. I have already touched on most of these but they are important enough to repeat for emphasis:

(1) Avoid inexcusable inaccuracy. Know your case, and know the facts.

(2) Don't exaggerate: if a lawyer exaggerates the facts he is simply asking for trouble

(3) Keep emotional content to yourself: it is unnecessary to involve the Court on an emotional level directly. Strong facts will speak for themselves, particularly if they are shocking. In particular, emotive language is frowned upon in appellate courts.

(4) Avoid involving the Court in collateral inquiries as to the personality or conduct of lawyers on the opposing side. This will generally embarrass a judge. If the issue is there the Court will identify and raise it.

(5) Do not waste time in emphasising elementary propositions. Allow the Judge some intelligence.

(6) Do not magnify trivia.

(7) Abandon wherever possible weak propositions or questions in which you have no faith. The ability to discern weak points and the willingness to discard them constitutes the mark of a really able lawyer.[32] It requires real courage and self-confidence as an advocate to dispense with weaker points, particularly where your client wants you to press everything, or where you hope the Court will not spot the weakness. Their inclusion only serves to weaken the rest of your argument: to include a weak point is virtually certain to dilute every strong one.

(8) Try not to evade difficult issues, either by not mentioning them at all or by relegating them to footnotes.[33] You cannot expect a central issue in a case to be glossed over. Do not ignore portions of opposing counsel's argument or his authorities on the basis that they are unfavourable to you. Deal with them. Grasp your nettles firmly.

(9) Don't use arguments that appear to be those of last resort. They send a signal to the Court that your case is hopeless.

(10) Avoid an out-and-out request to overrule an unhelpful precedent: ask for the case to be distinguished on one of many bases.[34] Courts are reluctant to say, in terms, that previous cases were wrongly decided, because continuity in the law or at least the appearance of continuity is important; Judges are much more inclined to distinguish in order to do practical justice. This is one of the few occasions in which it profits you for your advocacy to be oblique.

---

[31] Weiner *op.cit.* 61.
[32] *Ibid.* 96.
[33] *Ibid.* 104.
[34] See Andrew Goodman *How Judges Decide Cases: Reading, Writing ad Analysing Judgments* xpl 2005 p. 146-151.

(11) Do not attack or criticise previous counsel. It does you no credit, and is a matter for the Court to raise if it wants to.

USING A CONCLUSION

Write a conclusion that is powerful and assertive. You need to close in a strong way, rather than formulaically, with a weak phrase such as 'for the above reasons.' It is tempting to do so and close the piece of work, but it wastes an opportunity to say something memorable by way of a summary of your case. If the Court is pressed for time it may be one of first things the Judge reads; if you are unlucky it may be the only thing he has time to read. So don't be afraid to summarise and make it long enough to be effective. Use two or three sentences to remind the Judge of your reasoning, and why it should prevail. Make it as appealing as possible, going beyond a mere assertion, although it should be a synopsis and not say anything new. For that reason you should compose it last of all.

Make sure that you end your document by telling the court precisely what relief you seek so the Judge never has to ask. Be specific about it, so that the Court's order will be likewise.

CHAPTER 7
THE ART OF PRÉCIS
FOR LAWYERS

Under the rules of case management argument today seems to be hedged about by strict limitations on time. At every level of jurisdiction Judges feel the pressure of business and the desire for economy by advocates. The rapid pace of change in the law, and particularly procedural law, appears to limit what the judicial eye and ear is prepared to absorb. So there is a real need for the use of précis by lawyers – the method of preparing a salient summary of the points - at a time when that exercise in the use of written English is no longer taught in our schools.

The art of précis is not merely a method of shortening a piece of writing. It is a technique for improving clarity by condensing the amount of prose without losing its meaning.

You should plan to edit written submissions twice, once for substance and once for style. Good editing is very important. Sometimes you will find annoying errors even when reading through for a third time. If you are able to do so, leave some time between editing and your final read through. Come back to it with a fresh critical eye.

WHAT TO DO IF YOUR DOCUMENT IS TOO LONG

You should not shorten an essay by hacking out pieces in a way that destroys the meaning. Instead, see if you can improve the meaning by making the essay less verbose and more precise. This is entirely consistent with the message of chapter 6: try to replace clumsy or dull prose with shorter, snappier words to hold the reader's interest. Persuasive writing must grab the court's attention and hold it for the duration of the argument:

- Be precise
  Do you always know what you are saying, or are there places where you are just throwing words in? Replace vague passages that do not say anything important, and passages that ramble, with sentences that are to the point.

- Focus

  Try focusing your writing more on the title, headings or sub-headings of the document, and then check to see that the body of the text sticks to what you focused on and does not wander all over the place. Remove material that is not relevant to what you say you are doing.

- Understand what you write

  As a general rule, do not write anything you do not understand. If you fully understand what you are writing, you should be able to control it. This should include being able both to expand it and make it more concise. If you write what you do not understand, in the hope that that is the right thing to say, you will have lost control of your writing. Some arguments are difficult to follow because authorities have been relied upon with no true understanding of their meaning. Passages cited are often too long as well, as the writer does not know what to cut out. If this is what you do, remember - you need to think the problem through and plan before putting pen to paper.

- Use effective literary techniques

  Omit surplus words.[1] Use the active not passive voice. Avoid compound constructions. Remove common word wasters – 'the fact that', 'the question as to whether' 'there is' or 'there are', 'it is', 'there have been,' 'I might add,' 'it is interesting to note,' 'it is important to bear in mind,' 'it should not be forgotten' – and hackneyed and unnecessary phrases, such as 'at this point in time' (now), 'take action' (act), 'make an assumption' (assume). Use short words as well as short sentences: e.g. 'use' not 'utilise'. You want to end up with clear, crisp, economical writing.

    - Avoid lawyerisms – 'hereinafter' 'heretofore' 'on point' 'on all fours' 'may I respectfully suggest'.

    - Remove double negatives

    - If short, related sentences are kept to one main thought they may be combined.

    - Minimise the use of adjectives and adverbs. Use strong descriptive nouns and verbs.

    - Avoid long conjunctions: 'nevertheless' 'notwithstanding' 'furthermore' 'inasmuch as' 'howsoever' 'consequently'. Garner says[2] is it really necessary to have four syllables? They are old fashioned, stilted and pompous.

    - Simplify wordy prepositions:[3] 'with respect to,' 'as to,' 'in order to,' 'in connection with,' 'as regards to,' 'in respect of,' 'according as to whether.'

---

[1] "Unnecessary words waste space and the reader's time and they make strong writing weak" *The Elements of Technical Writing* 65 (1993) Gary Blake and Robert W. Bly.

[2] *The Winning Brief op.cit.* Ch.45.

[3] *Ibid.* Ch.46.

Using ways like this should improve the skeleton argument and shorten it at the same time.

THE PRÉCIS EXERCISE

Précising and paraphrasing are good practice for any lawyer, and any piece of writing can be reduced by this exercise. Lawyers in fact do use précis often, since they almost always create a summary of the facts of the case and an abstract of their client's position or argument.

In the traditional précis students reduce a passage of writing to a third or a quarter of its original length by taking these steps:

   (i)   Read through the whole passage to get an overall view;
  (ii)   Read it through again, underlining each point that needs to be included;
 (iii)   Write a summary of the passage with all the underlined points in the appropriate order, omitting all unnecessary matter;
  (iv)   Compare the summary with the original and add anything of importance that has been left out;
   (v)   Check the approximate length to see how close to the length aimed at has been achieved;
  (vi)   Re-read carefully to see if the summary flows smoothly and is grammatically correct.

CHAPTER 8
TASKS BEFORE LODGING

You have completed your document. You have printed it out. You have expended your effort. You are ready to send it off. But you have not finished.

CHECKING FOR ACCURACY

However mundane you feel the task to be, you must check meticulously all materials for accuracy and completeness:

- that the citation references are correct;
- that statutes have not been amended and provisions relied on are in force;
- that you have not misquoted *dicta* or legislation, or, for example, missed out a line;
- that you are not relying upon a case which was scrutinised on appeal, or was criticised or even overturned by a case in this morning's case alerter or *The Times*; and
- that references to exhibits and pagination in the trial, application or appeal bundle are correct.

A skeleton argument or written submissions in any form can not be proof read too often or too carefully, because nothing quite so destroys a court's confidence in a lawyer or in his argument as when it finds he has made inaccurate statements, either through carelessness or through design.[1] If at all possible find a willing (or not so willing) assistant, pupil or colleague to check citations, quotations and references for accuracy 'as your eye is likely to see what you intended, not what's on the page'.[2]

---

[1] Garner *The Winning Brief op.cit.* Ch.7.
[2] Weiner *op.cit.* at p.203.

FILING

Regard the Judge as a consumer. Offer him written submissions on a disc from which he can take parts of the key judgments or statutes you cite, and hopefully incorporate your submissions into his findings. Providing your document in electronic form is essential when producing closing submissions for a trial and for appeals where judgment is likely reserved. Remember, if the Court asks for electronic transmission of your skeleton it is for use, not for record keeping.

TAKING A STEP BACK

There are two exercises that may help your final overview of the document you have produced.

- First, read it out aloud. You will get a better sense of how you want readers to hear what you have to say.
- Second, read the argument without reference to the authorities, examples, or evidence to see whether your discussion is convincing by itself.

THE CLARITY TEST

Get others to help you assess the clarity of your argument. Try to explain it orally to a non-lawyer. If you cannot give an easy explanation, your writing will probably reflect that. Try this out on your partner or spouse - they are secure enough to offer honest critiques.

IMPRESS YOURSELF

The effective skeleton is one that puts you in a winning position before the Judge enters the court. It persuades the court to follow your analysis of the problem and rely on the authorities you have cited. It must be sufficient by itself to convince the Judge, so that if other side does not file one, you should win: you will have satisfied any doubt the tribunal may have and sated its appetite for asking questions.

So finally stand well back, metaphorically speaking, as you consider the overall impact of what you have created. Allow yourself to be impressed. If you feel not just happy with what you have produced, not merely that it will pass muster, but that you have fashioned a really good piece of work, so will the Judge.

There are a number of occasions when you are required to settle and file your written skeleton well in advance of the hearing. It is when you come to read it through again, not having seen it for some weeks or months, that there will be instances when you stop and think 'Wow! Did I write that!'

So try to impress yourself!

Often.

PART 3
WHAT SUCCESSFUL ADVOCATES PROVIDE: WORKED EXAMPLES

CHAPTER 9
INTRODUCTION

In order to establish what successful advocates provide I considered the views and work of six highly respected silks (QCs), and the equivalent number of juniors, some of whom worked with the same leaders. This was not a focus group, and those members of the Bar concerned were highly individualistic and strong willed. They knew what they wanted to do. The question of compliance, whether strict or otherwise, with the requirements of the CPR Practice Directions did not arise. However for our purposes, we should take it as read that successful advocates will not deliberately risk antagonising a Judge by failing to comply with recognised rules of practice. Even with considerable stylistic differences it became possible to connect their experiences, and to find some commonality of approach in preparing their written advocacy. Each was asked about methodology, style, format and content and, of course, what it is that makes a skeleton argument succeed.

I am extremely grateful to the following for having provided samples of their written advocacy and kindly granted me permission to select from among these worked examples: Edward Faulks QC (with Andrew Warnock, Charles Brown, Sarah Paneth and David Thomson), Simeon Maskrey QC, John Norman, David Pannick QC (with Dinah Rose), Michael Pooles QC, Spike Charlwood, Roger Stewart QC, and Jonathan Sumption QC (with Guy Philipps QC, David Anderson QC, and Jemima Stratford).

In some cases they were concerned to protect the identity of their lay clients, or specific witnesses and locations, and accordingly I have concealed such information. However in cases where this material has been used in open court and any appellate process has been exhausted, and where no objection is taken, I have used the material *verbatim*. I have provided a very brief introduction, which gives the outcome in each case and says where, if at all, it has been reported. I have indicated the total length of each document since in some examples I have used extracts only, but also to impress upon you how short a good skeleton may be.

The brief commentary I have added in annotated form is intended to highlight the points made earlier in the main text. The use of white space is also intended to enable you to add your own notes, which you should feel free to do, particularly where it is helpful for you to refer back to pages in Parts 1 and 2. At the conclusion of each example I include in bold type a concise 'good practice suggestion' which I hope will be something you either carry out already or may wish to. While there is no standard approach to preparing written submissions, these are matters which, if omitted, the Judge is likely to notice.

These are examples of what is essentially an art. They are not intended to be models or precedents, nor could they be. I wanted to show good advocacy in a reasonably wide range of different but effective personal styles of writing, which deal with both facts and law at different levels of tribunal. I have included examples of representation for different sides.

Please remember neither my interviewees nor I can offer a template. Why? Because skeleton arguments are significantly different depending on what they are being prepared for. That which is required for a case management conference with contested directions will not be the same as one supporting or opposing an application for summary judgment. Written submissions to open or close a trial will not be the same as those needed when the time comes to appeal the outcome of that trial. And in each of these the perspective from the viewpoint of the claimant or defendant is different. These differences in scope and approach are seen in the worked examples from actual cases.

VISUAL ADVOCACY AT TRIAL

One of the advantages of putting submissions into writing, even if skeletal, is the medium of communication itself. It may be that some of the points being advanced are better expressed when reduced to writing, matters which may be difficult to convey in the course of oral argument. Naturally the reverse is true. So, at an early stage of preparation, trial counsel may wish to consider whether the points available are more easily communicated in written or oral form.

At this juncture the Judge can be made to use his eyes as well as his ears to promote the better understanding of a case. For example, the use of visual aids - fairly common in the United States - can be a significant tool. Judges do tend to think in literary terms but diagrams are occasionally effective, as has been the experience in construction, technology and admiralty claims, particularly when a method, process or mechanism and its failure, or a very precise course or passage has to be shown. In clinical negligence claims a diagram of parts of the human body, now available on CD-Rom with digitally-enhanced 3D imagery is often used to enable Judges to see how bodily functions work, and where and how the problem in issue has occurred.

THE TRIBUNAL IN QUESTION

Good advocates have a healthy regard for the capability, background and former practice, likes and dislikes of the particular Judge before whom they appear and try to cater for anything specific of which they are aware in pursuing their client's case. Since the essence of advocacy - *ad vocare* - is to call the tribunal towards a particular viewpoint, it makes sense to do so. However, in most trials and appeals the advocate will rarely know the composition of the tribunal before the skeleton is to be filed. Chancery, Family and Queen's Bench Judges and their Deputies, and members of the Court of Appeal operate in a general pool system which may make it impossible to customise a skeleton argument, much as he might wish to.

Where the courts have a much closer case management system in which a trial Judge is designated at the outset of proceedings, for example in the Technology and Construction Court or the Commercial Court, the likes or dislikes of a particular Judge can be catered for insofar as to do so is consistent with the case. Counsel will be most often in a position to do this at the conclusion of any trial where he is asked to provide closing submissions in writing, or if he has a substantial interim hearing before an assigned Master, and will welcome the opportunity of being able to tailor argument to the particular Judge. By likes or dislikes, I refer to submissions which the individual Judge is more likely to find attractive or unattractive given his background or past expressions on the law. For example, if it is known that a certain Queen's Bench Master will not accept a skeleton argument of more than two sides in length, that is how the submissions must be compressed; equally if a trial Judge encourages an advocate to provide as full a closing submission in writing as he may wish, he need not worry unduly about the strictures of the practice rules and the costs implications. He is being asked to contribute to no small part of the Judge's judgment.

Customising is even more important when one has to try to cater for a Judge's likely familiarity with the particular area of law with which the case is concerned. The Department for Constitutional Affairs make its judges as generalist as possible. This is good both for the Lord Chancellor, who wishes to ensure that Judges are always fully occupied, and, to an extent, for cohesion in the law, since Judges will apply first principles to areas outside their immediate discipline.

Even within the divisions of the High Court, the deputy system means that one may have a trial Judge with no experience of the law in the particular case. You can try to accommodate this by preparing a short appendix to your skeleton,[1] which sets out the existing law and most recent authorities as neutrally as is consistent with your case. This sits well with the idea of counsel acting as a judicial assistant helping the court, rather than necessarily being a partisan figure

---

[1] See the example provided at Part 3 C *Martindale* and J *Phelps*.

EXAMPLE A

Queen's Bench Trial – Personal Injuries – Quantum only – Plaintiff's skeleton opening by Edward Faulks QC in 1998 – 10pp.

Brittle v Chief Constable of South Yorkshire Police was an action arising from the Hillsborough disaster of April, 1989. The Defendant admitted liability. At the trial for the assessment of damages, the live issues concerned the nature of the Plaintiff's injuries and causation.

The writer uses a relaxed narrative style with short sentences, and commands great simplicity of expression, much desired by most trial judges. The effect is not unlike a judgment by Lord Denning. As a skeleton it is almost entirely fact orientated. There is no separate chronology and no summary, as these are encompassed in the narrative, although the issues are set out at paragraphs 17 and 18. The facts are all laid out for the judge, and while the Plaintiff's case is asserted, note that it is deliberately understated. The technique of being undemonstrative is effective: the writer is telling the judge that the facts speak for themselves, subject to what he will find.

The action settled at the door of the court.

PLAINTIFF'S SKELETON OPENING

1. The Plaintiff, Robert Brittle, was born on the 7th March 1962 in Walsall. West Midlands. On the 15th April 1989, when he was 27, he attended Hillsborough Stadium to watch Liverpool versus Sheffield Wednesday in the semi-final of the FA Cup. He suffered physical and psychological injuries as a result. The Defendant has admitted liability and the Court is concerned with the assessment of damages only. A chronology is available with this skeleton opening.

2. *Bundles*
   A master index of bundles will be provided to the Court. The bundles are as follows:

Bundle 1 (red) -	pleadings
Bundle 2 (blue) -	witness statements
Bundle 3 (green) -	medical reports
Bundle 4 (grey) -	accommodation and needs reports
Bundle 5 (black lever arch) -	GP/Hospital/Clinic Notes
Bundle 6 (black) -	miscellaneous correspondence
Box 7 -	various videos

   (References in this skeleton opening
   are to the Bundles eg. 6.1
   (Bundle 6, page 1).

3. *The Facts*

   The Plaintiff was crushed against a perimeter fence. Many of those around him were killed or seriously injured. He suffered from a prolonged crush and probably lost consciousness. On examination at the Northern General Hospital, Sheffield immediately after the event he had signs of diminishing air entry on the left side of his chest. He had a small right pneumothorax, which required a chest drain. There was also air in the pericardium. He was transferred to the Intensive Care Unit and required a considerable amount of intravenous pain relief. His mental state was such that the Plaintiff was transferred to the Psychiatric Department. His lack of orientation was attributed partly to crush asphyxia and partly due to an acute stress reaction. By the 19th April his pain relief was reduced and chest drains were removed. It was noted that he was unable to bear his own weight and clinical examination showed weakness in both arms and legs. X-rays showed no fractures. It was originally thought that he might have had hypoxic spinal cord damage. A consultant in A & E, Mr. Wardrope (1.18), considered that the extent of his chest injury and muscle enzyme increase showed that he had suffered prolonged crush for some time. The weakness experienced in the muscles of the arms and legs was considered to be unusual although previously described in traumatic asphyxia.

4. On the 26th April 1990 the Plaintiff was transferred to Manor Hospital, Walsall. A physician treating him (report at 1.10) noted that he had not walked in the Northern General Hospital and that he still did not do so. On observation muscles of the lower limbs were moderately tender on pressure. Muscle tone was normal. Muscle power in the lower limbs appeared to be diminished considerably although this was attributed to severe pain caused by movement to the limbs. Both tendon and superficial reflexes were normal. There was subjective diminution of appreciation of sensations over the left arm. There was no obvious wasting of any muscle group. The physician referred the matter to a neurologist who could find no neurological problem and to a psychiatrist who thought that the problems were attributable to depression and acute grief following a massive traumatic experience superimposed on an emotionally immature personality. The Plaintiff was still not mobile when discharged on the 2nd June 1989 and left in a wheelchair.

5. He was seen by a neurologist in November 1989 (1.16). The Plaintiff was still completely unable to walk. The neurologist also reported stiffness and aching in the right shoulder, pins and needles and numbness in the right hand, and widespread emotional problems of the kind often associated with post traumatic stress disorder. He said: "Despite the virtually normal signs on examination on the bed, he was completely unable to walk. Even the prospect of walking made him agitated. When he was stood up at the side of the bed he started shaking and

clung on to people or objects around as would a drowning man. He was unable to make even small steps and, unless supported, would have fallen to the floor." The neurologist was in no doubt that all the symptoms were a direct result of the injuries sustained at Hillsborough Stadium. This emotional state was entirely explicable by reference to other survivors of horrific disasters. He considered that the characteristics of the Plaintiff's inability to walk indicated the problem was of a psychological origin and due to his emotional state.

6. Since 1989 the Plaintiff has been seen by a number of doctors instructed by solicitors on either side. Their reports are in bundle 3 (green). The medical notes themselves are in bundle 5 (lever arch black). It has been agreed between counsel that all medical notes in relation to the Plaintiff can be admitted into evidence without the need to call the authors of any notes and the Court is entitled to attach such weight if any as to the contents of the same as the Court thinks proper in the circumstances. The parties' expert witnesses who are called can comment upon all medical notes and draw such inferences from them as they consider appropriate. The relevant experts are:

For the Plaintiff -   Dr. Robin Jacobson (psychiatrist) and
                         Dr. David Park (neurologist).
For the Defendant -   Dr. J. Swift (psychiatrist) and Surgeon
                         Captain O'Connell (psychiatrist)

7. It is the Plaintiff's case that he was confined to a wheelchair until about the middle of 1996. He became able to drive a car and to swim. He could even stand up in a swimming pool because of the buoyancy of the water. However, he was unable to walk unaided; this he found frustrating and upsetting. He attempted suicide on one occasion.

8. He has had a number of the problems generally associated with post traumatic stress disorder such as depression, intrusive thoughts, nightmares, sleeping difficulties, irritability, hypervigilance and poor concentration. He has shown some obsessional features.

9. Dr. Jacobson saw him in July 1991 and then again in January 1993. By the latter date there was some sign of improvement in his symptoms of PTSD. Although he was still confined to a wheelchair with the aid of physiotherapy he was beginning to be able to stand for a few seconds. Otherwise he continued to crawl around the house and was unable to weight-bear or walk. Dr. Jacobson's view of his prognosis was that there was some sign of improvement of his hysterical conversion reaction (i.e. his inability to walk) but that he required more intensive rehabilitation.

10. He received rehabilitation at the instigation of the Defendant's insurers who paid for him to attend a course at the Department of Psychiatry, Royal Naval Hospital, Gosport administered by Surgeon Commander O'Connell. The Plaintiff attended the course, living

in a complex of flats away from the hospital with other members of the group. He apparently came to be less reticent as the course proceeded but remained in a wheelchair and still pre-occupied by the Hillsborough Disaster. Dr. O'Connell concluded in April 1984 that he continued to display the symptoms of post traumatic stress disorder. (3.104).

11. In January 1995 he went to RAF Headley Court, once again under the auspices of the Defendant's insurers, who paid for the course. Whilst at Haslar the emphasis was on post traumatic stress disorder. At Headley Court the Plaintiff was an in-patient at the Rehabilitation Unit. Attempts to mobilise him apparently caused him anxiety and a tendency to hyperventilate. It is said that he did not wish to co-operate with certain assessments proposed and he discharged himself after 13 days.

12. When Dr. Swift saw the Plaintiff in January 1996 he concluded that there was an unwillingness to give up what has been described as a "sick role" he said: "My impression is that he has made a good adjustment to the sick role and is not sufficiently discontented with his limitations to bear the emotional discomforts associated with change." (3.97). He considered that Mr. Brittle might actively resist change until there had been a financial settlement of his claim. He described his motivation as "suspect".

13. In his report of 1st May 1997 Dr. Jacobson also concluded that any residual temporary increase in symptoms was likely to diminish on resolution of his Court case. By the time Dr. Jacobson saw him Mr. Brittle was able to get around with crutches and for short periods without any crutches.

14. Dr. Jacobson has recently reviewed his opinion in the light of video evidence, the Defendant's exchanged medical reports and certain documents (viz the RAF Headley Court notes) and is now of the view that there is a deliberate element in Mr. Brittle's continued inability to walk normally which may well be motivated by a desire for financial gain.

15. The most recent reports of Dr. Swift (dated the 15th September 1997) and Dr. O'Connell (dated the 16th September 1997) indicate a hardening of their views of the Plaintiff's genuineness. Dr. Swift concluded that rhe Plaintiff was able to walk at some time between the accident and April 1993. He concludes (3.69) that the inability to walk initially was genuine "i.e. an unconscious process, conversion hysteria, associated with psychological trauma" but this has changed over the years and "that there is now a conscious element determining the maintenance of a state of invalidity." Similarly Dr. O'Connell concludes that "at a very early stage he developed a sick role, in part reflecting guilt, however I would say that the major reason that he continued to present with the bizarre symptoms of a physical nature was with a view to achieving financial compensation - in other words he was malingering." (3.108)

16. The only neurological evidence comes from Dr. Park who saw the Plaintiff for the second occasion in June 1995. He noted that his legs were weak but that there was no evidence of disability from the neurological point of view. He concluded; "I have discounted the possibility that the disability is factitious or feigned, and I believe it to be a consequence of a neurotic disorder, which is a direct consequence of the incident at Hillsborough."

17. *The Issues*

The principal issues concern the nature of the Plaintiff's disability and its causation. The Plaintiff had a vulnerable personality as is evidenced by his personal and medical history. He was undoubtedly involved in a horrific incident in which he might well have died. It is also common ground that he has suffered from post traumatic stress disorder albeit that this has improved. It is further accepted that at least initially the Plaintiff's inability to walk was genuine i.e. caused by some form of hysterical conversion and was not; a deliberate attempt to feign disability.

18. Where the issue lies is when, if at all, he was in fact able to walk but deliberately did not do so. The Plaintiff maintains that his disability has been entirely genuine and that his improvement, also genuine, is something that he has welcomed. In the medical reports there is reference to malingering, hysterical conversion and a "sick role". The difficulty in this case may be disentangling the relative contribution of any of these factors. Specifically the doctors disagree as to when there was a conscious element on the Plaintiff's part, involved in his failure to improve.

19. *Damages*

General Damages

Tlie Plaintiff is entitled to general damages for post traumatic stress disorder.

The JSB Guidelines suggest that the brackets are;

(a)	Severe -	£27,000 to £37,500
(b)	Moderately Severe -	£11,000 to £21,500
(c)	Moderate -	£ 3,250 to £ 8,000
(d)	Minor -	£ 1,600 to £3,250

It is the Plaintiff's case that (even apart from the inability to walk) his problems can probably be described as severe. The inability to walk is clearly an aggravating feature. It affected every aspect of his life and for a period of approximately 7 years he was confined to a wheelchair. He is now only able to walk with crutches. The Court will award an appropriate sum to reflect his physical disability. Account will also be taken of his undoubted physical injuries in the incident, the period of hospitalisation and the continued pain and discomfort in various parts of his body since the accident.

20. *Loss of Earnings*

The Plaintiff's early life was unpromising. But when he came out of prison in 1983 he began to settle down. From 1983 to 1989 he lived with his girlfriend and kept out of trouble. He had various forms of employment, mostly on a cash basis until 1988 when he obtained full-time employment with Mr. Owen. This was a highly satisfactory period of his life. Mr. Owen speaks highly of him (2.18). He was earning £154.62p net. Unfortunately he was made redundant towards the end of 1988 through circumstances unconnected with any dissatisfaction on his employer's part with the Plaintiff. His employment consisted of driving substantial goods vehicles around the country. The Plaintiff had a provisional HGV licence. He had taken his test once and failed and was due to take it again shortly after the Hillsborough Disaster but was unable to do so. Although he was unemployed when the accident took place, he had been offered a job by Peter Marriott which would have started in 1989 (2.31) at the rate of £300 per week for a 5½ day week. On any view of the evidence the Plaintiff was out of work as a result of the accident. The Defendants suggest the relevant period is 18 months (1.62). The Plaintiff says it was for much longer.

21. Employment: consultants have analysed Mr. Brittle's prospects now (see Keith Carter's updated report dated 28th October 1997 Bundle 1). The Plaintiff must now expect a difficult and lengthy job search having regard to his limited physical ability, his moderate ability generally, the job market and the period for which he has been out of work. The Plaintiff has made a few attempts to obtain employment but it is submitted that given the extent of his disability there was never any realistic chance of his obtaining a job.

22. It is the Plaintiff's case that the accident happened at a crucial time in his life when he was beginning to sort himself out. The likelihood is that be would have obtained work and continued working had it not been for the accident. That he has not been able to do so has been as a result of the accident which has also affected his position on the labour market for the long-term. The Plaintiff has provided a Schedule of Loss of Earnings to assist the Court. (1.30).

23. *Care*

The Court is referred to the report of Rachel Bush (4.28) and in particular page 35 and the following. The costing of the Plaintiff's care is contained at page 53 and reflected in a voluntary schedule (1.58).

24. *Other Losses*

The Schedule at 1.58 refers to the cost of a gardener/handyman. The Plaintiff was effective with his hands before the accident. There are also references to the need for physiotherapy, aids and equipment, travel cost, holidays and the need for investment advice.

GOOD PRACTICE SUGGESTION

WRITING STYLE

Style[2] may be unimportant where your aim is to bring the attention of the judge directly to the relevant matter or point. However in a longer document, particularly where the facts need explanation, the use of a narrative style in good English is most effective. You should avoid defined terms and use the language one would find in a novel in a straightforward story telling technique. In this way you reduce the case to its essence and arouse the human interest of the judge. If you use short sentences, words that are not too long (which makes the occasional lengthy word stand out), non-legal words and adjectives from other sources (but not clichéic or slang expressions) you will capture the attention of the reader and carry him forward to your argument expeditiously and confident of his understanding of your position.

---

[2] See also Examples at F, H and M.

EXAMPLE B

Queen's Bench Trial – Clinical Negligence – Quantum only – Claimant's skeleton opening by Simeon Maskrey QC in late 1998 – extract from 15pp.

Newton v Hereford Hospitals NHS Trust was an action for damages for 'wrongful birth' arising from a failed sterilisation. The Defendant admitted liability. At the trial for the assessment of damages, the parties filed a schedule that summarised their respective contentions. The Claimant's skeleton is specifically produced to highlight the major differences between the parties and summarise their rival contentions (para 3). As an exercise it is worth contrasting the style with the preceding case of Brittle.

The writer uses the technique of close comparison throughout. Although you may find defence counsel using this it is unusual in a claimant's opening, and therefore very specific to the situation. Its particular strength is clarity: the judge can focus directly on the issues to be decided without diversion.

The language is informal. Paragraphs are single issue and generally kept short. Key financial figures and citations are put in bold font. Much use is made of white space.

The action was compromised during the hearing.

CLAIMANT'S SKELETON OPENING

INTRODUCTION

1. This is a claim for damages for "wrongful birth". Liability has been admitted and interlocutory judgment entered on the 21st July 1998. The action proceeds as an assessment of damages. Put shortly, the claimant was sterilised on the 10th April 1995. The sterilisation failed because the left fallopian tube was not occluded properly. In August 1995 the claimant discovered she was pregnant with her 5th child. She declined the offer of an abortion. C was born on the 15th February 1996.
2. The rival contentions of the parties are summarised in the revised schedule served on the 11th January 1999 (page 52 bundle A) and the undated counter-schedule in reply (page 86 bundle A).
3. The purpose of this opening is to highlight the major differences between the parties and summarise the rival contentions.

PAIN AND SUFFERING

4. The claimant seeks £40,000. The defendant admits £20,000 (page 91 bundle A). The claimant relies on the following matters in support of her contention.

    4.1 The pregnancy was complicated (report from Mr. Jarvis dated 3rd September 1998 (page 102 bundle B)).

    4.2 The labour and delivery were difficult although in the event the baby did not suffer HIE (page 103, bundle B). An episiotomy was required.

    4.3 The claimant was obliged to undergo a re-sterilisation under general anaesthetic on the 26th September 1996. She suffered vomiting as a consequence of the anaesthetic (page 104, bundle B).

    4.4 As a consequence of the pregnancy and birth of C the claimant suffered "notable and disabling evidence of depression" (report from Dr. Seifert dated 26th October 1998 (page 86, bundle B). "severe depression" (report from Dr. Bradley dated the 2nd November 1998 (page 231, bundle B).

    4.5 By July 1999 the claimant's psychiatric symptoms had lessened and both experts felt that there was no psychiatric reason why she should not return to work (page 236, bundle B).

    4.6 The court should take account of the recommendations contained in the Law Commission's Report, Law Com No. 257 that such awards should be increased by a factor of between 1.5 and 2.0 and that it is open to the courts (albeit via court of appeal guidelines) to do so. *Alsford v British Telecommunications plc* (1986) CA October 30th is not authority to the contrary.

LOSS OF CONGENIAL EMPLOYMENT

5. The claimant seeks £5,000. The defendant concedes £1,000 (page 91, bundle A). The claimant will rely upon *Hay v Ministry of Defence* in support of her contention.
   She has had to give up employment that she enjoyed and that provided her with stimulation and social intercourse. It is unlikely that she will ever return to work of a similar nature.

EXPENSES TO DATE OF TRIAL

6. The claimant has sought:

    6.1 £3,773 in respect of "recorded expenses"

6.2 **£1,192** in respect of estimated expenses

6.3 **£3,813** in respect of general household expenditure.

See pages 56 and 81 Bundle A

7. The defendant has allowed £4,611 + £1,080 = £5,691 (page 92, bundle A). The defendant has reached this figure by reference to NFCA rates, reduced by one-third and child benefit received. Apparently this has been done because Mrs. Convey has not seen the claimant's supporting documentation. She makes much complaint about the failure to "release" documents (see page 113, bundle B for example). The complaint is misconceived (see pages 87 and 15 -in that order-bundle F).

8. The reduction of one-third from the NFCA rates has been made because the defendant contends that the Newton family's income and expenditure was below the average used by the NFCA (see page 121 bundle B). The claimant does not accept this contention and it amounts to one of the significant disputes between the parties. The claimant contends that the NFCA rates are appropriate for future expenditure and is prepared to rely on the rates for past expenditure. However, she does not accept a one-third deduction. Therefore the claimant will accept £5,691 × 133.3% = £7,586 under this head of claim.

FUTURE MAINTENANCE COSTS

9. The claimant seeks £64,085 under this head of claim (page 57, bundle A). The defendant allows £26,759 (page 93, bundle A).

10. The claimant has used the NFCA rates to the age of 18 (page 7 bundle B). It is accepted that no allowance has been made for accelerated receipt. Accordingly the claimant is prepared to accept the multipliers put forward by the defendant (page 110, bundle A) provided that the correct up to date NFCA rates are used (page 7, bundle B). Thus, the claimant seeks £44,058.

11. The defendant relies upon Mrs. Convey's report in order to establish that NFCA rates are inappropriate. In essence it is said that the family income in 1999 would have been £17,717 pa; that £7,269 would have been spent on the adults and running the car; thus leaving £10,447 for the children or £2,089 pa for each child (page 141, bundle B). As NFCA rates amount to an average of £4,336 pa spent on each child it can be demonstrated that they are an inappropriate benchmark in this case.

12. The claimant contends that Mrs. Convey's approach is misconceived. First, one has to look at the likely expenditure by the Newtons in 1995. Prior to C's birth the claimant had resumed full time work. Her

net income was £8,931. Her husband earned £10,715 net. The family received £1,859 pa child benefit. Thus, £21,505 was available for the family. If NFCA rates for 1995 are used it can be seen that £12,780 would be spent on the 4 children, leaving £8,725 pa for the two adults (see page 11B, bundle B)(the witness evidence supporting these figures is at pages 4 and 51, bundle C. The documentary evidence is at pages 35 and 37 of bundle E and page 139, bundle B). Therefore it can be demonstrated that the family expenditure on the children was at or about the rate used by the NFCA. The same exercise can be carried out at 1999 rates assuming that C had not been born. Once again, the family income would have been sufficient to spend the NFCA average figure on each child (page 11C, bundle B).

13.   The errors made by Mrs. Convey can thus be summarised;

13.1   Using the RPI to reach the assumed 1999 income of Mr & Mrs Newton.

13.2   Assuming that Mrs Newton would have remained in part time work but for C's birth.

13.3   Dividing the money available for the children by 5 rather than by 4.

LOSSES CONSEQUENT UPON FORCED HOUSE MOVE

14.   As a consequence of the birth of C (a) the claimant had to give up work (b) her husband was unable to earn at previous levels and (c) there was additional expenditure. In order to make ends meet the claimant was forced to sell her house at The Haven, Green Lane, Eardisland, near Leominster, and the building plots that went with the house (see page 12, bundle C). The need to sell quickly meant that the sales were at an under-value (see page 13, bundle B).

15.   Moreover, the claimant incurred expense moving from The Haven to 'X' Avenue, Leominster (page 29, bundle C).

16.   The move to 'X' Avenue was forced upon the claimant by the birth of C. As soon as she is in a position to do so she will move back to accommodation of a comparable standard to The Haven and which will be large enough for the whole family. costs associated with running a larger house (page 81, bundle A). Furthermore the cost of such a property has increased more rapidly than the value of The Haven (page 53, bundle B).

17.   The claimant abandons the claim for the cost of a further move back to a smaller home (page 98, bundle A). The claim therefore amounts to £62,936 (plus interest)(page 57, bundle A).

18. The defendant's approach has been to accept the costs of moving from The Haven and the costs of moving to a larger house insofar as it is established that it has been necessitated by C's birth (page 97, bundle A). The sum admitted on that basis is £15,169. No other costs are accepted. In particular it has been denied that the sales of The Haven and the building plots were forced or were at an under-value (see page 184, bundle B) and it is denied that it was in fact necessary to sell The Haven (see page 191, bundle B).

19. The observation that it was unnecessary for the claimant to sell The Haven is based upon a misapprehension of the claimant's case. It was necessary to sell and then buy a cheaper property so as to pay off debts which had accumulated and to be closer to the amenities of Leominster (see pages 5 and 13, bundle C).

CLAIMANT'S LOSS OF EARNINGS

20. But for the birth of C the claimant would have continued working for Barclays Bank on a full time basis (pages 36 & 37, bundle E)(pages 4, 11, 12, bundle C). The calculation is at page 64, bundle A. The claim amounts to £34,109 to date.

21. The defendant appears to accept that but for C's birth the claimant would have remained in employment with Barclays (page 88, bundle A). Therefore the claim has been admitted (page 99, bundle A) but presumably with the caveat that she would have incurred child care expenditure.

22. The claimant says that she would have worked full time at Barclays Bank but for C's birth; that she would probably have worked in the customer and sales department at a net salary of £11,650 pa rising each year for 5 years (page 65, bundle A); that she has been prevented from doing so; and that her earning potential has now been reduced by (a) her child care commitments and (b) her absence from the labour market. A multiplier of 17.17 is sought which reflects a working life to age 65. The claim on that basis amounts to £145,386.

23. The defendant has accepted that but for C's birth:

    23.1 the claimant would have been able to work full time at a net salary of £10,590 pa (pages 112 and 114, bundle A) until the year 2003. A loss of earnings for that period (subject to child care costs) is therefore accepted with a multiplier of 4.

    23.2 From the year 2003 to 2014 the defendant accepts a partial loss of earnings on the basis that the claimant will now only obtain part time work (pages 113 and 114, bundle A). A multiplier of 8.5 is used. However, the defendant concedes that in order to work the claimant will incur child care costs for C's and will make an additional payment in respect of such costs.

23.3   From 2014 to 2018 (the claimant's 60th birthday) a small loss of £582 pa is accepted on the basis that the claimant would by then have been able to work full time work at a comparable salary. A multiplier of 2.5 years is accepted.

24.   On this basis the defendant concedes a loss of earnings of £77,093.

25.   The major dispute between the parties is, therefore, (a) the extent to which it is likely that the claimant will be able to obtain work from 2003 and (b) what her likely salary will be (c) what it would have been had she remained at Barclays and (d) whether she would have worked to age 65 but for C's birth.

26.   The claimant accepts that her psychiatric condition is unlikely to prevent her from working from the year 2003. It is highly unlikely that she would be able to obtain work in the banking sector (report from Keith Carter page 80, bundle B). It is possible that she could obtain part time clerical work at a salary of £4,385 gross (say £4,000 net) and the claimant is prepared to revise her claim accordingly (page 72, bundle B; page 214. bundle B). It is accepted that after 2 years her income would begin to rise as she gained in experience and worked longer hours. From 2005 she could be expected to earn £8,723 gross (say £6,990 net) and from £2014 she could earn £10,815 gross (say £8,100 net) (see page 72, bundle B). On that basis the claim falls to £137,204.

27.   The claimant disputes the assertions contained in the defendant's employment report that (a) she would not have been a candidate for promotion within Barclays (page 204, bundle B) (b) she could expect to earn the median salary of a counter clerk on her return to full time employment (page 213, bundle B) (c) she would probably have retired at the age of 60.

MR. NEWTON'S LOSS OF EARNINGS

28.   The claim to date is £12,124 (plus interest). The future claim is £8,030 (pages 58 and 82, bundle A).

29.   The claimant does not understand the defendant to be challenging the fact of this loss or that it flows from the birth of C. As the claimant understands it the defendant disputes the claim simply because it is the loss of Mr. Newton and not hers.

30.   The claimant accepts that her husband left his job because he was unable to work shifts following the birth of C. She accepts that this is his loss rather than hers. However, his loss of overtime to the date of trial and into the future is a consequence of (a) assisting the claimant whilst she suffered from severe depression and (b) assisting her with child care in the future. Therefore this is a loss sustained by Mr. Newton in order to assist the claimant and it is recoverable

according to ordinary *Housecroft v Burnett* principles. Thus the claimant reduces her claim to £5,900 (plus interest) to the date of trial and £8,030 until 2003 (see page 82, bundle A).

LOSS OF PENSION AND OTHER BENEFITS

31. The claimant abandons her claim for loss of preferential borrowing and disability on the labour market. However, she maintains her other claims and awaits the response of the defendants in respect of the loss of pension claim (see page 104, bundle A).
32. The claimant abandons the claims made in respect of her husband's losses.

CARE OF C

33. The claim amounts to £57,822 to date and £48,241 for the future (page 59, bundle A). The defendant admits travel costs paid to Mrs. Newton senior (£427) but has denied all of the other claims (page 105 & 106, bundle A). The denial is based upon the premise that the claimant is not entitled to the cost of caring for C as this is counterbalanced by the positive elements of bringing up a child (see *Thake v Maurice* [1986] QB 644)(page 90, bundle A).
34. The claimant asserts that the cost of caring for C is recoverable provided that there is no double recovery when also claiming loss of earnings.
35. That the claim is allowable in principle is clear from the court of appeal decision of *Emeh v Kensington AHA* [1985] QB 1012. See, in particular, the judgment of Waller LJ @ 1022. In *Thake v Maurice* [1986] QB 644 the court of appeal agreed that the joy of having a healthy child could cancel out the time and trouble spent looking after that child (see, for example, page 683). But (a) these cases were decided before *Housecroft v Burnett* [1986] 1 All ER 332 and the modern practice of evaluating care provided by family by reference to commercial care costs, discounted by 20-33% (see Kemp 5-025) and (b) there can be no doubt that in this case the birth of C did not result in joy and comfort, but in severe depression that is still continuing. Moreover it is illogical to allow a loss of earnings claim and not a gratuitous care claim.
36. The claim made in respect of care provided by Mrs. Newton senior is recoverable subject to the normal *Housecroft v Burnett* principles.
37. The claim for the care provided by the claimant is subject to a deduction in respect of the loss of earnings claim. Thus the claim should be reduced by (say) 50 hours per week and the calculation should be as follows:

168-50 =118 hours per week × £1.80 per hour × 177 weeks = £37,595 (see page 8. bundle B and page 83, bundle A).

38. For the future the claim is based on the report prepared by Mrs. Sweeting (see page 9, bundle B).

TRANSPORT

39. The claim is for the cost of a VW Sharan at £18,587. The defendant argues that a set off is required in respect of the sale of two old vehicles. The principle of the contention is accepted but the discount sought of £11,000 is too high (see page 107, bundle A). The claimant is prepared to concede a discount of £5,000 reducing the claim to £13,587 plus interest for past losses and £13,587 for the future.

FINANCIAL ADVICE

40. If multipliers are assessed on the basis of a 3% discount rate when a net return of 2% is all that has been achievable for the past 12 months it is appropriate to seek financial advice and assistance. The claim is therefore maintained. The cost of £1,200 pa represents 10 hours advice each year and is a modest claim. Therefore the claim remains £32,219 (see page 83, bundle A).

CONCLUSION

41. The defendant admits by its counter-schedule £197,404 plus interest and pension loss but subject to (a) an adjustment for child care costs and (b) proof that moving from The Haven was justified. As amended in this opening the claimant seeks an award of £546,990 plus interest.

GOOD PRACTICE SUGGESTION

Try to break down issues into small bites.[3] Make issues as simple as is consistent with accuracy – but be wary of oversimplification. In doing so try to avoid stylised language. Accuracy in dealing with the facts and the case is more important than worrying about simplification.

---

[3] See also Example J

EXAMPLE C

Queen's Bench Trial – Employer's duties – Defendant's skeleton opening by John Norman in July, 2004 – 6pp together with appendix on the law of 12pp.

Martindale v Oxford County Council was a stress at work claim brought by a teacher. The Defendant contested liability on the issues of breach of duty and causation.

In his overview of the facts the writer uses short sentences in non-legal language with few technical terms. He has a narrative style which contains cross-references to the trial bundles. A close perusal of the document reveals that the defence case is not actually stated in terms; the ground is merely laid under paragraph 3. This gives defence counsel considerable flexibility depending on how the evidence comes out.

The opening contains an integrated chronology. The events of four years are confined to three-quarters of a page. Key dates are selected and highlighted with bold face.

Analysis of the law is relegated to a separate appendix. This enables the narrated opening to be advanced as unbroken prose. It is designed to assist a judge who may be unfamiliar with – or have no knowledge at all of - what is a specialist area. This is a useful technique when you want to compartmentalise the facts and the law.

At trial the claim failed and was dismissed. Permission to appeal was refused by the Court of Appeal.

OPENING SUBMISSIONS OF THE DEFENDANT

At Trial: 8th July 2004

1. **Overview**

    1.1 This is a stress at work claim. Liability and quantum are in issue. The focus of events is really in the early part of 1999, although there are elements of the history which are important.

    1.2 The Claimant was an experienced teacher at X Middle School. His subjects were Art, and Design and Technology ("D&T"). He first went sick with depression in September 1997, and although he complains that he was 'bullied' by Mr Y (Particulars of Claim §15 – p.5) he makes no claim in respect of that episode (Particulars of Claim §18 – p.5).

    1.3 He returned to work in May 1998, with a structured return starting with part time work. Almost exactly a year later, in April

1999 (the beginning of the summer term), and long after he had returned to full time working, he went sick again. He was then 43 years old. He claims damages only in respect of this episode. The report of the Defendant's psychiatric expert, Prof. F, is agreed (p.93). The condition was an adjustment disorder, with anxiety and depressed mood (p.109).

1.4   The essence of his pleaded case is that the pressures of work were too great for him, the Defendant knew this (or ought to have known this), and the Defendant ought to have reduced them. The Claimant also characterises the Head's executive decision in 1998 as to what he should teach in the coming year as 'bullying' (p.7 §24) – but no adverse consequence comes from this. Those pressures in part seem to be related by the Claimant to difficulties which the school was having generally – despite the 'new broom' introduced in April 1997. He disagreed with the management decisions on allocation of resources. There is no recognisable overwork claim pleaded. Although breaches of the Working Time Regulations appear in the immensely lengthy list of broken duties, no facts in support are pleaded – i.e. it is not said he had to work too many hours, merely that those hours limited what he could usefully achieve. His witness statement makes complaint about the hours worked, but does not reach any relevant threshold.

1.5   The Defendant's pleaded case is that the Claimant returned to work after careful discussion with the Defendant, the Defendant also spoke to his GP, and took advice from Occupational Health. In short, the Claimant returned to work with advice that he was fit. He retained ready access to suitable sources of medical/welfare advice, including counselling, and his return to work went well - with support from his Head Teacher and from LEA advisers. His sudden illness immediately after the Spring holiday was unexpected and was not caused by any breach of duty. The Claimant had made an appointment to seek advice from Occupational Health shortly before this (p.9, §32). It appears that neither he nor his advisers foresaw impending illness – or, as he had done before, the Claimant chose to ignore either his own view and/or the advice he was receiving.

1.6   It is apparent from the history given that there was a conflict between the Defendant's managerial decisions and what the Claimant felt ought to have been done. See also Prof F on p. 108-9. This appears to be at least partly related to his union activities. He was unable to accept the decisions of the new Head and failed to adjust or cooperate fully. Although he knew he could not and would not get his way, he chose to ignore the situation and stay put, but built up enormous anger over this. Worse, he had no medical support: his own GP was pleased with the progress he made after returning to full time work. The Defendant involved the Claimant's own GP and the Occupational Health adviser, but made it clear that the Claimant's job could not and would not be adjusted, and that the Claimant had to be fit for the job he would be required to do before he would be allowed back. Once the Claimant decided to return and started work the Defendant was not advised that he had to have any special regime. Although some 9 months later in March 1999 he had concerns about his health (see GP notes), but he fell ill before any material advice could be given to the Defendant (apparently he received none either), and well before any advice could have been effectively acted upon.

<u>Key Dates:</u>

20.10.95 GP Note: heart / palpitations; v anxious; change of routine – chat [described as 'sea-change' – F p.7]

20.9.96 GP Note: exhausted, work – **'stress / burnout' diagnosed** *[semble, ignored by the Claimant – no time off]*

Sept '96 re-monitoring of C; upset, proposed leaving; job applications unsuccessful;

Apr '97 Change of management. Acting Head = Mr R; Dep = Mrs S

2+5.6.97 review meetings with R; request for C's 'back of envelope' plans for new workshop layout for Sept;

?6.6.97 to GP; told he should take time off for stress; **rejected GP advice** [F p.3]

30.6.97 referral by D for health monitoring (headaches; 11 days off this year)

1.9.97 C off sick from beginning of term – 7m – cut hand + reactive depression; Occ H and **offered free [confidential] counselling** – which he took up

8.10.97 GP Note: 'constructive dismissal, lawyer'

Nov '97 Ofsted – D&T unsatisfactory, Art satisfactory

17.3.98 note: S and OccH (J A) interview C with John L, Paul Mc, George H and C's friend R S; make it clear he is not to return until he is fit.

Apr 1998 GP to Ms T (Snr Educ Officer) = 'fit as anyone + fit as he'll ever be' (recorded in letter 1.5.98 to Head, Mrs S)

May '98 C returns to work – support and short hours;

25.11.98 GP Note – much better; medication to continue for 3m

5.3.99 GP Note: 'work pressures again', possible depression – prescribed Temazapan [not sleeping]

"consulted union rep. who told him work pressures were excessive

23.3.99 meeting with Head

12.4.99 training day (day before term starts); request from Head for scheme of work – C felt he could not cope and went to GP *[F p.5]*

13.4.99 first day sick

2. Preliminary Matters

2.1 The Claimant has very recently served a report from Prof. G. The substance as well as the flavour of the report is not appropriate for forensic circumstances. It improperly attempts to address many issues which are the exclusive province of the trial Judge.

2.2 It may greatly assist if some of the witness statements were simply excluded. Several of the Claimant's witnesses do not address pleaded issues, but rather make complaints or give histories of quite different matters. In particular events prior to 1998 would seem wholly (or largely) irrelevant {W, Ws, L, A, S}. Ms T seems to have a different agenda – her own complaint. A great deal of the matters referred to by the Claimant's witnesses do not appear admissible, in particular the Claimant has neither sought nor obtained permission to adduce the extensive opinion evidence.

2.3 The Claimant also proposes to call his solicitor, Ms N. The wrong statement appears in my bundle – p.386. The statement relied upon appears to go to the credit of a witness the Defendant may call, Mr P. The Defendant submits this evidence is inadmissible – it seeks to impugn the credit of a witness. In any event the Claimant can call Mr P if he wants to, or can cross-examine him if and when the Defendant calls him. Further:

    a. it is accepted that he would not sign the statement prepared for him;

    b. he was expressly told he could alter or amend what the Claimant prepared as he saw fit;

    c. Ms N's evidence of what he meant cannot be admissible.

3. Legal Principles

3.1 In stress cases there are some important differences or additions to the standard approach to the duty of care owed by an employer to an employee. These can easily be overstated. To assist there is an annexe to these submissions dealing with recent cases and the overall approach in this area of the law.

3.2 Whether the issue is the first episode of stress or, as here, a return to work, the standard of care is the same: to take reasonable steps to avoid exposing the Claimant to unreasonable risk of injury because of the requirements of his work.

3.3 Once there has been an extended period of psychiatric illness all sides recognise that there is a significant risk of relapse. There may be just as much (or more) adverse psychiatric influence from not working, or from seeking a new job, as there may be from returning to work. The options are usually for the Claimant to remain off work, to be a part timer or subject to special duties (with reductions in pay and status), or getting back to full time work with no special restrictions.

3.4　The fact that a relapse may occur does not in any way mean there has been a breach. It is the nature of the Claimant's condition that relapses are likely, and are not readily avoidable, but that the risk for the Claimant is worth taking. The employer does not underwrite the risk any more than the Claimant's medical or other advisers warrant that the risk is low.

3.5　The risk is kept within reasonable bounds partly because the alternatives carry similar risks, and partly because the Defendant has ensured that the Claimant has ample means of avoiding pressures when they get too much – i.e. not just unpleasant, but where he can see the build up of a pathological reaction. He can take days off, he can return to his GP for treatment or advice (or seek and follow advice from any other relevant source), he can approach his counsellor. What he cannot expect to do is to impose a special regime on his employer. That sort of claim falls exclusively within the jurisdiction of the Employment Tribunal under the Disability Discrimination Act.

3.6　The primary responsibility for an individual's health lies on the individual himself. This is particularly so where the person concerned is mature, educated and responsible, and where the subject condition is one which necessarily he will be best placed to assess and address – and one which many people wish to keep confidential. "People must accept responsibility for their own actions and take the necessary care to avoid injuring themselves or others" – *Gorringe v Calderdale BC*, 2004 UKHL; *Tomlinson v Congleton Borough Council* [2004] 1 AC 46.

4.　Quantum: it is the nature of cases with psychological injury that there is often a great number of variables which need to be resolved. Stress cases particularly give rise to these problems. It may be helpful to resolve the primary issues before addressing the detail of issues on quantum.

APPENDIX

Actions for Stress at Work – a Summary of applicable Law

1. Although claims of this character are essentially the same as any other claim concerning occupational injury, there are a number of important and unavoidable special factors.
2. The material factors and principles have been summarised by the Court of Appeal in *Hatton*[1], whose conclusions in turn have been approved (with a small distinction) by the House of Lords in *Barber v Somerset CC*[2]. The detail of these decisions appears at the end of this summary.

THE DUTY OF CARE

3. It is essential to bear in mind in every case that the employer's duty is not simply to take care, and is not proved to have been broken simply because someone becomes ill because of his or her work.
4. The employer's duty is to take reasonable care to ensure that the Claimant is not exposed to unreasonable risk of injury by reason of the requirements of his/her work – see *Hatton* §43(7)+(8). The material duty relates to health and safety. It is no good identifying stress generated by a breach of some obligation which is not within the scope of any arguable duty of health and safety (e.g. non-payment of wages, lack of promotion, selection for transfer).
5. There are many competing duties owed by employers, especially public bodies, and these competing duties inform the nature and limits of the relevant duty of care owed to the Claimant. Conflicts between employees, or between employees and customers, are likely to bring into play a whole range of competing contractual and statutory duties. The public duty to fulfil certain statutory requirements regardless of resources can also give rise to difficulties.
6. For example, seen only from the Claimant's position it may be wholly unreasonable to keep the irritating Mr. Bloggs in the same post, or even to keep on employing him at all, but Mr Bloggs has his own rights, many imposed on the employer by statute, all of which the employer must also honour. While it may be upsetting to the Claimant not to get the changes he or she thinks would best assist, the employer may quite reasonably consider that the Claimant's special demands are bad for morale (and for the stress of other employees), or may reasonably value Mr Bloggs' contribution far more highly than the Claimant's (indeed the employer's obligation to his shareholders or to good financial conduct may oblige him to do so). In any event most employees agree that conflicts at work will be resolved by various types of grievance procedures. This in itself not only serves to reduce the risk of injurious conflict, but may be said to inhibit both the

---

1 *Hatton v Sutherland* [2002] 2AER 1 CA (Brooke, Kay, Hale LJJ) – comprising 4 appeals: *Jones v Sandwell MBC*; *Bishop v Baker Refractories*; *Barber v Somerset CC*.
2 *Barber v Somerset CC* [2004] UKHL 13

employee's right to claim and the employer's scope for response. See *Hatton* §43(9).

7. The reality of many situations is that even if there is something that the employer can do, he has a wide discretion as to how he manages his employees and especially how he manages an individual employee, and if the Claimant does not like it he/she is always free to leave the job and seek other employment. It is a false submission that this is not merely 'unfair' but actionably so:- fairness is material to unfair dismissal only. See *Hatton* §43(8),(9)+(10).

8. It also has to be borne in mind that Parliament has expressly provided for the sort of 'accommodation' which an employer is obliged to provide in response to an employee's health problems – and has specified the remedy available where he fails to do so. The Disability Discrimination Act 1995 applies to defined health problems, mental health only being included where particular criteria are met. Breaches of duties under the Act lie within the exclusive jurisdiction of the Employment Tribunal and have very tight time limits – 3 months[3]. It is submitted that:

   a. the common law had provided no significant remedy in relation to mental health caused by stress at work prior to 1995 (*Walker v Northumberland*[4] was reported in 1995);
   b. it would be unusual if Parliament had provided for an unnecessary remedy;
   c. employment law is a closely regulated and highly sensitive political area; the common law should be very slow to impose any obligation or confer any remedy which Parliament has not thought appropriate when addressing the material area of activity (cf. the House of Lords' decision in *Johnson v Unisys*[5]).

FORESEEABILITY

9. Mental health issues necessarily give rise to special problems of foreseability. Employment problems will be included in almost any list of potential injurious stressors, thus there will rarely be any issue that psychological injury is a foreseeable consequence of stress at work. However, that does not address the issue of foreseeability with which the law is concerned. What has to be foreseeable by the employer is that the combination of this employee and this job is such that there is an unreasonable risk of injury – see *Hatton* §43(3). Until that stage is reached the employer can have no obligation to investigate steps to

---

[3] section 8, applying to discrimination in the employment field.
[4] *Walker v Northumberland* CC [1995] 1AER 737
[5] *Johnson v Unisys* [2001] UKHL 13; [2001] 2WLR 1076

reduce the particular and unusual risk back to a reasonable level, still less to have put them into place.

10.   All health matters are necessarily personal, and are usually confidential. People tend to be particularly sensitive about mental health matters, both employers and employees. Employees may react very badly to any suggestion that their mental health is not good. Conduct by an employer even by concerned inquiry about mental health may be characterised as intrusive and wrongly critical, and may provoke allegations of breach of the underlying duty of trust and confidence, or of discriminatory conduct. Merely revealing to an employee that the employer is concerned about his mental health may itself be stressful and corrosive to an effective working relationship.

11.   An employer may well be best advised to rely upon the employee to be responsible enough to seek and follow their own medical advice, and at most to do little more than suggest that if they have any health concerns they should seek advice from their own GP. If there are employees who cannot be treated as responsible enough to look after their own health and/or to take their own decisions about it, good or bad, this will be an extremely rare situation. See *Hatton* §43(6). An employer who provides an independent confidential counselling service will usually have discharged any material duty of care - see *Hatton* §43 (11); necessarily this is an effectively passive arrangement on the part of the employer, which reflects the employee's primary responsibility for his own health.

12.   As Lord Reed put it in *Rorrison v West Lothian College* 1999 Ct of Sess [an application to strike out the action - "debate on Procedure Roll"] :

> "I can find nothing in these matters (or elsewhere in the pursuer's pleadings) which, if proved, could establish that Andrews and Henning ought to have foreseen that the pursuer was under a material risk of sustaining a psychiatric disorder in consequence of their behaviour towards her. They might have foreseen that she would at times be unsatisfied, frustrated, embarrassed and upset, but that is a far cry from suffering a psychiatric disorder. Many if not all employees are liable to suffer those emotions, and others mentioned in the present case such as stress, anxiety, loss of confidence and low mood. To suffer such emotions from time to time, not least because of problems at work, is a normal part of human experience. It is only if they are liable to be suffered to such a pathological degree as to constitute a psychiatric disorder that a duty of care to protect against them can arise; and that is not a reasonably foreseeable occurrence (reasonably foreseeable, that is to say, by an ordinary bystander rather than by a psychiatrist) unless there is some specific reason to foresee it in a particular case. I can see no such reason in the present case."

13. In *Petch v Customs & Excise* [1993] ICR 789 CA – the Claimant clerk of many years had a "mental breakdown" (manic depression) in 1974. He returned to work and then suffered an episode of "hypomania" in January 1975. In 1983 to 1986 he was ill again. His employers were aware of his health history. He complained that his episodes of illness were caused by improper pressure of work. His claim was dismissed, Dillon LJ stating:

> "*I take the view .. that, unless senior management in the Defendant's department were aware or ought to have been aware that the Plaintiff was showing signs of impending breakdown, or were aware or ought to have been aware that his workload carried a real risk that he would have a breakdown, then the Defendants were not negligent in failing to avert the breakdown.*" [p.796H].

PARTICULAR DUTIES – E.G. TO DIAGNOSE PROBLEMS; TO GIVE SYMPATHY, ETC.

14. It was also argued in *Petch* that the employer had a duty to counsel or give sympathetic support. Dillon LJ said:

> "*[the Plaintiff] submits that [his manager's] duty .. was to have counselled him, and endeavoured by leisured discussion to soothe away his worries ..... For my part I do not believe that there was any such duty in law on Mr Woolf.*" [p.799D].

15. On the submission that the employer owed a duty to give special weight to the views of the Claimant in making executive decisions when he knew that the employee was vulnerable:

> "*I cannot think that the duty of care owed to the plaintiff required that the chairman should subordinate his own views on the correct tactics to the plaintiff's views ... But I cannot see what other outcome from the impasse favourable to the plaintiff there could have been.*" [p.800C]

16. This decision was approved by CA in *Garrett v LB Camden* [2001] EWCA Civ 395 where Simon Browne LJ observed:

> "63. *Unless, however, there was a real risk of breakdown which the claimant's employers ought reasonably to have foreseen and which they ought properly to have averted, there can be no liability.*"
> "67. *It seems to me hardly surprising that Mr Garrett's claim should in those circumstances be held to fail. The combined effect of those twin findings was that he knew materially more than his employers about his propensity to work-related stress and*

breakdown, and can hardly, therefore, blame them for not recog-
nising the particular difficulties attendant upon his continued
employment."

17. Accordingly, although there may well be concurrent duties upon the employer and on the Claimant himself, the Claimant cannot simply refuse to take responsibility for his own health. Where he chooses to work knowing that his work puts his health at risk he will be accepting the risk of injury at work, and his employer may well be in no position to deny him the opportunity to take that risk. If the employer were to do so he not only would risk a claim for injury from the stress of stopping the Claimant from working, but would also risk claims in respect of unfair dismissal, discrimination, and defamation : *Spring v Guardian Assurance*[6].

THE DUTY AFTER MEDICAL ADVICE IS DISCLOSED

18. Whether the material duty has been breached is tested by asking whether the Claimant has proved that the Defendant obliged him/her to suffer an unreasonable risk of injury – i.e. an unreasonably high risk. If the employer has medical advice that the employee is at special risk from certain factors at work, and then imposes those factors regardless, he will often be in breach, but not necessarily so.

19. First, what is the nature of the medical disclosure? It is a matter of fact and degree whether there has been sufficient disclosure. An employee may claim a need for special treatment because of his health, but an employer who has no medical report is hardly obliged to comply with the employee's request - it may be common for employees to try to get light or favourable duties in this way. The employee may be vague in his description, or he may agree to do the very work which on one view he has suggested he should not be doing. An employer with clear advice directly from a medical source is much more likely to be obliged to respond – see *Hatton* §43(10).

20. However, the response which the law requires is not necessarily to follow the medical advice – as the above passages cited from both *Petch* and *Garrett* demonstrate. If it is evident to the employee that his employer cannot or will not put the special measures in place, the employee must still decide (i) whether he is prepared to risk his health by continuing to work in the known adverse conditions, (ii) whether he should go to his GP to obtain a sick certificate (i.e. unfit at this time to work in this job), or (iii) whether he should seek a different job. Many disputes involve questions of this kind.

---

[6] [1994] 3AER 129; [1995] 2AC 296

21. There are also cases where the employer agrees to act in a particular way aimed at reducing the adverse factors at work. Mostly this is by giving an employee a graduated return to work. Sometimes some quite specific steps are agreed. The question then often arises: "When are the steps to be taken?" or "How long are these steps to remain in place?" In *Walker v Northumberland CC* [1995] 1AER 737 Colman J rejected a claim for damages for injury arising from fairly extreme pressures upon an employee who was contemporaneously complaining to his employer that those pressures would injure his health. However, he awarded damages in respect of the injury arising after Mr Walker's return to work. On his return there was specific medical advice as to what was needed, and the employer agreed to put the necessary structure in place. Having done so for a brief period, the employer then reverted to the pre-existing system and the Claimant had a further breakdown. This decision has been regularly referred to and either approved or not criticised in the Court of Appeal

OVERWORK

22. To a degree psychological stress injuries can readily be compared to physical ones. There are recognised limits to physical endeavour, and if an employer asks an employee to lift too great a weight he will be liable for ensuing damage. Similarly if an employer obliges someone to work too hard and causes injury thereby, he will be liable.

23. In lifting cases there is a quite specific statutory threshold – albeit relaxed in cases of farm labourers. The corresponding regulation for stress may be said to be the Working Time Regulations 1998: an excess of 48 hours per week on average for over 17 weeks breaches the regulation, unless the parties have contracted out. Of course in both cases the coincidence of a breach of duty and an injury does not prove causation, that is quite a separate matter.

24. It must also be borne in mind that there is no such thing as an impossible job – see *Hatton* §43(4) – it is the combination of a vulnerable employee with an onerous job that may result in injury. To establish a breach of duty the Claimant must prove that the work demanded of this particular employee was such that he/she was foreseeably exposed to an unreasonable risk of injury (cf. *Walker,* above).

INJURY / CAUSATION

25. Lastly there are very complex issues of causation. It must be borne in mind that 'stress' is not a medical condition; it is the function of various factors in a given person's environment. 'Stress' at work is usually

considered to be beneficial: it focuses attention, promotes efficiency, and generally is therapeutic to mental health.

26. It is not enough for the Claimant to prove he has suffered an injury caused or contributed to by stress at work; he must prove it was caused by an identified breach - see *Hatton* §43(15). With a condition such as ptsd (post traumatic stress disorder) there is usually no great problem: there is an identifiable index event. However, psychological injury associated with 'stress' is a far more complex beast.

27. First, there is invariably a problem in that the psychiatrists relate the cause to the Claimant's perception of the material events, as opposed to the events themselves. This is a perception which in many cases will have become distorted by reason of the psychological condition – i.e. both after the onset of the condition and in the prodromal state individuals tend to have a heightened and unreliable or unrealistic perception of events.

28. Second, the events referred to at work as the source(s) of the injurious stress almost invariably include matters which are not-actionable (such as personality conflicts; disappointment at the way resources are administered, frustrations at an inability to do one's job in a different way, resentment at more favourable treatment of other employees, etc.).

29. Third, there is usually a catalogue of stresses which exist outside work, whether emotional, financial, environmental, or otherwise (although many of these may not be revealed and/or may prove difficult to discover).

30. Another common problem is that one of the important stressors identified by the Claimant and/or her psychiatrist is often the employer's response to the primary complaint, rather than the subject matter of the complaint itself. For example, the conduct of another employee may well have been upsetting – albeit not pathologically so – but the Claimant may be even more upset by the grievance procedure and the ensuing decisions, although it will be very rare that the employer's conduct in this regard is actionable in the civil courts (as opposed to the Employment Tribunal).

31. The Claimant then has to unravel all the concurrent stressors and prove on the balance of probabilities that a stressor which the court holds to have amounted to a breach of duty has actually caused an injury - see *Hatton* §43(15). This is not straightforward. The concurrent factors may be such that the material stressor (i.e. that which flows from any breach that the Claimant may have proved) simply cannot be identified with sufficient certainty as a potential and separate stressor. Even once identified, it is usually still difficult to prove causation to the necessary standard: psychiatrists often do not feel able to say with any certainty that the removal of this stressor from the environment would probably have left the Claimant in good health, or to a measurable degree in better health. This is not a *Fairchild*

problem, there is only one Defendant – all the other stressors tend to be non-actionable.

32. That is not the end of the problem. The Claimant also has to prove that, absent the proven breach of duty, some different and more beneficial consequence would have ensued. In many cases the options for the employer would in fact have made no material difference (cf. Dillon LJ's comments in *Petch*, above). In some cases the options will have been such although it is possible that the employer might have acted in a way which would have helped avoid some or all of the subject injury, the *likely* non-tortious alternative course that the employer would have taken would also have made no difference. In many cases the best solution would have been for the employer to have dismissed / retired the Claimant for incapacity / ill-health before the injury arose. Not only is there no duty to do this - see *Hatton* §43 (12) – but where this feature is present it will often reflect the fact that this is the course that the Claimant ought to have taken – impacting on questions of *volenti* or on contributory negligence, or both.

EXTENT OF INJURY

33. Once an injury is proved to have been caused by the identified breach, there is also the question of how significant or persistent it is. Psychological injuries from stress often simply reveal a vulnerable personality. Current thinking is that vulnerability to many psychological disorders is usually a constitutional matter, even where there has been no reported (or recorded) psychological problem before. In short, the employee will often be increasingly at risk of developing psychological problems – whether in response to work or to other factors – and the condition for which damages are claimed may be seen either as an acceleration of the onset of the condition, or one which would in any event have been superseded by a subsequent episode within a given period. In *Hatton* the problem was resolved in one case in this way – see §43(16).

THE RECENT CASES: *HATTON,* AND *BARBER*

34. The Court of Appeal in *Hatton* conveniently set out a list of key features:

"43. From the above discussion, the following practical propositions emerge:

(1) There are no special control mechanisms applying to claims for psychiatric (or physical) illness or injury arising from the stress of doing the work the employee is required to do (para 22). The ordinary principles of employer's liability apply (para 20).

(2)   The threshold question is whether this kind of harm to this particular employee was reasonably foreseeable (para 23): this has two components (a) an injury to health (as distinct from occupational stress) which (b) is attributable to stress at work (as distinct from other factors) (para 25).

(3)   Foreseeability depends upon what the employer knows (or ought reasonably to know) about the individual employee. Because of the nature of mental disorder, it is harder to foresee than physical injury, but may be easier to foresee in a known individual than in the population at large (para 23). An employer is usually entitled to assume that the employee can withstand the normal pressures of the job unless he knows of some particular problem or vulnerability (para 29).

(4)   The test is the same whatever the employment: there are no occupations which should be regarded as intrinsically dangerous to mental health (para 24).

(5)   Factors likely to be relevant in answering the threshold question include:

(a)   The nature and extent of the work done by the employee (para 26). Is the workload much more than is normal for the particular job? Is the work particularly intellectually or emotionally demanding for this employee? Are demands being made of this employee unreasonable when compared with the demands made of others in the same or comparable jobs? Or are there signs that others doing this job are suffering harmful levels of stress? Is there an abnormal level of sickness or absenteeism in the same job or the same department?

(b)   Signs from the employee of impending harm to health (paras 27 and 28). Has he a particular problem or vulnerability? Has he already suffered from illness attributable to stress at work? Have there recently been frequent or prolonged absences which are uncharacteristic of him? Is there reason to think that these are attributable to stress at work, for example because of complaints or warnings from him or others?

(6)   The employer is generally entitled to take what he is told by his employee at face value, unless he has good reason to think to the contrary. He does not generally have to make searching enquiries of the employee or seek permission to make further enquiries of his medical advisers (para 29).

(7)   To trigger a duty to take steps, the indications of impending harm to health arising from stress at work must be plain enough for any reasonable employer to realise that he should do something about it (para 31).

(8)   The employer is only in breach of duty if he has failed to take the steps which are reasonable in the circumstances, bearing in mind the magnitude of the risk of harm occurring, the gravity of the harm which may occur, the costs and practicability of preventing it, and the justifications for running the risk (para 32).

(9)   The size and scope of the employer's operation, its resources and the demands it faces are relevant in deciding what is reasonable; these include the interests of other employees and the need to treat them fairly, for example, in any redistribution of duties (para 33).

(10) An employer can only reasonably be expected to take steps which are likely to do some good: the court is likely to need expert evidence on this (para 34).

(11) An employer who offers a confidential advice service, with referral to appropriate counselling or treatment services, is unlikely to be found in breach of duty (paras 17 and 33).

(12) If the only reasonable and effective step would have been to dismiss or demote the employee, the employer will not be in breach of duty in allowing a willing employee to continue in the job (para 34).

(13) In all cases, therefore, it is necessary to identify the steps which the employer both could and should have taken before finding him in breach of his duty of care (para 33).

(14) The claimant must show that that breach of duty has caused or materially contributed to the harm suffered. It is not enough to show that occupational stress has caused the harm (para 35).

(15) Where the harm suffered has more than one cause, the employer should only pay for that proportion of the harm suffered which is attributable to his wrongdoing, unless the harm is truly indivisible. It is for the defendant to raise the question of apportionment (paras 36 and 39).

(16) The assessment of damages will take account of any pre-existing disorder or vulnerability and of the chance that the claimant would have succumbed to a stress related disorder in any event (para 42)."

35. In *Barber* the House of Lords unanimously held that these propositions were correct, but the majority held that the Court of Appeal had misdirected itself in applying them in the case of Mr Barber. The majority held that the findings of fact which the trial judge had made were within the range of findings he could properly have made, without any of the House observing that they would have found the facts in the same way. It is difficult to divine any material proposition of law which alters the concise direction given by the Court of Appeal; at this stage the commentators do not appear to have found any.

GOOD PRACTICE SUGGESTION

- THE BRIEF CHRONOLOGY[4]:- The essence is to keep it brief, aiming for no more than a half to three-quarters side of A4. If possible never create a chronology which the judge has to turn over. To succeed in this you must be highly discriminating with the facts, so that only the dates and events with which the hearing is concerned are listed. If it is reliable the judge is likely to prefer to use the shorter chronology should both sides produce one.

- Do not hold back any of your basic argument – certainly never anything essential. Retain some colour to bring it to life orally. Oral argument is for dialogue, explanation, and amplification but the court should receive no serious surprises. Withhold any particular angle of an argument which may be received better if advanced orally.

---

[4] See also Example J

EXAMPLE D

Chancery Division Trial of Preliminary Issue – Limitation – Defendant's skeleton argument by Michael Pooles QC and Spike Charlwood in July, 1999 – 16pp.

Abbey National Plc v X was a solicitor's negligence claim in which the bank alleged that its conveyancing solicitors had failed to notify matters which would have alerted the bank to the existence of fraud by mortgage applicants. The issue for the court was to assess the date of the bank's subsequent knowledge of the fraud under s.14A Limitation Act 1980.

The language used throughout is fairly formal and legalistic. There is a strong emphasis on detail. Extensive citation is given within the text with substantial quotes from the key authorities. Considerable use is made of footnotes, mainly to cross-refer to the evidence contained in the trial bundles. This document could be used as the basis for a judgment without the judge having recourse to anything other than the referenced evidence.

At trial the claim failed as being time barred and was dismissed. Permission to appeal was granted but the appeal was later abandoned. The case is reported at Times 30th August 1999; [1999] EGCS 114 and Lawtel AC9200139.

SKELETON ARGUMENT ON BEHALF OF THE DEFENDANTS

1. This is the trial of a preliminary issue of limitation pursuant to the order of Master Moncaster made on 18 September 1998 [A/2/46-48].[1] A chronology and *dramatis personae* accompany this skeleton argument.

BACKGROUND

2. This is one of a large number of claims issued by Abbey National plc ("Abbey") against firms of solicitors who acted for it in relation to purchases of residential property in the late 1980s and early 1990s. This claim concerns 20 Upbrook Mews, Bayswater, London W2 ("the Property"). The purchaser and mortgage applicant to Abbey was R S and completion took place on 15 December 1989 at a price of £330,000. The complaint now made against the Defendants ("X") is that they failed to report to Abbey that Ms S's purchase was taking place by way of back to back transfers under which (i) W M

---

[1] References in square brackets are to the trial bundles. Thus, this is a reference to binder A, tab 2, pages 46-48. The core bundle is given the reference "CB".

transferred the Property to F W for £210,000 and (ii) F W transferred it to Ms S for £330,000 (SoC, para. 10 [CB/1/6]).

3. The history of the loan to Ms S after completion is a sorry tale of default (by Ms S) and delay (by Abbey). Ms S defaulted immediately and possession was obtained on 24 January 1991. Despite this, the Property was not sold until 3 May 1995. In the interim Abbey took steps to investigate AB, its valuers, but, it is alleged, it never once occurred to any of its employees or agents that a claim might exist against X.

4. Notwithstanding the fact that Ms S's purchase completed on 15 December 1989, the Writ herein was not issued until 14 August 1997 [CB/1/1-2]. Accordingly, it is the X's case that Abbey's claim is barred by the Limitation Act 1980 ("the Act"). It having been conceded by Abbey that (i) its equitable claims are not tenable and (ii) its Writ was issued more than 6 years after the accrual of its common law claims,[2] the sole issue for the Court is the determination of the starting date for the purposes of s.14A(4)(b) of the Act. The crucial date, of course, will be 14 August 1994 and we refer to this date below as "the Cut Off Date".

THE PARTIES' POSITIONS

5. Although its Writ was issued on 14 August 1997, Abbey claims that it did not have the knowledge required by s.14A of the Act until 19 September 1997[3] when it received notification from the Land Registry that the transfers from W M to F W and from F W to Ms S had been sent by X to the Land Registry at the same time.[4]

6. This assertion – which must be wrong even as to actual knowledge – represents an overly simplistic approach which focuses too much on actual knowledge. X submits that Abbey obtained at least constructive knowledge of its claim significantly before the Cut Off Date as a result of one or more of the following:

(i) information concerning mortgage fraud and the potential involvement of professionals in such frauds received from external bodies such as the Building Societies Association, the Council for Mortgage Lenders and the Law Society;[5]

---

[2] Affidavit of Andrew Whitmore, paragraph 2 [A/3/88].

[3] Affidavit of Andrew Whitmore, paragraph 4(h) [A/3/91].

[4] AW1, page 1 [A/3/95].

[5] Which material was disseminated fairly widely (see, for example, [F/13/2252, 2259, 2261 and 2286-9]) although not, it seems, to any of those giving evidence in this case. The documents in binder F, tab 13 were not disclosed in the present action, but in Abbey National v Forsyths (unreported, 11 June 1997, QBD (OR), HHJ Fox-Andrews QC).

(ii) the realisation that it had, would or was likely to suffer a significant loss on its loan to Ms S;

(iii) its investigation of AB;

(iv) its receipt from X of the Schedule of Deeds [CB/4/1697]; and

(v) discussions with other lenders and any investigations consequential upon those discussions.

PRELIMINARY MATTERS

7. Three preliminary matters arise in relation to s.14A of the Act:

   (i) the correct approach to it;
   (ii) upon which party does the burden of proof lie; and
   (iii) the application of the concept of knowledge to Abbey.

(i) The correct approach to s.14A

8. X submits that the correct approach to the issues raised by s.14A of the Act is that set out by Sir Thomas Bingham MR (as he then was) in *Spencer-Ward v Humberts* [1995] 1 EGLR 123 at 126L:

> "It is, I think, necessary that issues on this section should be approached in a broad common-sense way, bearing in mind the object of the section and the injustice that it was intended to mitigate.[6] There is a danger of being too clever and it would usually be possible to find some fact of which a plaintiff did not become sure until later. It would be a pity if a desire to be indulgent to plaintiffs led the court to be unfair to defendants."

(ii) The burden of proof

9. X submits that the burden of proof rests with Abbey. X having raised the issue of limitation, it is for Abbey to prove that its claim is not barred by the Act; i.e. it must, in the context of this case, show that "the earliest date on which [it] had ... the knowledge required for bringing an action for damages in respect of the relevant damage"[7] was on or after the Cut Off Date. See:

   (i) *London Congregational Union Inc v Harriss & Harriss (a firm)* [1988] 1 All ER 15 at 30d-g *per* Ralph Gibson LJ:[8]

---

[6] As to which, it should be noted that the protection of defendants from stale claims was seen as equally as important as avoiding claimants being statute barred before they were aware they had a claim. See the 24th report of the Law Reform Committee, paragraphs 4.2 and 4.4.

[7] S.14A(5) of the Act.

[8] With whom (on this point at least) both Sir Denys Buckley and O'Connor LJ agreed. See 34f and 37f.

"The onus lies on the plaintiffs to prove that their cause of action accrued within the relevant period before the writ. ... Counsel for the plaintiffs argued that the plaintiffs had proved 'an accrual of damage' within the six-year period before the writ by proving the existence of damage within that period and that, on tendering that proof, the burden passed to the defendants 'to show that the apparent accrual of a cause of action is misleading and that in reality the cause of action accrued at an earlier date'. I cannot accept this contention. It confuses the existence, or continued existence, of damage or its consequences with accrual of damage, which is the coming into existence of damage. In my judgment, the burden on a plaintiff is to show that, on the balance of probabilities, his cause of action accrued, ie came into existence, on a day within the period of limitation. If he shows that, then the evidential burden would, as stated by Lord Pearce, pass to the defendants to show, if they can, that the apparent accrual of the plaintiffs' cause of action was misleading etc."

(ii) *Campbell v Meacocks* (unreported, 26 July 1995, CA) at page 7 of the transcript *per* Otton LJ:[9]

"Thus the Campbells, upon whom the burden of proof lies, must show that the 'starting date' occurred within three years of the issue of their writ."

(iii) *Abbey National v Forsyths* (unreported, 11 June 1997, QBD (OR), HHJ Fox-Andrews QC) at page 26 of the transcript:

"... the law is well settled that the onus at all times is on the society to show that the earliest date when it had knowledge (including knowledge within sub-section (10)) occurred on or after the 29th April 1993."

(iv) *Paragon Finance plc v DB Thakerar & Co (a firm)* [1999] 1 All ER 400 (a case concerning s.32 of the Act) at 418b *per* Millett LJ:[10]

"The question is not whether the plaintiffs *should* have discovered the fraud sooner; but whether they *could* with reasonable diligence have done so. The burden of proof is on them. They must establish that they *could not* have discovered the fraud without exceptional measures which they could not reasonably have been expected to take."

(iii) **Abbey's knowledge**

---

[9] With whom Hirst and Nourse LJJ agreed. See page 12 of the transcript.
[10] With whom Pill and May LJJ agreed. See pages 419b and 420h.

10. There can be no doubt that s.14A applies to corporate entities such as Abbey.[11] In this case information was acquired by Abbey in a number of different ways: some, such as the knowledge relating to Ms S, was specific to this transaction; some, such as that relating to AB, whilst not specifically concerning this transaction, was related to it; and some, such as the information gained from other lenders and external bodies, was generic. X submits that:

   (i)   Abbey's actions are to be judged by looking at all the information it had and asking what steps it ought to have taken. There is no need or requirement to delve into questions of who had what knowledge when and what ought to have been done with it; or
   (ii) all knowledge gained by employees of Abbey acting in the course of their employment is relevant knowledge of Abbey; or
   (iii) it was for Abbey to ensure (or to have in place systems to ensure) that:

      (a) an individual or department was responsible for taking decisions as to whether to sue professionals; and
      (b) all relevant knowledge was passed to that individual or department.

See *Finance for Mortgages Ltd v Farley* [1998] PNLR 145, *Meridian Global v Securities Commission* [1995] 2 AC 500, *Lennard's Asiatic Petroleum* [1915] AC 705, *El Ajou v Dollar* [1994] 2 All ER 685, *Abbey National v Wilkin & Chapman* (above) and *Birmingham Midshires Building Society v Infields* (unreported, 20 May 1999, QBD (TCC), HHJ Bowsher QC).

SECTION 14A OF THE ACT: MATTERS IN ISSUE

11. The matters in issue are, it is submitted, limited as follows: what was the earliest date upon which Abbey had (actual or constructive) knowledge that the loss caused by the loan to Ms S was "attributable in whole or in part to the act or omission which is alleged to constitute negligence"; i.e. the failure to report that Ms S was purchasing the Property by way of a sub-sale.[12]
12. It is presumed that Abbey does not contend that its damage was ever such as not to be "sufficiently serious to justify instituting proceedings for damages".[13] If it does, it is submitted that its loss was

---

[11] For examples of s.14A of the Act being applied to such entities, see: *Abbey National v Forsyths* (above), *Abbey National v Wilkin & Chapman* (unreported, 7/10/97, QBD, HHJ McGonigal) and *Finance for Mortgages Ltd v Farley* [1998] PNLR 145.

[12] S.14A(8)(a) of the Act. X were the only possible solicitor defendants and Abbey at all material times had the right to bring any action which might exist against X as a result of their conduct of Ms S's purchase of the Property.

[13] S.14A(7) of the Act.

clearly sufficiently serious by February or May 1991, at which points it was anticipating a loss of £21,000 [CB/4/1122] and £74,000 [B/6/1151].[14]

SECTION 14A(8)(A) OF THE ACT: ATTRIBUTION

13. Section 14A(8)(a) (together with s.14A(10)) of the Act requires that Abbey should have known (actually or constructively) "the facts which can fairly be described as constituting the negligence of which [it] complains."[15] Thus, the facts of which Abbey must have had actual or constructive knowledge are that:

   (i)   the Property was purchased by way of a sub-sale; and
  (ii)   that fact was not reported to Abbey.

14. As to (ii): first, this would have been immediately apparent from Abbey's underwriting files; and, secondly, given that it is Abbey's case that report of the sub-sale would have caused the withdrawal of the offer to Ms S (SoC, para. 11 [CB/1/7-8]), it must follow that it accepts that, once it is aware that there was a sub-sale, it also becomes aware that that fact was not reported. Thus, the issue is simply: when did Abbey first have (actual or constructive) knowledge that the Property had been purchased by way of a sub-sale?

CONSTRUCTIVE KNOWLEDGE[16]

15. Knowledge that the Property had been purchased by way of a sub-sale was or could have been gained:

   (i)   from the information contained in Ms S's application form [CB/4/1022-1025] when combined with the Land Registry documents sent to Abbey;[17]

---

[14] That this loss had not crystalised is, it is submitted, irrelevant. See *Nykredit Mortgage Bank plc v Edward Erdman Group Ltd* [1997] 1 WLR 1627. To suggest otherwise would be to confuse the issues when loss is suffered and its quantification. Abbey's apparent reliance on the need to establish the economic viability of a raft of claims is misconceived. No construction of the Act is apt to found an additional consideration of whether Abbey wishes to institute other proceedings.

[15] *Hallam-Eames v Merrett Syndicates* [1995] 7 Med LR 123 at 126, col. 2 *per* Hoffmann LJ (giving the judgment of the Court).

[16] S.14A(10) of the Act.

[17] The application form gave the vendor as V [CB/4/1024]; the proprietorship register stated that the person registered as the proprietor of the land immediately prior to Ms S was Mr M [CB/4/1697]. NB that, in addition to receiving the Schedule of Deeds from X, Abbey carried out its own search of the register on 29 August 1990 [CB/4/1083]. As well as being considered by Abbey, the deeds were considered by both firms of solicitors instructed by Abbey in relation to the sale of the Property. See [CB/4/1140] (Mendel Hazan & Co) and [CB/4/1548] (Tucker Turner Kingsley Wood & Co, who were asked specifically whether the completing solicitors – i.e. X – might be sued [CB/4/1658]).

    (ii) by contacting X;

    (iii) by calling for X's file in good time; or

    (iv) by obtaining the relevant information or transfers from the Land Registry.[18]

16.   It is, therefore, X's case that:

    (i) Abbey had the requisite knowledge from July 1990 (the date of receipt of the Land Registry documents); or

    (ii) could have gained that knowledge at any time by the making of one or more of the simple enquiries mentioned in paragraph 15 above.

The next section of this skeleton argument sets out in summary the matters upon which X rely as showing that Abbey ought to have made those enquiries long before they did and in any event prior to the Cut Off Date.

MATTERS WHICH ABBEY KNEW OR OUGHT TO HAVE KNOWN FROM WHICH KNOWLEDGE WAS OR OUGHT TO HAVE BEEN OBTAINED

17.   The matters set out below should (together or separately) have alerted Abbey to the potentially disastrous nature of the loan to Ms S or suggested that the underlying transaction may not have been as Abbey believed and to the need to investigate the transaction, including X's role in it, further.

    (i) Ms S's failure to supply a MIRAS 70 form [CB/4/1058 and 1061].[19]

    (ii) Ms S fell immediately into arrears, necessitating the sending of a "final notice" only three months into the loan period [CB/4/1076] and the cheque sent to clear those arrears [CB/4/1076] failed to clear [CB/4/1081] It was noted on 25 June 1991 that "The reason for the arrears are unknown and arrangements to clear them were not adhered to." [CB/4/1162]

    (iii) The discrepancy between the employment details given by Ms S in her application form [CB/4/1022] (and confirmed by a reference [B/6/1037]) and the information obtained upon the making of enquiries in early April 1990 [CB/4/1077-81] (which discrepancy was sufficient to prompt a referral to Abbey's Securities and Investigations Department [CB/4/1077 and 1080]).

---

[18] The means by which Abbey now asserts it did gain knowledge (affidavit of Andrew Whitmore, paragraph 4 [A/3/88-91]).

[19] The Council for Mortgage Lenders' guidance notes: "Where an applicant appears to be eligible for MIRAS and has not returned his MIRAS form further checks should be made about the applicant." [E/8/2075]

(iv) The notification on 5 April 1990 that the Property was to be sold [CB/4/1079].

(v) The property was unoccupied when repossessed and peaceable possession taken [CB/4/1601].

(vi) In early February 1991 Abbey received repossession valuations at £225,000-£230,000 and £175,000-£180,000 [CB/4/1102-1105], leading to an anticipated loss of £21,000 [CB/4/1122]. On 8 July 1991[20] a sale at £195,000 was approved, accepting a loss of in the region of £89,000 [CB/4/1168]. The position as regards loss deteriorated thereafter.[21]

(vii) From November 1990 onwards Abbey carried out a detailed investigation into AB, the firm which provided the mortgage valuation. Action was contemplated against that firm by August 1991 and it was believed to have been guilty of a fraud by 31 January 1992 [CB/5/1977]. By no later than August 1991, Abbey was on notice that: (a) the true value of the Property at the time of Ms S's purchase was "closer to £200/225,000"; (b) the Property had been on the market for some considerable time at that price; and (c) it seemed that none of the group of properties of which the Property formed part had ever achieved a price of £300,000.[22] If Abbey believed that AB was a party to a fraud, any consideration of the nature of the underlying fraud involved ought to have given rise to consideration, and investigation, of the existence of a link between Ms S and her vendor and whether, prior to completing Ms S's purchase, X had or ought to have had any material indicative of that link or otherwise suggestive of price inflation.

18. Clearly, therefore, Abbey was or ought to have been aware from a very early stage (and certainly no later than February 1991) that they had suffered a substantial loss in relation to the loan to Ms S. It is submitted that that, of itself, was enough to require Abbey to take steps to investigate the cause(s) of that loss and that that investigation should have included one or more of the enquiries set out in paragraph 15 above. See *Forbes v Wandsworth Health Authority* [1997] QB 402 at 412C and 413F *per* Stuart-Smith LJ:[23]

"Turning to the words of s 14(3), it is clear that the deceased could reasonably have been expected to acquire the relevant knowledge with the help of suitable medical advice. The real question is, whether it was reasonable

---

[20] The asking price having been reduced from £245,000 to £207,000 in early May 1991 [CB/4/1151].

[21] See, for example, [CB/4/1209 and 1391].

[22] See the report of Barnard Marcus entitled "Abbey National plc v AB Partnership" [CB/4/1185-1191].

[23] Although doubting the correctness of viewing the matter in terms of a decision, conscious or unconscious, by the claimant, Evans LJ agreed that the claimant should have taken a second opinion "soon after the amputation, if he ever intended to do so" (at page 423F). Roch LJ dissented.

for him to seek that advice. If it was, he took no steps at all to do so. One of the problems with the language of s 14(3)(b) is that two alternative courses of action may be perfectly reasonable. Thus it may be perfectly reasonable for a person who is not cured when he hoped to be to say 'Oh well, it is just one of those things. I expect the doctors did their best'; alternatively the explanation for the lack of success may be due to want of care on the part of those in whose charge he was, in which case it would be perfectly reasonable to take a second opinion. And I do not think that the person who adopts the first alternative can necessarily be said to be acting unreasonably. But he is in effect making a choice, either consciously by deciding to do nothing, or unconsciously by in fact doing nothing. Can a person who has effectively made this choice many years later, and without any alteration of circumstances, change his mind and then seek advice which reveals that all along he had a claim? I think not. It seems to me that where, as here, the plaintiff expected or at least hoped that the operation would be successful and it manifestly was not, with the result that he sustained a major injury, a reasonable man of moderate intelligence, such as the deceased, if he thought about the matter, would say that the lack of success was 'either just one of those things, a risk of the operation or something may have gone wrong and there may have been a want of care; I do not know which, but if I am ever to make a claim, I must find out'.

In my judgment, any other construction would make the 1980 Act unworkable since a plaintiff could delay indefinitely before seeking expert advice and say, as the deceased did in this case, I had no occasion to seek it earlier. He would therefore be able, as of right, to bring the action, no matter how many years had elapsed. This is contrary to the whole purpose of the 1980 Act which is to prevent defendants being vexed by stale claims which it is no longer possible to contest. The primary limitation period in personal injury actions is therefore three years from the date when the cause of action occurred. This is modified when the plaintiff does not know, and could not reasonably discover with the assistance of expert advice, matters essential to his cause of action. If he can bring himself within the provisions of ss 11 (4) and 14 he has an absolute right to bring the action and no question of discretion arises. Section 33, in my opinion, is designed to give the court an ultimate discretion in cases such as this, so that it can allow the plaintiff to sue if it is equitable to do so.

...

In my judgment, a reasonable man in the position of the deceased, who knew that the operation had been unsuccessful, that he had suffered a major injury which would seriously affect his enjoyment of life in the future, would affect his employability on the labour market, if he had any, and would impose substantial burdens on his wife and family in looking after him, if he is minded to make a claim at any time, should and would take advice reasonably promptly."

19. In further support of the submission that loss alone is sufficient to require investigation, X relies upon the fact that this appears to be the approach eventually adopted by Abbey once it did begin to review claims.[24] For the avoidance of doubt, should it be suggested that there was insufficient knowledge of loss until the sale of the Property by Abbey, X will contend that:

  (i) that is incorrect. The fact of sale does no more than crystallise a loss which already exists; see *Nykredit Mortgage Bank plc v Edward Erdman Group Ltd* [1997] 1 WLR 1627; and

  (ii) in any event, the sale should have been completed long before 3 May 1995. See *Bristol & West Building Society v Fancy & Jackson* [1997] 4 All ER 582 at 623e-f *per* Chadwick J:

> "It is, I think, beyond argument that such part of the loss as is attributable to the society's failure to realise the mortgaged property at a proper price or within a reasonable time cannot be regarded as having been caused by the breach of the retainer or the breach of the warranty of authority. That part of the loss has been caused by the society's own conduct in failing to mitigate."

Similarly, an unreasonable delay in the sale cannot put back the date of Abbey's knowledge. In particular, the gain realised by refusing the offer of £130,000 made in May 1992 [CB/4/1315] (£22,000) was substantially outweighed by the additional losses suffered between May 1992 and May 1995 (being of the order of £60,000-£70,000 plus some proportion of the management, etc costs of £43,080.90).

20. If, however, the mere fact of the loss was insufficient to require Abbey to make such investigations, it is submitted that Abbey had ample further information which required the making of further enquiries. That information falls into three categories:

  (i) information gained by Abbey whilst administering the loan to Ms S or obtained during investigations relating to that loan and AB;[25]

  (ii) general information gained from external bodies;

  (iii) information gained from other lenders and the investigation undertaken by FIS; and

  (iv) information held by Abbey's legal department as solicitors.

---

[24] Affidavit of Gary Black, para.s 10-11 [A/3/136-7].

[25] With whom there was said to be "a definite problem" by 26 November 1990. AB were suspended from Abbey's panel on or about 27 November 1990 and Abbey knew by 30 November 1990 that AB had been reported to the police [CB/5/1705-7]. By 21 August 1992 at the latest the Property had been associated with other AB properties [CB/5/1719].

21. Information falling within sub-paragraph (i) above is largely dealt with in paragraph 17 above. In addition, the title deeds received in July 1991 [F/14/2391] showed that the person registered as the proprietor of the Property prior to Ms S's purchase was not the person believed by Abbey / represented by Ms S [CB/4/1024] to be the vendor. Schedule 1 to this skeleton argument summarises the material received by Abbey from external sources. As to this, it is noteworthy that by April 1992 Abbey was aware of the significance of and acting upon sub-sales [F/13/2286]. As to sub-paragraph (iii) of paragraph 20 above, the timing and scope of the knowledge obtained will be a matter for investigation with Abbey's witnesses. As to sub-paragraph (iv), see the recognition of the significance of mortgage fraud, reporting obligations and sub-sales found in binder F, tab 13 (the *Forsyths* file).

THE CORRECT APPROACH TO THE QUESTION OF REASONABLENESS

22. S.14A(10) of the Act states that "... a person's knowledge includes knowledge which he might reasonably have been expected to acquire - ..." and then sets out two matters from which knowledge might be acquired. As is implicit in the above submissions, it is X's case that the issue of what knowledge Abbey might *reasonably* have been expected to acquire is to be determined by reference to the specific facts of this case. By contrast, Abbey's case appears to be that:[26] (i) it was not, prior to the Cut Off Date, aware of the possibility of successful recovery actions against solicitors; (ii) it was reasonable for it to investigate the economics of suing solicitors generally before making enquiries in any specific case; and (iii) without the knowledge gained by carrying out that investigation, there was nothing to alert it to the fact that X's role in the loan to Ms S ought to be investigated.

23. As to this, X submits as follows:

    (i)   it should be remembered that it was not the investigation of the position vis-à-vis solicitors generally that allegedly alerted Abbey to the present claim, but the investigations which it carried out into transactions involving AB in 1996 and 1997.[27] Those investigations could and should have been carried out as part of Abbey's investigations of such transactions in 1990-1992;

    (ii) a case specific approach is consistent with the approach taken by the courts in *Abbey National v Forsyths, Abbey National v Wilkin & Chapman* and *Birmingham Midshires Building Society v Infields* (above);

---

[26] See, in particular, the evidence of Gary Black [A/3/131-53].
[27] Affidavit of Andrew Whitmore, paragraph 4 [A/3/88-91].

(iii)   the economics of investigating and suing solicitors generally are irrelevant to whether the questions thrown up during the administration of the loan to Ms S should have been investigated;

(iv)   Abbey was well aware as early as January 1991 of the possibility of making claims against solicitors who had been negligent and that a failure to pass information on to Abbey might amount to negligence;[28]

(v)   even if it was not so aware, the additional knowledge obtained by Abbey which it says prompted the realisation that solicitors might successfully be sued went simply to the legal consequences of facts already known to it, a matter which is irrelevant to s.14A of the Act;[29]

(vi)   it needed no general investigation to realise that this case ought to have been investigated. In particular, by no later than August 1991[30] Abbey knew or ought to have known that: (a) the Property had been over-priced; and (b) their borrower, Ms S, had disappeared, and it was incumbent upon Abbey to make enquiries as to the mechanism by which the over-pricing had occurred;

(vii) the need to consider the economics of pursuing solicitors arose only out of Abbey's failure to consider the issue at the time each individual file had been dealt with and is no answer to the allegation that this transaction should have been considered properly during its lifetime; and

(viii) even if it was, in the circumstances of this case, reasonable to carry out fairly general investigations prior to investigating this case, that investigation should have been completed no later than the beginning of 1994.[31] The following matters, in particular, are relied upon:

    (a)   significant losses were experienced by Abbey from 1990 onwards;[32]

    (b)   substantial amounts of information concerning solicitor involvement in mortgage fraud had been received by Abbey from 1988 – 1992;[33]

---

[28] See Mrs H's memo of 14 January 1991 [F/13/2260-2]. Similarly, the material summarised in schedule 1 to this skeleton argument is quite explicit as to the potential involvement of solicitors in mortgage fraud. There should have been no need, as late as 1994, to train staff as to ways in which this might occur.

[29] See s.14A(9) of the Act and HF Pension Trustees Ltd v Ellison [1999] TLR 159.

[30] See paragraph 17 above.

[31] Thus leaving sufficient time before the Cut Off Date for any case specific enquiries to be made.

[32] See paragraphs 3 and 4 of Gary Black's affidavit [A/3/132-3] and paragraph 5 of Geoff Skelton's affidavit [A/3/105].

[33] See schedule 1 to this skeleton argument.

(c) Abbey had received, and taken steps to circulate, draft guidance relating to the reporting of sub-sales in April 1992.[34] This led to the amendment of their certificate on title;[35] and

(d) in any event, Abbey took too long over its general investigations.

CONCLUSION

24. The various matters which were or ought to have been known to Abbey were clearly such as to require it to take steps to investigate X's role in the transaction. The steps required were not complex and for Abbey to suggest that it remained ignorant of the possibility of recoveries against solicitors until after the Cut Off Date is incredible. The words of HHJ Bowsher QC, giving judgment in *Birmingham Midshires Building Society v Infields* (above) are apposite:

> "… someone in the claimants' office should have said, 'We employ solicitors to protect us against fraud and to prevent our loans being used to buy property for rent, what was this solicitor doing?'
>
> …
>
> I find it hard to believe that those responsible for the management of Building Societies in general or this Building Society in particular were ever so naïve as to think that solicitors can do no wrong. If they were so naïve, I do not believe that assists them with regard to section 14A of the Limitation Act. The reasonable man is not naïve."

GOOD PRACTICE SUGGESTION

- Overview - always provide a succinct history of the action thus far and the core issues.[5]

- Never create issues which are not pleaded.

- Use propositions of law to identify the issues: get authorities that fit and apply these to your facts, in order to create a legal framework for your argument.

- Be cautious about anticipating arguments from the other side, especially if there is nothing in the statements of case to alert you. Do not identify weaknesses the other side may not have seen or, at least, have not properly formulated. If there is any serious prospect of your opponent and the court not taking a point that damages you, don't deal with it.

---

[34] See Steve Reading's memo of 24 April 1992 [F/13/2286-96].

[35] [F/13/2333].

[5] See also Examples C and J.

- If you are defending keep out of your skeleton argument the detail of points and material you intend to use in cross-examination. Do not over commit yourself in argument – leave room to manoeuvre depending on how the evidence comes out. You will otherwise find yourself a hostage to fortune.

EXAMPLE E

Chancery Division Trial – Defendant's skeleton argument by Spike Charlwood in April, 2003 – 18pp.

Z v X was a solicitor's negligence claim arising out of the conveyance of a house purchased by the claimant at auction for more than it was worth. The issues at trial concerned the nature and extent of the professional retainer and what duties were owed under it, breach, causation, quantum and failure to mitigate loss.

There is a strong emphasis on detail and cross-referencing to the five trial bundles. The text is de-cluttered by placing heavy reliance on footnotes. The language used is not formal, occasionally idiomatic but not conversational. There is a real sense of completeness – the judge can base his entire judgment on this written skeleton should he wish to. As a document it is designed for the judge to take away and use to formulate his opinion after the evidence has concluded. The writer uses a chronological narrative that is sufficiently detailed to avert the need for a separate chronology.

Note that the writer deals with the Claimant's pleaded case without pre-empting the way evidence may come out in relation to certain issues. No formal conclusion is offered.

At trial the claim succeeded but only to the extent of 10% of the value of the claim pleaded.

SKELETON ARGUMENT

on behalf of the Defendant

INTRODUCTION

1. This is an action alleging professional negligence against the Defendant, a solicitor. It arises out of the Claimant's attempted purchase of 10 Chestnut Road, South Tooting, London SE29 ("the Property") and follows litigation between the Claimant and Lambeth Council relating to the Property.
2. There are 5 trial bundles: A – statements of case and evidence; B1-3 – Claimant's disclosure; and C – Defendant's disclosure (his file). The Court is respectfully asked to pre-read the skeleton arguments and the documents identified in the agreed reading list.

THE FACTUAL BACKGROUND

3. On 20 February 1996 the Claimant attended a property auction. He had previously decided to bid for lot 101, the Property, which had been described in the auction particulars [B2/386] as freehold. A correction at the auction [B2/399] stated that in fact only a leasehold interest[1] in the Property was being sold and that the unexpired term was only about 30 years. The Claimant nonetheless successfully bid £44,500 for the Property and paid a 10% deposit.

4. On 23 February 1996 he, together with DS and VC, two property-developer friends of the Claimant, attended at the Defendant's offices. The Defendant's attendance note of that meeting appears at [C1]. It is the Defendant's case[2] that: (i) this was his first contact with the Claimant;[3] (ii) at that time the Claimant was, to all intents and purposes, proceeding as a nominal purchaser on behalf of M Properties Ltd;[4] (iii) he advised that the Property would need to be occupied by an individual, rather than a company; (iv) the Claimant believed at that stage that the freehold was owned by Lambeth; (v) the Claimant had "problems with m[or]t[ga]ge"; and (vi) he was asked to obtain further information as to the Property and to liase with Lambeth in connection with the proposed purchase of the leasehold and freehold interests in the Property.

5. The Claimant did not at that meeting ask the Defendant to take the necessary steps to complete.[5] He did not at that time have finance in place, did not know who the freeholder was and wanted, if possible, to acquire the freehold in addition to the leasehold interest which he had purchased at the auction. In any event, these matters meant that completion could not have been effected at that time.

6. On 27 February 1996 the Defendant discovered that the freeholder was not Lambeth, but B Engineering Ltd.[6] He wrote to B's parent company on 1 March 1996 [C10]. They responded via their management company, XX Management Ltd, on 14 March 1996 and indicated a willingness in principle to sell the freehold [C13]. VC confirmed on 19 March 1996 that it would be in order to arrange an

---

[1] The lease appears at [B2/376]; Lambeth's title at [B2/382].

[2] See paragraphs 6-8 of his statement [A123-5].

[3] There is a dispute as to whether there was any prior contact between the Claimant and the Defendant. See paragraph 5 of the Claimant's first witness statement [A69] and paragraphs 6-7 of the Defendant's statement [A123-4]. As the Claimant contends only that "limited and informal advice" was given before 23 February 1996 and makes no complaint about that advice, the dispute appears to be relevant only (and only peripherally) to the question of how far the Claimant was prepared to act under his own steam and/or without legal assistance. See further paragraphs 26 and 27 below. The Defendant's evidence (which is supported by his attendance note [C1] and his diary entry [B3/1087]) should be preferred.

[4] Thus: the Defendant's attendance note [C1] gives the name of the client as "M Properties"; Messrs DS and VC were connected with M Properties; and M Properties and/or VC continued to be referred to / involved until at least 15 March 1996 [C3, 4, 9, 13 and 15].

[5] C.f. paragraph 11 of the Claimant's statement [A74].

[6] Statement, paragraph 10 [A125]; note dated 27/2/96 [C3]. Andrews & Robson, Lambeth's estate agents, described the freeholders as having "some unusual ways of dealing with individual transactions." [B2/438]

inspection by XX [C15]. On 20 March 1996 the Defendant made an appointment for the inspection to take place on 27 March 1996 [C15].[7] Shortly after 4 April 1996 the Defendant received a schedule of dilapidations from B's solicitors [C19]. The total value of the works set out was some £40,261.37 [C25A]. This was almost three times the £15,000 that the Claimant had expected to spend on the Property.[8] The Defendant sent a copy of the schedule to the Claimant on 13 April 1996 [C19].[9]

7. In the meantime, the Property had on 1 March 1996 been valued and the valuation [B1/414-414b[10]] showed that the Claimant had paid more for the leasehold interest in the Property than it was worth.[11] The Claimant does not say when he received this, merely that he did.[12]

8. As at early April 1996, therefore, the transaction suffered from the following features:

    8.1.   the interest in the Property purchased by the Claimant was lease-hold, not freehold;

    8.2.   the unexpired term of the lease was only about 30 years;[13]

    8.3.   the Claimant thought that enfranchisement would be "costly";[14]

    8.4.   the freeholder was an unconnected third party who wanted £20,000 for the freehold interest in the Property;[15]

    8.5.   if he could not buy the freehold interest, the Leasehold Reform Act 1967 would not assist him for 3 years and only then if there had been individual residence;[16]

    8.6.   substantially more needed to be spent at the Property than the Claimant had anticipated; and

    8.7.   the Claimant had, or believed he had, overpaid for the Property.

---

[7] See, in general, paragraph 12 of his witness statement [A125].

[8] See paragraph 6 of his statement [A70].

[9] See, in general, paragraph 13 of the Defendant's statement [A125-6].

[10] NB that part of this document is missing from the trial bundles.

[11] In its present condition the freehold value of the Property was put at £47,000, the estimated restricted realisation price ("ERRP") of the freehold at £45,000 and the ERRP of the leasehold at only £35,000. No non-ERRP value for the leasehold was given, but the Claimant read the report as valuing the lease at £35,000 [B2/375A]. In any event, by analogy with the freehold figures it would have been no more than £37,000.

[12] See paragraph 9 of his first statement [A72]. He also says that he is "sure" that he showed the report to the Defendant. This is disputed. Neither the finances nor the economics of the deal were discussed with the Defendant in any detail. See paragraphs 32, 34 and 35 of the Defendant's statement [A130-1]. The clear evidence of the Defendant on this point should be preferred to the uncertain evidence of the Claimant.

[13] A term so short that it was given as the reason by the valuers for their valuation of the leasehold interest (which was some £10,000 lower than the freehold price) [B2/414a-b].

[14] See his note at [B2/364] (typed copy at [B2/375A]). Some of the figures which the Claimant had in mind for other aspects of the matter are set out at [B2/375B] and bear out his assessment.

[15] See the Claimant's draft letter at [C29].

[16] See s.1 of the Act.

9. In other words, the Claimant had every incentive at that time to try to improve his position if he could. Indeed, unless the Claimant could improve his position, the transaction did not make economic sense.

10. Unsurprisingly, therefore, the Claimant opened negotiations with both Lambeth[17] and the freeholders[18] in an attempt to improve his position. Initially it seemed that, at least as far as Lambeth were concerned, this might bear fruit. They did not simply reject the idea that they should deal with the dilapidations, but referred the question to the Borough Valuers [C28].[19] Lambeth did not reply substantively until 18 September 1996 [C43-4]. They apologised for their delay (about which the Claimant had complained on at least 3 occasions[20]), but refused to reduce the purchase price. Nothing had happened with the freeholders in the interim. As at September 1996, therefore, the transaction retained all of the unattractive features set out above.

11. Despite this, the Claimant's letter to the Defendant of 23 September 1996 [C42] reads in part:

    "Now that we are (hopefully) near to completion I shall seek the funds for the purchase and contact you shortly about this."

12. In fact, no such contact was received. It is the Claimant's case[21] that he also orally instructed the Defendant in September 1996 to "proceed with completion as quickly as possible". The Defendant denies this and relies in particular on the fact that this assertion is inconsistent with the Claimant's letters of 23 September 1996 (above) and 17 November 1996 (below) and is unsupported by any documentary evidence.[22]

13. The Claimant next wrote to the Defendant on 17 November 1996 [C45], following service of a Notice to Complete by Lambeth [C47]. His letter reads:

    "Please find enclosed a letter I have received from Lambeth and a notice to complete. I would be grateful if you could write to them with a new date – how about 22/23rd December? [I need at least a month to finalise the funds][23]
    Please let me know if there is any problem."

---

[17] See, for example, paragraph 21 of the Claimant's first statement [A82]. It is denied that the Claimant negotiated with Lambeth because of anything the Defendant did or did not do.

[18] See, for example, his letter to CHP Management [C29].

[19] See also [B2/451 and 454].

[20] 20 August and 6 and 11 September 1996 [B2/460, 463 and 467].

[21] See paragraph 32 of his first statement [A92].

[22] Including the telephone logs recently disclosed by the Claimant [B3/1082-6].

[23] Emphasis added.

14. Again, it is the Claimant's case[24] that he also orally instructed the Defendant to "complete the purchase as soon as possible", but again this is inconsistent with his letters and is unsupported by any documentary evidence[25] and is denied.

15. As at September / November 1996, therefore, the Claimant had been unable to improve the transaction, was still stalling and still did not have the funds in place. Indeed, this funding issue was never solved during the Defendant's retainer. Thus, on 10 February 1997 [C71] the Claimant again raised the issue of finance:

> "… for now, I'll work on the financial arrangements and contact you again in a couple of weeks."

16. On 28 November 1996 [C56] the Defendant sent Lambeth a letter designed to hold things up. On 12 December 1996, following discussion with the Claimant, the Defendant sent to Lambeth an offer that the Claimant would pay a further £25,000 for the leasehold interest in the Property [C59-60].[26] This offer was chased (by the Defendant resending the letter with a fax cover sheet [C62]) on 6 January 1997. By letters dated 3 and 5 February 1997 [C66-8], Lambeth reiterated their position and stated that the contract had been rescinded, but offered to refund the Claimant's deposit.[27]

17. On 6 February 1997, the Claimant and the Defendant met at the Defendant's offices. The Defendant's attendance note of that meeting appears at [C69-70]. As is clear from that attendance note: (i) the Defendant made it clear that the legal position relating to the Notice to Complete was not clear;[28] (ii) the Claimant for the first time informed the Defendant that he had been carrying out works at the Property; (iii) the Claimant knew that he had taken a risk; and (iv) it was agreed that the Defendant would write a holding letter whilst a plan of action was decided.

18. The Claimant terminated the Defendant's retainer by letter dated 18 March 1997 [C91-2]. In the meantime he had written to the Defendant on 10 February 1997 [C71], sent the Defendant £200 without being asked [C79] and thanked the Defendant a number of times [C71, 79

---

[24] See paragraph 38 of his first statement [A94].

[25] Again, including the telephone logs.

[26] There are two disputes in relation to this. First, as to whose idea the further offer was. See paragraph 43 of the Claimant's first statement [A98] and paragraph 46 of the Defendant's statement [A/135]. Secondly, as to when the letter dated 12 December 1996 was sent. See paragraph 44 of the Claimant's first statement [A99] and paragraphs 17 and 18 of the Defendant's statement [A127]. The Defendant's evidence on both points should be preferred. The second issue is dealt with in more detail in paragraph 36 below.

[27] An offer they had in fact previously made. See paragraph 11 of the Claimant's first affidavit in the claim against him by Lambeth [B1/74].

[28] A position which he reiterated in his letter of 18 February 1997 [C75] and which reflected his advice in his letter of 24 June 1996 [B2/453] that the Claimant was in "a very unusual situation and the legal ramifications have to be thought through very carefully."

and 88]. There is no letter of complaint from the Claimant. His letter of 18 March 1997 acknowledges that:

18.1. he had originally instructed the Defendant "to deal with the matter of the *conveyance* of 10 Chestnut Road"[29] and that that had been expected to be "a relatively straightforward matter";

18.2. he had taken "an expensive gamble";

18.3. the Defendant would have advised against spending money on the Property;

18.4. the responsibility for his "'risky' venture" was his;

18.5. he was happy with what the Defendant had done; and

18.6. he had been consulting his college tutors about the case.

19. Various other factual assertions are made by the Claimant, including that he was advised on various occasions that Lambeth was not in a position to complete and as to the Notice to Complete.[30] This is denied. The Defendant will rely, in particular, on his letters of 24 June 1996 [B2/453] and 18 February 1997 [C75] and his attendance note of 6 February 1997 [C69-70] and the inconsistency of the Claimant's assertions with the careful approach disclosed by those documents.

20. The Claimant's new solicitors, HAW, wrote to Lambeth only 2 days after the Defendant's retainer had been terminated [B2/590]. They asserted that Lambeth's Notice to Complete had not been valid because Lambeth did not have a sealed transfer. Despite all that had happened, negotiations continued[31] and on 6 November 1997 Lambeth remained willing to sell to the Claimant at the original price [B2/626].[32]

21. Lambeth eventually issued proceedings against the Claimant for possession of the Property on 2 April 1998 [B1/67]. On 22 May 1998 Master Moncaster refused to order possession because of the discrepancy between the transfer and the contract [B1/174]. On 14 December 1999 the Claimant was advised that his prospects of a successful outcome were 60-80%, although perhaps at the lower end of that bracket [B3/1039]. On 13 January 2000 that assessment was slightly improved [B3/1072]. On 17 February 2000 judgment was entered for Lambeth, the Claimant's case having wholly failed [B1/263].

22. Despite the advice that he had received, and notwithstanding the fact that his failure in the Lambeth litigation was not caused by the Defendant, the Claimant issued proceedings against the Defendant on 28 February 2002 [A1], just inside the limitation period.

---

[29] Emphasis as in the original.

[30] See paragraphs 16 [A78], 18 [A80], 38 [A94-5], 41 [A96] and 43 [A98].

[31] See, for example, [B2/620 and 624].

[32] It is not clear why this led nowhere. It does, however, demonstrate that Lambeth at all times remained amenable to dealing with the Claimant at the original price and that they did not consider the Notice to Complete the be all and end all.

THE ISSUES

23. The detailed issues in this case are set out in the agreed list of issues. In essence, however, this is a case about failure to respond to a Notice to Complete. The Claimant says that completion should have been facilitated in about November 1996 and would have occurred if this had happened. The Defendant denies this. The Notice to Complete is a short and straightforward document, sent direct to the Claimant. He did not ask for advice about it and it is incredible to suppose that he did not understand it or that his conduct was determined by the Defendant.

THE CLAIMANT, THE TRANSACTION AND ITS FINANCING

24. Breach of duty and causation in this case both need to be considered against its particular and peculiar background. This was not a straightforward conveyancing transaction.[33] It was removed from the run of the mill by three features in particular: (i) the nature of the transaction itself; (ii) the Claimant's experience and actions; and (iii) the financing of the transaction. It is the Defendant's case that these features are not only the background against which the Defendant's retainer and duties are to be assessed, but also show that the transaction did not complete for reasons unconnected with the Defendant and that it would never have completed. Each of the specific matters referred to above is dealt with in turn below.[34]

i. **The transaction itself**

25. The relevant features of the transaction are largely set out under the heading "The factual background" above. They include: the change from leasehold to freehold; the length of the unexpired term of the lease; the Claimant's desire to acquire the freehold; the freeholder's countervailing desire to acquire the leasehold; the economics of the transaction; and the cost of the works required. As a result (and as set out above), the Claimant made a number of attempts to improve the transaction from his point of view and continued to attempt to improve it long after he had ceased to instruct the Defendant.

---

[33] Indeed, the Claimant described it in his letter of 18 March 1997 as "a major saga" [C91].

[34] For the avoidance of doubt, the Defendant does not contend that these are necessarily all of the reasons why the matter did not proceed (although they may be). The Defendant is, and was, not privy to all that was happening. They do, however, demonstrate that there was much more to the transaction than the Claimant suggests and provide the, or an, alternative explanation for what happened that the Claimant is unable satisfactorily to deal with.

ii. The Claimant's experience and actions

26. The Claimant was not an innocent abroad. He had, for example, previously been employed in the advice and housing service sectors, had worked for a London Borough (Southwark), in September 1996 began legal studies at South Bank University,[35] consulted his tutors about the case and had connections with a property development company and/or persons involved in property development (M Properties and VC / DS).

27. Perhaps reflecting that experience, the Claimant was prepared to take important decisions (such as the decisions to proceed with the purchase even though only a leasehold interest was on offer and to renovate the Property prior to completion) on his own. His works at the Property, of course, fundamentally altered the economics of the Claimant's situation and his relationship with the transaction. No longer could he walk away from the transaction for the loss of his deposit; the money he had spent on repairs would also be lost.

iii. Financing the transaction

28. The Defendant denies that the Claimant was at any relevant time ever willing or able to finance completion of the purchase of the leasehold of the Property at the price agreed. He was unemployed or a student at the material times, has produced no documentary evidence that such finance was available,[36] could not have relied on the Leasehold Reform Act 1967 to support an application for finance,[37] never managed materially to improve the transaction, continued to negotiate with the freeholders long after terminating the Defendant's retainer[38] and the very fact that he never obtained finance strongly points to its non-availability. Either he could not get finance or, if finance from H and F was available, it was on terms that, prior to the termination of the Defendant's retainer, he was unwilling to accept.

29. Quite apart from that, he never indicated to the Defendant that such finance was available. Indeed, all of his correspondence[39] to the Defendant proceeds on the basis that it was not. In September 1996, for example, he promised to revert to the Defendant about the funds for the purchase [C42], but never did. His next letter [C45], in November, stated that at least another month was required and, in any event, he has provided no evidence of having taken any steps relating to finance after that month.

---

[35] See paragraph 8 of his second statement [A110] and paragraphs 2-3 of his first statement [A67-8].

[36] The only offer during the Defendant's retainer is dated 27 February 1997 [B2/566]. It is for 3 months only and charges interest at 24% APR for those 3 months and at 37.25% APR if the loan is continued. It is, to say the least, hardly an attractive offer. A similar offer was made on 15 November 1999 [B2/654].

[37] Because the rights conferred by that Act cannot be exercised until after 3 years' residence.

[38] See paragraph 20 above.

[39] See paragraphs 11, 13 and 15 above.

iv. **Conclusion**

30. It is therefore the Defendant's case that: (i) the Claimant did not need, or instruct the Defendant to provide, much of the advice he now says that he ought to have been given; and (ii) the Claimant's position was far more complicated than he now seeks to portray. As to the former, the Claimant drove the transaction, took many important decisions on his own and was not reliant on the Defendant in the way he now asserts. His true views of the Defendant's services and what he wanted from the Defendant are best ascertained from the correspondence towards the end of the Defendant's retainer and, in particular, his letter of 18 March 1997.[40] That correspondence, unsurprisingly, is uniformly positive. As to the latter, the Claimant cannot now seek to pretend that those other difficulties did not exist and to blame the Defendant for matters in fact caused by his own actions and/or the situation in which he found himself.

BREACH OF DUTY

i. **Introduction and summary of the Defendant's case**

31. The Defendant denies that he acted negligently, in breach of contract or in breach of duty as alleged or at all. In short, he did what he was asked to do, did not mislead the Claimant and the attempt to blame him for not doing more takes his retainer out of its context.

32. In substance, the Particulars of Claim[41] contain four allegations of negligence against the Defendant. All are denied.

32.1. That he failed to facilitate or effect completion of the Claimant's purchase of the Property (on or before 29 March 1996 or after September 1996, alternatively November 1996).[42]

32.2. That he failed to advise as to the Claimant's contractual position.[43]

32.3. That he failed to act promptly to make an offer to Lambeth.[44]

32.4. That he failed to advise the acceptance of Lambeth's offer to refund the Claimant's deposit.[45]

---

[40] [C91] See, more generally, paragraph 18 above.

[41] As set out below, it is far from clear that the third and fourth allegations are pursued.

[42] PoC.34(1), (2) (5) and (6) [A/14-15].

[43] PoC.34(3), (4) and (7)-(10) [A/15-16].

[44] PoC.34(11) [A/16].

[45] PoC.34(12) [A/16].

ii. The first and second allegations of negligence

33. The Defendant's answers to these allegations are threefold. First and most generally, it is his case that, against the background set out above, he was not required, and/or not instructed, to advise or act in the ways alleged.[46] The Defendant will, if necessary, rely on *Caradine Properties v DJ Freeman* [1999] Lloyd's Rep PN 483.

34. Secondly, there are more specific answers to each of the allegations. Thus, for example:

34.1. negotiations, particularly with Lambeth (who might have been willing substantially to reduce the price), between March and September 1996 make it wholly unrealistic to suggest that completion should have taken place before September 1996;[47]

34.2. at the time, the Claimant blamed Lambeth and not the Defendant;[48]

34.3. by the Claimant's letter of 23 September 1996 [C42] the Defendant was instructed that the Claimant would contact him about finance;

34.4. again, finance was still an issue in November 1996 [C45];

34.5. the Defendant was never instructed to complete and the background to the transaction was such that he was not required to take any step to prompt completion;

34.6. the Defendant did not advise that the Notice to Complete was not valid[49] and was not required to give any advice he did not give;[50] and

34.7. the Claimant did not need, and/or instruct the Defendant to give, advice about the contract or Special Conditions.

35. Thirdly, advice that Lambeth was not in a position to complete would not, had it been given, have been negligent. Thus, for example, Master Moncaster dismissed Lambeth's Originating Summons on the basis that there was a discrepancy between the transfer and the contract,[51] the Claimant's new solicitors put forward the view that the Notice to Complete was not valid in their letter of 20 March 1997 [B2/590] and the Claimant's present legal team advised that he had a 60-80% prospect of establishing the Notice to Complete was not valid.

---

[46] See further paragraph 7 of the Defence [A46-7].

[47] In any event, Lambeth attested to the fact that "Completion did not take place [prior to 29 March 1996] as [Lambeth] experienced a delay in preparing the deed of assignment." See paragraph 6 of the affidavit of J C dated 2 April 1998 [B1/3].

[48] See Lambeth's note of his complaints to them on 20 August and 6 September 1996 [B2/460 and 463].

[49] See paragraph 19 above and paragraph 36.2 of the Defence [A53].

[50] In particular, it was not negligent not to raise any of the points dismissed by the Court in the Lambeth action [B1/266].

[51] See [B1/174], para.10.

iv. The third allegation of negligence

36. It is far from clear whether this allegation is pursued as a causally relevant allegation of negligence. It is dealt with at paragraph 44 of the Claimant's first witness statement [A99], but no evidence of any causative effect is given. If it is pursued, the allegation is denied. In particular: it is denied that the offer was not made promptly; and, in any event: (i) a delay between 12 December 1996 and 6 January 1997 (i.e. over the Christmas and New Year period) would not have been negligent; and/or (ii) the Defendant had no reason to suppose that any further offer was time critical.

v. The fourth allegation of negligence

37. Again, it is far from clear that this allegation is pursued. At paragraph 47 of his first statement [A101] (the only part of the statement which deals with this issue), the Claimant merely asserts that the Defendant did not tell him to accept the offer. He does not say why such advice should have been given, especially against the background that the Claimant had by then spent some £25,000 repairing the Property. If it is pursued, it is denied. In particular: the Claimant knew of Lambeth's offer, which was in any event a repeat of an earlier offer rejected by the Claimant without reference to the Defendant [B1/74]; it was not for the Defendant to advise him to take it; the Claimant does not say in his evidence that he would have accepted such advice; and, in any event, he would not have done so, if for no other reason than because of his expenditure on the Property.

CAUSATION

38. Even if (contrary to his case) the Court concludes that the Defendant acted in breach of duty, it is denied that that breach caused any loss to the Claimant. It will be assumed in the remainder of this section of this skeleton argument that some breach of duty has been found against the Defendant.

39. There are two aspects to causation in this case:

   39.1. first, but for whatever breach of duty is found, could the Claimant have completed a purchase of the Property and, if so, would he have done so – this is dealt with in this section of this skeleton argument; and

   39.2. secondly, if these questions are answered in favour of the Claimant, were the various individual heads of loss claimed caused by the Defendant's breach of duty or within the scope of his duty – this is dealt with in the next section of this skeleton argument (under the heading "Quantum").

40. In short, it is the Defendant's case that the Property was never on offer to the Claimant on terms, or in a form, which would have been acceptable to him. He had made a bad bargain at auction and was never able to row himself out of it. In any event, he did not have available to him the funds necessary to complete the purchase. See further paragraph 23ff above.

41. Further or alternatively, the true cause of any loss he suffered was the unauthorised work he carried out at the Property and/or the unusual features of the transaction as set out above.[52] Given in particular that Lambeth twice offered to repay his deposit,[53] had he not done that work, he could at any time have resiled from the transaction without loss (and it is implicit in his alternative case that he would).

42. As to the third allegation of negligence – alleged delay in offering Lambeth £25,000 – there is simply no evidence that this would have made any difference to their position or that it caused the Claimant to litigate with Lambeth.[54]

43. Causation in respect of the fourth allegation – failure to advise acceptance of Lambeth's offer to repay the deposit – is dealt with in paragraph 37 above.

QUANTUM

i. Introduction and summary of the Defendant's case

44. Four heads of loss are set out in the Particulars of Claim: (i) various alternative differences in the value of the Property at different dates; (ii) rental income; (iii) liability to Lambeth; and (iv) the deposit.

45. Even if (contrary to his case) the Court concludes that the Defendant was negligent, it is denied that the Claimant is entitled to damages. In short: the Claimant made a bad bargain for which the Defendant was not responsible; was not prevented by the Defendant from renting the Property out; litigated with Lambeth for his own reasons and with the benefit of independent legal advice from lawyers other than the Defendant; and rejected Lambeth's offer to repay the deposit for his own reasons.

46. Alternatively, for the reasons given below, any award of damages should be limited to the difference between: (i) the amount which the Claimant agreed to pay for the leasehold interest in the Property; and (ii) the true value of that interest as at the date of the

---

[52] See paragraph 23ff above.
[53] See paragraph 16 above.
[54] C.f. the alternative claim at paragraph 35(B)(2) of the Particulars of Claim [A18].

auction, alternatively the date of the Defendant's breach. That difference was negative (i.e. the amount paid was less than the value of the leasehold) or nil at the date of the auction and was never more than £5,000.

ii. The difference in value claim

47. There is no reason in this case to depart from the general rule.[55] The Claimant is (if he is entitled to anything) entitled to the value of the Property, less the amount he would have had to pay for it. The Defendant's primary case is that this results in no award of damages: the value of the interest purchased by the Claimant, which was the only interest in respect of which the Defendant was retained, was £35,000;[56] and the Claimant paid £44,500 – i.e. £9,500 more than its value – for it. Alternatively, if the value of the Property is to be assessed at the date of the Defendant's (assumed) breach,[57] the difference in value was never more than £5,500.[58]

48. The Claimant is not entitled to take into account any benefit which may have accrued by reason of any works at the Property or any possible acquisition of the freehold.

   48.1. The Claimant purchased the Property in an unrepaired state and retained the Defendant in relation to the Property in that state.

   48.2. The Claimant did not inform the Defendant that he intended to carry out works at the Property and was aware that the Defendant would have advised against such works.

   48.3. The Claimant purchased only a leasehold interest in the Property, never acquired the freehold interest and retained the Defendant in relation to the leasehold interest.

   48.4. In any event, the Claimant has not sought to contend that he was prevented from acquiring alternative property by reason of any default of the Defendant.

49. Accordingly, any loss consequent on either matter was not caused by the Defendant, was too remote and/or was outside the scope of the duty of care he owed and/or the contemplation of the parties.

---

[55] See *Jackson & Powell on Professional Negligence* (5th edn, 2002; update 2003), para.10-264. In particular, there is no basis for awarding damages for the loss of the Claimant's bargain, if by that phrase the Claimant means anything other than the measure of damages set out here. (C.f. paragraph 35(A)(1) of the Particulars of Claim [A16].) The Defendant did not guarantee any result, but merely to use reasonable skill and care.

[56] See Colleys' valuation of 1 March 1996 [B2/414] and paragraph 7 above.

[57] There is no basis for any other date and, in particular, for March 2000.

[58] See paragraph 8.03 of Mr G's report [A145].

iii. The letting claim

50. See paragraph 56 of the Defence [A59]: the Claimant's damages are limited as set out above; the loss is too remote; the Defendant was not informed of the Claimant's intention to rent out the Property;[59] he was not prevented from doing so by the Defendant; and was the author of his own misfortune. In any event, his claim that he would have let the Property is inconsistent with his desire to use the Leasehold Reform Act 1967 to acquire the freehold interest in it.

iv. Liability to Lambeth

51. See paragraph 57 of the Defence [A60]. The attempt to differentiate between mesne profits paid to Lambeth and the interest accruing on any loan the Claimant would have taken out to finance a purchase is an attempt to relitigate issues raised and settled with Lambeth.

v. The deposit

52. The quantum of the deposit is agreed. For the reasons already given, it is denied that it is recoverable.

GOOD PRACTICE SUGGESTION

- Length
  You should be very conscious of length.[6] Make sure the document is not too long. While it may be that some cases demand skeletons in excess of the 20-page guidance, more often than not the longer the written submission, the less well received it will be. As a suggestion, be as brief as you sensibly can. It should not be necessary to re-write to reduce length, but do so where you can.

- Abbreviations
  Most advocates dislike the use of abbreviations and use them only because they believe (wrongly) that the court wants them, or they are under pressure to shorten their written submissions and this feels like a way of helping to do so. In fact abbreviations interfere with the readability of the text because, unless the reader is very familiar with their use, he must make a mental note to stop and check to whom the contraction is referring. Sometimes a judge will physically have to stop and look back some pages. It is irritating to have to do so.
  You should distinguish between skeleton arguments, where brevity is expected in the form of abbreviated parties, personal names – particularly

---

[59] See paragraph 36 of his statement [A131].
[6] See also Example N

corporations – and statutes, and fuller written submissions, where these are not. Use only familiar or recognised short forms. Do not create your own abbreviations or create new terms of art. The court will not appreciate it. Where being concise is important you should use established nomenclature, contract full names, and refer to parties' status or occupations, such as 'the complainant', 'the donor,' 'the driver,' 'the doctor.' After first setting out the full title of a piece of legislation or delegated legislation, reduce it to 'the Act' or 'the Rules'; contracts, disciplinary codes or proposals can be 'the Code' or 'the Scheme'. If parties' names are being used, do not use initials but do give a title.

- Textual Emphasis
  No consensus has emerged on the question of textual emphasis, although opinions extended only between those who advocate none at all (preferring headings and subheadings) and those using bold or italic type very sparingly. The overuse of textual enhancement may be seen by some judges as an intellectual challenge to their ability to spot the point. They think it is spoon-feeding a little too far. Some advocates wish to use italics only for sub-headings or the citation of authority
  Ideally you should use bold only for topic headings, the title, and central dates and events in the chronology. Use italics very sparingly as a contrast to impress something on the judge.

EXAMPLE F

Queen's Bench application to strike out claim as disclosing no cause of action - Applicant's skeleton argument by Edward Faulks QC and Charles Brown in July, 1997 - 6pp.

Beasly v Buckinghamshire C.C. was an action by foster carers against their local authority for personal injuries suffered by them in the course of caring for a teenage boy who suffered from cerebral palsy and epilepsy.

The brief introduction to the case is in non-legal and non-technical language. There is a logical progression to the argument in which the points raised are separated out and each is made succinctly.

All citations made are within the text – there are no footnotes used – but this does not inhibit the readability of the prose or impede the flow of the argument.

The strike out application failed, the judge holding that the claim was arguable. The case is reported at [1997] PIQR P473.

SKELETON ARGUMENT ON BEHALF OF THE DEFENDANT

INTRODUCTION

1. The Plaintiff and her husband agreed to provide long-term foster care for Mark Simpson, a teenage boy suffering from cerebral palsy and epilepsy. A written agreement was entered into on or about March 14th 1991. Mark came to live with the Plaintiff's family in June 1991. The Plaintiff claims that she injured her back in the course of looking after Mark. The allegations of negligence are that the Defendants did not make a proper assessment of the Plaintiff's suitability to look after Mark, they failed to monitor the placement and to provide appropriate support and equipment. The Plaintiff's back condition is said to have resulted in the termination of the placement and various consequential losses.

2. The Defendants' Summons is to strike out the Plaintiff's claim as not disclosing a cause of action (RSC 0.18 r.19). The Defendants do not oppose the Plaintiff's Summons to amend the Particulars of Claim or the service of a Reply, albeit out of time.

THE DEFENDANTS' SUBMISSIONS

3. The Defendants are unaware of a decided case where foster carers have sued a local authority for injuries sustained by them in looking after

foster children. The case of *White v Essex County Council* raises a similar (but not identical) point. Mr. Justice Hooper is handing down judgment in the High Court on the 7th July. A copy of the judgment will be made available.

4. The leading case on local authorities' liability when performing a social services function is *X v Bedfordshire County Council* 1995 2 AC 633. The House of Lords decided that local authorities were immune from claims in negligence arising out of decisions made in the course of investigating sexual abuse or in relation to the taking of children into care. In subsequent cases it has been argued that claims arising out of the breakdown of fostering arrangements fall outside the scope of the decision in X. The Court of Appeal in two cases (*H v Norfolk County Council* 10th May 1996 and *Barrett v Enfield* 25th March 1997) decided that the reasoning in X provided the basis for immunity from claims in negligence for local authorities arising out of claims made by children in foster care.

5. In deciding whether there is a duty of care in a novel situation, a Court has to decide:

    (a) that damage to the plaintiff is reasonably foreseeable;
    (b) that there is sufficient proximity between the plaintiff and defendant; and
    (c) that it is fair, just and reasonable to impose a duty of care, as a matter of policy.

(See *Caparo Industries v Dickman* 1992 A.C.605). It is submitted that, having regard to the decision in X, it is not appropriate to undertake a Caparo 3 stage analysis on the facts of this case in that the Defendants are a local authority who do not owe a duty of care "in relation to the administration of a social welfare scheme" (ibid 751 C to D), which is designed to protect the welfare of children. It is certainly clear that no duty will exist in relation to decisions made by social workers or in relation to the consequences of such decisions when:

    (i)   children who should have been taken into care are not (*X v Bedfordshire*);
    (ii)   children are taken into care when they should not have been (*X* (the *Newham* facts));
    (iii) a child is wrongly allowed to stay in a foster home with an abuser (*H; Barrett;*);
    (iv)   a child in care is consistently sent to inappropriate homes/placements (*Barrett*).

6. Even if the Court decides that X is not binding on the facts of this case, it is submitted that there are cogent reasons why it would not be fair, just and reasonable to impose a duty of care on the facts of this case.

(i) The nature of the relationship between the local authority and the foster parents is based on statute. Detailed provisions are contained in the **Children Act 1989, Arrangements for Placement of Children Regulations 1991**, the **Foster Placement (Children) Regulations 1991** and the **Guidance to the Children Act 1989.** The provisions govern the respective rights and obligations of the local authority and foster parents, the emphasis being always on the local authority's overriding duty to the child for whom it is responsible. Any "agreement" (as is the case here) is not a legally binding document but simply an aid to the successful fostering of children by foster parents.

(ii) There is no claim here for breach of statutory duty. The Courts will not normally superimpose a common law duty of care in these circumstances (see *X* and *Stovin v Wise* **1996 AC 923**).

(iii) The reasons militating against there being a duty of care imposed on social workers, can appropriately be transposed from *X*;

    (a) Cutting across the statutory system for the welfare of children. The choice of foster parents and the placement of a particular child involve schools, doctors, the police, health visitors and a number of different social workers. It is thus a multi-disciplinary process.

    (b) The task is extraordinarily delicate.
It involves trying to reconcile the welfare of adolescents often with severe physical or mental difficulties who would benefit from fostering with the interests of prospective foster parents and their family. These are matters of fine judgment and with "difficult" children no solution is straightforward, or without some risk.

    (c) The defensive approach.
The imposition of liability might result in less frank and full discussion about placements with prospective foster parents. Communications between local authorities and foster parents would be cautious and hedged about with disclaimers. The spectre of litigation is a real one. Time and money will be expended on investigating and defending often unjustified claims. The allegation here is of a physical injury; there could equally be allegations of psychological damage caused by fostering troublesome adolescents. Some of the claims would be wholly unjustified but would nevertheless involve expense in their investigation and time in defending them adequately.

    (d) The availability of complaints procedures under the **1980 Child Care Act** and the **1989 Children Act.**

    (e) The undesirability of imposing a duty on a regulatory system for social welfare. The local authority have a facultative role. It provides assessment and support pursuant to its statutory obligations. The common law should not create a duty of care which may create difficulty in the discharge of statutory functions.

7. The only case which can provide any encouragement to the Plaintiff in this case is *Barrett v Enfield*. The Master of the Rolls made certain (obiter) comments to the effect that there might be some liability on the part of local authorities for certain operational matters notwithstanding the general immunity in relation to decision-making functions. It is submitted that the Master of the Rolls did not mean operational in the policy/operational dichotomy sense. (This distinction has been disapproved of by the House of Lords in *X* and *Stovin and Wise*). It may be that there might be some residual liability for mundane negligence, not deriving out of the discharge of statutory functions. Such liability would not apply here where the Defendants' assessment, placement and supervision of that placement falls plainly within the scope of the discharge of their discretionary statutory functions.

8. The employer/employee analogy is not appropriate. A care assistant engaged by the local authority is owed a duty of care by his or her employer, who can control, as is the case with any employee, what work is done and how it is done. The essence of fostering is that the foster child becomes part of the fostered family. It is plain that the foster parents are not the agents of the local authority (see *S v Walsall Metropolitan Borough Council* 1985 3 All ER 294). The Foster Carers Handbook is a useful guide to fostering and is designed to help foster parents. Its provision does not alter the fundamental relationship between the local authority and foster parents.

9. If a foster child cannot sue because the imposition of a duty of care would not be fair, just and reasonable, a foster parent should not be in a better position. The policy reasons in favour of immunity have equal force regardless of the identity of the Plaintiff.

GOOD PRACTICE SUGGESTION

* Submissions
  Break these down into numbered issues if possible.[7] Try to resist using sub-paragraphs.
* Try to build a coherent whole.[8] Move submissions around – particularly factual submissions - and see how they work best.

---

[7] See also Example O
[8] See also Example J

EXAMPLE G

County Court application – Wasted Costs - Preliminary issues – Skeleton argument of the Non-party by Spike Charlwood in October, 2003 – 10pp.

In A v B application against X wasted costs were sought against a former legal representative. The application notice did not specify in which capacity costs were sought against him, whether under CPR 48.7 as legal representative or under CPR 48.2 as a non-party, and X took the issue of jurisdiction as a preliminary point.

The skeleton arguments were sequential: here X responds to that of the applicant.

The language is formal but not overly legalistic. The argument is detailed – the submissions are set out as a list. The key authorities are dealt with in the text, but use is made of additional argument and citation in footnotes.

As a result of the arguments raised here the application was withdrawn.

SKELETON ARGUMENT OF X (A Solicitor)

INTRODUCTION AND SUMMARY

1. This skeleton argument deals with the Claimant's application for wasted costs against Mr X issued on 3 October 2003. It has been agreed between the Claimant and Mr X that the hearing on 10 October 2003 will deal with the first stage of the Claimant's application only.

2. As to that, Mr X's position is in summary that:

    2.1. he doubts whether the hour set aside to deal with post judgment matters on 10 October 2003 is sufficient to deal with all of the matters raised by the Claimant and, more particularly, the costs issues against him; and

    2.2. in the light of the matters which have to be considered at the first stage of the application, the Claimant's application should be dismissed at that stage.

TWO PRELIMINARY ISSUES

(i) Lack of evidence

3. Despite the period of time between the giving of judgment (29 August 2003) and her application (3 October 2003), the Claimant's

application is unsupported by any proper evidence[1] and, in particular, any evidence going to the matters required to be considered by the Court as a pre-cursor to any wasted costs application.[2] It should therefore be dismissed for this reason alone.

(ii) Jurisdiction

4. The Claimant's application notice does not identify whether her application is made against Mr X as a legal representative (CPR Part 48.7) or as a non-party (CPR Part 48.2). Her skeleton argument suggests, in effect, that it does not matter. Mr X does not accept this. Different, albeit related, considerations apply and in order to succeed (which Mr X submits she cannot) the Claimant will need properly to establish her case on one or other basis. Each basis is therefore dealt with separately below.

WASTED COSTS / COSTS AGAINST MR X AS A LEGAL REPRESENTATIVE

(i) Introduction

5. In summary, any claim for wasted costs against Mr X on the basis that he was a legal representative must fail because:

   5.1. he was not, at the material times, acting as a legal representative within the meaning of the Supreme Court Act 1981 and/or the CPR;

   5.2. privilege has not been waived by the Defendant (whose legal representative Mr X is alleged to have been) and no exceptional circumstances justifying the order have been made out;

   5.3. no breach of duty to the Court has been identified;

   5.4. no explanation as to how wasted costs have been caused has been put forward;

   5.5. the costs in issue do not justify the costs of the wasted costs proceedings; and

   5.6. in any event, no factual basis has been put forward sufficient to satisfy the court that, if unanswered, it would be likely to lead to a wasted costs order.

6. In addition, the Court should bear in mind:

---

[1] In particular, part C of her application notice comprises in substance submission and not evidence.

[2] I.e. (i) that it has before it evidence or other material which, if unanswered, would be likely to lead to a wasted costs order being made; and (ii) the wasted costs proceedings are justified notwithstanding the likely costs involved. See paragraph 53.6(1) of the Practice Direction About Costs (p.1141 of the 2003 White Book).

6.1. that this is not a case in which any inference can be drawn from the Claimant's success – Mr X believes that the Defendant intends to ask for permission to appeal and, in any event, this was simply a case in which, at the end of the day, the Court preferred the evidence of the Claimant to that of the Defendant. As the Court itself observed,[3] there were "thoroughly good arguable points" open to the Defendant;

6.2. that, in any event, it is (as note 48.7.5 to the 2003 White Book observes) "rarely if ever safe for a court to assume that a hopeless case[4] was being litigated on the advice of the lawyers involved"; and

6.3. the risk that this application is motivated by the Claimant's likely inability to obtain a valuable costs order against the Defendant, who is publicly funded.[5]

(ii) Not a legal representative

7. If Mr X is to be made liable as a legal representative, then it must be as the legal representative of (and specifically as the solicitor to) the Defendant. But from almost the very beginning[6] of the litigation O's were the Defendant's solicitors. Thus they took the litigation forward after that and, for example: (i) must have obtained counsel's advice that there was "at least a moderate prospect of a successfuly (sic) defence";[7] and (ii) quite properly insisted in relation to discussions about mediation that it was they who would be in charge and who owed duties to the Legal Services Commission.[8] Similarly: (iii) both the Defendant and her husband state[9] that, "O's are acting for the administratrix in the pending civil proceedings"; and (iv) Mr X's evidence was to the same effect.[10]

8. Accordingly, Mr X was not a person "exercising a right of audience or right to conduct litigation"[11] and cannot therefore be liable as a legal representative.[12]

9. More generally, the above illustrates the fundamental and fatal (to the Claimant's application) divergence between:

---

[3] At p.8 of its judgment.

[4] The point is even clearer where the Court has accepted that the Defendant's case was not hopeless.

[5] See note 48.7.6 of the 2003 White Book.

[6] The Claim Form was issued on 6 August 2002. O's served a notice of change of solicitor [880] on 25 September 2002, the Defendant having acted in person in the meantime.

[7] See the legal aid certificate at [881].

[8] See, in particular, their letter of 12 May 2003. [492]

[9] At paragraph 5 of their statements. [144 and 214]

[10] See paragraph 1 of his statement. [328]

[11] Supreme Court Act 1981, s.51(13).

[12] NB that it is not relevant that the Claimant has referred in part C of her application notice only to matters prior to 25 September 2002 (the date when O's went on the record for the Defendant). At no time prior to 6 August 2002 were there any proceedings on foot and Mr X could not therefore at that time have been exercising a right of audience or conducting litigation.

9.1.   the periods during which: (i) the acts complained of by the Claimant took place (*viz.* 5 June 2000 – c. July 2002); and (ii) the costs which the Claimant seeks to recover were incurred (*viz.* 6 August 2002 onwards). She seeks, in other words, to recover costs incurred at a time when other solicitors and counsel, whose conduct is not impugned, were acting for the Defendant and must have been advising the legal services commission that she had a meritorious case; and

9.2.   the two capacities – (i) solicitor to the administratrix of the estate and (ii) witness / provider of practical assistance in the proceedings – in which Mr X acted.

(iii) **Privilege**

10.   The Defendant has not waived privilege in respect of this matter. Accordingly, Mr X is of necessity precluded from giving any account of the advice given to the Defendant or the basis on which the case was conducted. As a result, it cannot be assumed that: (i) Mr X was acting on his own initiative in any respect; or (ii) the Defendant acted as she did because of Mr X. Indeed, there is much (including, for example: the Defendant's financial position; the worth of the property; the Defendant's evidence as to her conversations with the deceased;[13] her evidence about missing money, the watch and jewellery;[14] and her duty as trustee for her mother) to suggest that the Defendant would have litigated in any event.

11.   More generally, the House of Lords confirmed in *Medcalf v Mardell* [2003] 1 AC 120 that it would require an "exceptional"[15] case before a wasted costs order could be made against an opponent's legal representative when privilege had not been waived and this is not such a case.

(iv)   **Breach of duty to the court**

12.   Further to the Court of Appeal's decision in *Persuad v Persuad* [2003] EWCA Civ 394, especially paragraphs 16-22, "it is a necessary requirement of any wasted costs application that there should have been a breach of duty to the court". As to this: (i) no such breach has been identified; and (ii) it reinforces the point made in paragraphs 7 to 9 above, namely that the order cannot be made because Mr X was not at the time acting as a legal representative and therefore owed no such duties.

---

[13] E.g. at [222].
[14] See [271].
[15] *Per* Lord Bingham at paragraph 23.

(v) Causation

13. The only acts identified in the Claimant's application notice are acts prior to the issue of proceedings. Nonetheless, she seeks as wasted costs the costs of the proceedings. This is despite the fact that O's and counsel acted almost throughout the proceedings and must have advised the legal services commission that the Defendant had a meritorious case. Accordingly, it is denied that any act or omission of Mr X can have caused the Claimant's costs of the proceedings.

14. Further or alternatively:

   14.1. the Court confirmed at p.8 of its judgment that the trial was conducted on "helpful and conventional lines";

   14.2. at no point did the Court intervene to limit the evidence of any witness;

   14.3. the decisions to call and cross-examine the Defendant and Mrs X were not made by Mr X; and

   14.4. the original time estimate for the trial was 3 days, and in the circumstances the Claimant's alternative claim for 2 days' trial costs cannot succeed.

(vi) Costs

15. The Claimant has failed to supply any evidence as to the likely cost of the wasted costs proceedings. As is always the case, however, when new lawyers (i.e. those representing Mr X) have to get up to speed on a case which has been ongoing for some time, the costs are likely to be substantial. Indeed, Mr X's costs already amount to some £6,880 and his solicitors estimate that a full hearing would involve further costs in excess of £20,000. Accordingly, and given that: (i) the Claimant seeks only £25,000 + VAT; and (ii) will incur further costs herself, the proposed proceedings would be disproportionate and should not be permitted.[16]

(vi) No factual basis for proceeding

16. In order to be permitted to proceed to the second stage of the process, the Claimant must persuade the Court not only that it would be proportionate to permit this,[17] but also that the Court has before it "evidence or other material which, if unanswered, would be likely to lead to a wasted costs order being made". In addition to the general points made above, Mr X will deal below with the specific matters set out in the Claimant's application notice, those set out in her skeleton argument and those referred to in the judgment.

---

[16] See *Chief Constable of North Yorkshire v Audsley* [2000] Lloyd's Rep PN 675.

[17] As to which, see paragraph 15 above.

The Claimant's application notice

17. Paragraph 1 – absent a waiver of privilege, these matters cannot be attributed to Mr X; Mr X offered to refer any matter upon which the Claimant's solicitors wanted to rely to counsel;[18] after O's were instructed, negotiation was a matter for them and mediation was attempted;[19] the Claimant's solicitors were not influenced by Mr X's view of Mr M;[20] and Mr X's view was that Mr M would be unpredictable under cross-examination.[21]

18. Paragraph 2 – any threat and/or accusation was ignored and had no impact on costs; otherwise, see paragraph 17 above.

19. Paragraph 3 – an independent firm of solicitors, O's, was instructed; otherwise, see paragraphs 17 and 18 above.

20. Paragraph 4 – these affidavits were relied on by O's and counsel and the witnesses called by them; the witnesses were heard; and it cannot be assumed that the text was Mr X's and not that of the witnesses.

21. Paragraph 5 – see paragraph 18 above.

The Claimant's skeleton

22. Paragraphs 6(a) and (b) – these are dealt with above.

23. Paragraph 6(c) – this cannot be relied on, and no inferences should be drawn, in the absence of a waiver of privilege.

24. Paragraph 6(d) – the assertion of none of these matters was improper.

Pages 6-9 of the judgment[22]

25. These cannot support an application for wasted costs. Indeed, the Court itself noted (at p.8) that:

25.1. the criticisms contained in pp.6-7 of its judgment were of "limited" direct relevance to its judgment; and

25.2. "despite the problems raised by the Witness Statements the case was conducted on helpful and conventional lines with a fair and searching cross examination and the proper points (many of them, right or not, thoroughly good arguable points) properly taken and explored."

Both of these observations, it is submitted, undermine the Claimant's case that costs, or trial costs, were wasted by reason of any conduct of Mr X.

---

[18] See [439].

[19] See [478]ff.

[20] See, for example, their letter of 1 May 2002. [441]

[21] See his attendance note of 18 April 2002. [407]

[22] By which reference it is assumed that the Claimant intends to refer to the passage headed, "X's conduct of the case and the form of the Defendant's evidence."

26. Further, and with respect to the court, Mr X responds to those matters as follows: Mr X did not have conduct of the case, O's did; absent a waiver of privilege, the Court could not properly conclude that Mr X was responsible for the Defendant's evidence; in any event, the state of the Defendant's evidence was explained in her opening statement; and even if a "dangerous" one, the course adopted in relation to the Claimant's original statements to Mr X was not improper, unreasonable or negligent.

27. As to the matters on p.8 of the judgment (and going on to p.9):

27.1. there is no suggestion in point (i) that the Claimant's costs have been increased;

27.2. in any event, it would be for the Claimant to establish that they had been and, as set out above, point (ii) does not support the view that this was the case; and

27.3. points (iii) and (iv) go to Mr X's position as a witness and not as a legal representative.

(vi) **Conclusion**

28. For all these reasons, therefore, the Court should not make a wasted costs order against Mr X.

NON-PARTY COSTS

29. *Symphony Group Plc v Hodgson* [1993] 4 All ER 143 remains the leading authority on non-party costs. The guidelines set out in that case are set out on p.1115 of the 2003 White Book and will not be repeated here. Most importantly, the Court of Appeal noted that such an order would be exceptional. Further, Mr X submits that: (i) the jurisdiction does not exist, as the Claimant appears to suggest, to fill gaps in the wasted costs jurisdiction; (ii) the Claimant has not set out any basis upon which Mr X might be held liable under a non-party costs order; and (iii) he is not within any of the categories of person (such as insurers, directors, etc) traditionally the target of non-party costs orders.[23]

30. In any event, even if the Claimant can overcome the hurdles set out above, then Mr X relies on the points made in relation to wasted costs in opposition to the claim for non-party costs.

---

[23] Mr X reserves the right to say more on this point and, in extremis, to ask for an adjournment should the Claimant seek to expand on her claim for non-party costs.

CONCLUSION

31. For the reasons given above, the Claimant's costs application should be dismissed.

32. If the application is not dismissed, then directions will be required for the second stage of the procedure. In that event:

    32.1. Mr X would ask for sufficient time to allow for transcripts to be obtained and evidence to be taken; and

    32.2. he would also ask for the matter to be referred to another judge.[24]

GOOD PRACTICE SUGGESTION

- Headings

  Topical headings and sub-headings should be used to break up significantly large portions of text. These offer useful guidance to the judge, since they act as signposts saying both that the skeleton is moving on and where it is progressing to. Subheadings should be used sparingly.

  Most advocates to whom I have spoken do not use argumentative headings, although you may wish to consider this technique, which I discuss at Part 2.

---

[24] In short, he would contend that: (i) comments already made by the Court mean that he has a legitimate fear that he would not receive, or would perceive that he had not received, an impartial hearing from the Court at the second stage; and (ii) accordingly, this is one of the rare instances where, if the matter is to proceed, it should be referred to another judge. As to the usual rule and the existence of the exception to it, see *In re P (a Barrister) (Wasted Costs Order)* [2001] TLR 482. For an example of the European Court of Human Rights holding that a judge's comments at a previous hearing made it a breach of article 6 of the European Convention of Human Rights for him to hear a subsequent hearing, see *Ferrantelli and Santangelo v Italy* [1996] 23 EHRR 288, esp. para.s 59-60.

EXAMPLE H

Queen's Bench Trial – Personal Injuries – Plaintiff's skeleton argument by Edward Faulks QC and Sarah Paneth in June, 1997 – 7pp – followed by and to be compared and contrasted with Plaintiff's closing submissions by Edward Faulks QC – 11pp.

Davies v Wyre Forest District Council was an action for serious personal injuries caused to the Plaintiff in his local authority's swimming pool when he slipped, struck his head and lost consciousness at the bottom of the pool. The trial dealt with liability, contributory negligence, causation and quantum.

The skeleton uses non-legal language with short sentences in an extended narrative style – it might come from a novel. It tells a human-interest story. It allows the facts to speak for themselves with almost no commentary. Note that the legal issues are also couched in non-legal language: the same literary style extends to the legal analysis of the Plaintiff's case, with short sentences, simple concepts and assertions which are neither formal nor stylised.

There is neither discussion of nor submissions on the law.

The written closing submission has no introduction. It has a narrative, almost lyrical style, which takes in both an analysis of the evidence and submissions. Again, the language is non-legal, fact led and legal argument is minimised.

Note the use of strategically placed questions that enable the court to focus on the issues and adopt the answers provided.

There is no assertive conclusion favouring the Plaintiff's case. The writer uses understatement to great effect.

The Plaintiff succeeded on liability and obtained a substantial award. The case is reported at [1998] PIQR P58.

SKELETON ARGUMENT ON BEHALF OF THE PLAINTIFF

1. **THE ACCIDENT**
    The Plaintiff (d.o.b. 10/6/72) will be 26 on the second day of the trial. He was 19 at the time of the accident. After leaving school at 16 with 4 GCE passes, he worked as a trainee draftsman and in steel fabrication production. At the time of the accident he was employed as a central heating engineer. He was about 6 ft. 5" tall and 12 stone. His hobbies included rugby, basketball, running and the Territorial Army.

On Sunday 16th September 1990 he went with a group of male friends to a swimming pool, which formed part of a leisure complex known as the Forest Glades Leisure Centre, Kidderminster owned by the Defendants. The pool included slides and a wave machine. The Plaintiff was in the course of getting out of the pool (the wave machine was on) via a recessed step when he slipped and fell in. He does not recall precisely what occurred as he fell and no one witnessed his entry into the pool. The overwhelming likelihood is that his head struck the bottom.

He was observed by some of his friends lying face downwards in the pool. Once they realised he was in serious difficulties (he was blue in the face) they began to drag him to the shallow end of the pool. A lifeguard attended him at the side of the pool after he had been removed from it and he was resuscitated. He was subsequently taken to hospital.

2. THE INJURIES

The Plaintiff was taken initially to Birmingham Accident Hospital and then transferred to the hospital at Oswestry. He was there found to have bruising of the scalp and a crush fracture of C5 vertebral body and virtually complete tetraplegia below T2. He was discharged from hospital after 5 months. There had been no substantial recovery of power and sensation in his lower limbs. After spending 7 months in Wolverhampton Young Disabled Unit he moved to a 2 bedroomed flat.

The Plaintiff is confined to a wheelchair. He cannot walk. He has to have his bowels evacuated manually. He needs personal and domestic care daily. There are gross restrictions on his independence. His life expectation is reduced. There is no prospect of any significant recovery.

3. THE TRIAL

The Court is concerned with liability only. An order for a split trial was made on 20th June 1995. Although originally listed for 5 days only, the service of further evidence (mainly by the Defendants) is likely to cause that time estimate to be exceeded. The Court has been informed.

4. BUNDLES

A (Blue)	-	Case Bundle of Pleadings
B (Yellow)	-	Witness Statements
C (Green)	-	Expert's Reports
D (Red) (large)	-	Discovery
(small)	-	Plans
E (Black)	-	Relevant inter partes correspondence
G (Blue)	-	Expanded Pleadings bundle with affidavits, orders etc.

5. THE ISSUES

(i)   How the accident happened. The Plaintiff says he slipped and fell. The Defendants have advanced no positive case to the contrary.

(ii)   What happened after the Plaintiff was seen face down in the water. There is a dispute as to where the lifeguard(s) were when the accident occurred, what role they played in the rescue and what precisely occurred by the side of the pool.

(iii)   Whether the recessed step was foreseeably dangerous to users of the pool, like the Plaintiff. The parties' experts disagree.

(iv)   Whether the rescue was incompetently managed having regard, in particular, to the risk of spinal injury. The parties' experts disagree.

(v)   Whether better handling of the Plaintiff after he was observed in the pool, would or might have resulted in less serious disability. The experts disagree.

6. THE PLAINTIFF'S CASE
(for a sketch plan of the pool see C.95).

(a)   The Plaintiff was a visitor within the meaning of the Occupiers Liability Act 1957. He had also paid to use the pool. The Defendants owed him a duty of care in tort, the common duty of care under the Occupiers Liability Act and a contractual duty to take reasonable care to ensure his safety.

(b)   The recessed step (illustrated at C.95, 119, 120 and 121) (also described variously as a stepped edge, a ledge and a stepper freeboard) was a highly undesirable feature. It encouraged access and egress to the deeper end of the pool (via the recessed step) from the sides. There should have been barriers to prevent this. Wave pools generate excitement. They also result in variable depths of water (the peaks and troughs of the waves). This necessitates a greater than usual "freeboard" (the vertical distance between still water level and the top of the pool side wall). The step becomes wet when the wave machine is on (as was the case here). The step appears to have been the idea of the Defendant's own (unspecialised) architects. Their reasons for its inclusion are inadequate. It is a feature which is *not* reproduced in any of the many leisure pools seen, researched and designed by the Plaintiff's experts. It should not have been part of the design or, at the least, barriers should have been erected around the deeper part of the pool. In either event the accident would not have occurred.

(c)   There should have been at the very least 3 lifeguards observing the pool. In fact there was probably one only effectively doing so. She (Tonia Solly) did not see the Plaintiff enter the pool nor did she observe him in the water until her attention was drawn to him by the Plaintiff's friends. Neither she not Todd Richardson, the other lifeguard, when he eventually appeared, treated the Plaintiff as having a possible spinal injury. Steps should have been taken to immobilize his neck in the course of extracting him from the pool and thereafter. Such steps would not have prejudiced his general resuscitation, including the freeing of his airways. It is apparent that the Plaintiff had an incomplete lesion of the spinal cord and that part of the spine must have been in continuity at the time of the accident. Incorrect handling (of which there is evidence here) can aggravate such an injury (see C.10). It is the Plaintiff's case that there would on the balance of probabilities have been a greater degree of recovery had there been proper handling. Even if the Court is only satisfied that the Plaintiff lost a chance of greater recovery because of the inadequate handling, he is entitled (in contract) to be compensated for the loss of that chance.

CLOSING SUBMISSIONS ON BEHALF OF THE PLAINTIFF

THE ACCIDENT

1. The Plaintiff fell into the pool whilst in the process of climbing out. Whether he slipped or over-balanced is unclear and unimportant in relation to the outcome of this case. He was attempting to get out via a recessed step in the deep end of the pool quite near to the steps. Although the Plaintiff and his friends were clearly in good spirits there is no suggestion that the accident was the result of any misbehaviour on his part. Various suggestions in documents that he dived or dive-bombed into the pool are not supported by any admissible evidence. The Court is asked to accept the Plaintiff's own account which is that he fell. It may be that in the course of falling he tried to correct his fall, as experienced swimmers will often do. The result is that his entry may have been quite like a dive.

2. Why did he fall? The ledge on which he was standing had only a 12 inch going (to use the language of the Building Regulations). The Plaintiff was a very tall and heavy man. The ledge was probably wet as a result of the operation of the wave machine and he may well not have wholly regained his balance whilst attempting to get out of the pool via an unsuitable mode of exit. The Plaintiff, although strong, was somewhat tired after an extensive period going up and down the water slides. No one saw him enter the pool but the Plaintiff's account has not been challenged and is likely to be right.

3. Why was he so gravely injured? This wave pool, in common with wave pools generally, had a high free board. The wave machine was

operating at the material time. It is likely that the Plaintiff fell into the water when there was a trough reducing the water level. The water level was already severely reduced (see Mr. Limbrick's drawing). The Plaintiff was heavy and would have travelled through a considerable distance into quite shallow water, striking his head on the floor of the pool with his head and neck in deadly alignment.

4. He sustained an incomplete lesion of his spinal cord as a result of the contact with the bottom of the pool. The Plaintiff's recollection thereafter is partial, though it is likely that he was unconscious, face down in the pool for some little time before his friends noticed him. By the time they did so he was blue. They thought he was joking but turned him over and started to drag him down the pool towards the beach end. Todd Richardson (one of the life guards on duty) came to assist. The precise point at which he entered the pool and lent a hand is in dispute. By the side of the pool resuscitation was given to the Plaintiff and he was put in the recovery position. The Plaintiff says that he was conscious and talking when this happened and had asked the lifeguard not to move him.

THE LIFEGUARDS

5. It is clear that the life guards had agreed amongst themselves to reduce their number from 3 to 2, contrary to the approved practice at the pool. Todd Richardson refused to accept that he had anything to do with the decision until his own inconsistent statements were put to him. Both Todd Richardson and Tonia Solly (the life guard in the pulpit) were qualified life guards and had knowledge of spinal injury. The relevant handbook which was disclosed in the course of the trial clearly shows the need for careful handling of suspected spinal injuries particularly the immobilisation of the neck. The accident was not witnessed by either of the life guards. If Todd Richardson had been sitting in his high chair at the beach end he should have seen the Plaintiffs entry into the water. There was nothing to prevent his doing so and few people in the pool to distract his attention. In an effort to explain his failure to notice the Plaintiff's fall, Todd Richardson invented considerable activity in the beach area by the Elephants. When he says that he did see the Plaintiff he described him as blue and not breathing. On Todd Richardson's account it was only 15-20 seconds or so when his attention was not on the area of the pool where the Plaintiff fell. The truth is that Todd Richardson was not on the high chair when the incident happened, nor was he near to it. Even on his account he was not sitting on the high chair. He said that after only 10 minutes he needed to stretch his legs. The documents disclosed at the very end of the trial indicate that in the post-accident investigation there may well have been acknowledgment that Todd Richardson was not in his post

or scanning the pool when the accident happened. This is the evidence of the Plaintiff's friend, Craig Swinney (Witness Statement - B15 and confirmed in evidence). The Court is asked to find that there was only one life guard in her post at the time, namely Tonia Solly. She did not see the entry into the pool either. Being in the pulpit she had to revolve around nearly 360 degrees in order to keep an eye not only on the pool but the slides. She had to alert Todd Richardson to the Plaintiff's presence in the water. Her evidence suggests that she turned the wave machine off after alerting him. Todd Richardson in an effort to explain his inattention suggested that the water was still when he saw the Plaintiff first. The delay in responding to the Plaintiff's desperate plight had a significant effect on what occurred. Had his fall been witnessed by one or other of the life guards there would have been early intervention. His mode of entry into the pool and subsequent immobility should and probably would have raised the suspicion of a spinal injury. Whilst spinal boards may not have been approved, the principle of immobilisation should have coloured the life guards' approach to the rescue. Expired air resuscitation could have been provided in the water and attempts made to float Richard Davies out of the pool and take him onto the poolside without risking aggravation of his injury. Tonia Solly's attempt to explain her delay in responding was unattractive. She has suggested that Richard Davies was "playing dead" on an occasion before his actual accident. This is rather a grotesque coincidence. In the witness box she said that she told him off for doing so. This is entirely inconsistent with what she said in her Health and Safety Statement and it is indicative of an attempt to cover up for her and her boyfriend's delay in responding to an emergency.

THE DESIGN OF THE POOL

6. It was completed in about 1986. Leisure pools have been built since about the middle of the 1970s in this country. The Wyre Forest Pool included an "innovative" (to use the words of the Defendant's expert Mills) feature namely the recessed edge. This feature is not and has not been reproduced in any leisure pool in this country or abroad. The only similar feature can be found in the Olympic Pool in Montreal. This is despite an extensive search by experts involved in this case to find one. The pool in Montreal (not seen by any of the experts in the case) is a conventional swimming pool and the design may have been to combat the effects of the wash caused by vigorous swimming. It certainly did not have a similar design function as that in the Wyre Forest Pool. The design was the exclusive responsibility of the Council's own architects. Mr. Graham, the Defendant's expert architect, said that "specialist advice should be sought". A senior architect was called to give evidence. In his witness statement it seemed to be

suggested that the feature was in some way the responsibility of Bywater who manufactured the wave machine, or even Ove Arup. But in the witness box it was clear that Mr. Steed acknowledged that the design came from him. Despite extensive requests by the Plaintiff's solicitors no documents were produced concerning the genesis of this design or its implementation. Whilst it was suggested that there was some implied endorsement by Bywater of the design, no evidence was adduced to support this contention. Bywater could have been called in evidence. It is surprising that no memoranda, correspondence or plans were relied upon in support of the inclusion of the design feature. The Defendant's approach to Discovery does not lead to confidence in the assertion that there were no documents. But a lack of documents does not suggest a careful assessment of the feature by the architects or anyone else involved in the construction of the pool.

7.   The Defendant's evidence was that the feature reflected a compromise. Was it a means of ingress and egress? The leisure pool had a high free board (necessary with wave pools). The proper practice (probably not followed here) was to announce to swimmers the imminent turning on of the wave machine, and to encourage weak or tired swimmers to leave via the beach end. There were conventional steps for use by swimmers. The recessed step was small (C93), probably slippery and required some considerable upper body strength to allow swimmers (particularly with the wave machine going) to haul themselves onto it. There was no rail of any sort to assist. It was an unsafe means of access and egress. Mr. Graham conceded that he would now include barriers "for his professional indemnity". And yet the Defendant continued to maintain that the design was a safe one.

It was said by the architect that it was partly designed as a rest. (This is illustrated at C119) but there was no foot rest (as is normal with a rest design) and in any event a rest feature could have been designed without the step being incorporated at all. It has been vaguely suggested that it was appropriate for swimmers to sit on when waves washed over them. The architect said as much but accepted in evidence that he had never seen any swimmers doing this. The other use was for swimmers to dive from when training or competing in conventional swimming events, traversing the pool.

Whilst it may sometimes be desirable to incorporate conventional swimming pool and design swimming pool features in one, the way this was achieved was at the expense of safety. A better compromise is illustrated in Mr. Limbrick's report (C157).

It is common ground that no leisure pool should now be built which permits ingress and egress from the sides. Thus the stepped edge design would contravene current thinking. It is accepted by all witnesses that there is a continuing duty to monitor leisure pools in terms of their safety, to react to current thinking and to learn from accident profiles.

(See (inter alia) para 3(2) of the Defendant's architectural witness Lambert).

8. It is the Plaintiff's case that the stepped edge was an inherently dangerous design feature. At the time of construction Mr. Limbrick (whose unchallenged expertise the Court is asked to accept) was partly responsible for the construction of three major leisure pools - all had barriers to prevent ingress and egress. It may be that some other leisure pool which was designed in the 70s or even the early 80s did not have barriers although now all would. But none had the stepped edge and no barriers. The Court should accept the evidence of Mr. Sanders and Mr. Limbrick then it was reasonably foreseeable that an accident would result from this design feature. It is further submitted that the Plaintiff would not have attempted to leave the pool had there been no recessed step. Thus causation is established.

9. Even if the Court is not satisfied on some *Bolam* argument that the recessed step was dangerous it is submitted that by the time the Plaintiff had his accident steps should have been taken to eliminate or reduce the risk presented by the unsatisfactory design feature. The *Bolam* analogy is in any event misconceived. In deciding whether a doctor has been negligent in 1976 one looks at the state of knowledge and practice in 1976. When deciding whether a swimming pool is safe in 1990 the Court should look at what steps should reasonably have been taken to ensure the safety of pool users, even if such steps involved modifying or eliminating a design feature which might have been considered acceptable at the date of construction.

10. The Defendants should have looked carefully at the use of the recessed step and the accident profile at the pool. Mr. Graham accepted the need for *retrospectively* introducing guidelines in S.I.S.P. It appears that the architect responsible for the design had no further role in assessing its usefulness and safety. The evidence from the Defendant (Mr. Dickens) was that there was some assessment of the accidents, albeit on a one by one basis. It is submitted that this approach is wholly inadequate to enable a clear picture of an accident profile to emerge. It was certainly not one favoured by Mr. Mills at pools he has run. Nor was it accepted as a proper approach by Mr. Sanders, who has had considerable experience of accident profiles. The evidence of relevant accidents was extremely hard to obtain from the Defendant (the Court has been referred extensively to relevant correspondence and summonses) (Bundle E). A large number of further documents emerged shortly before the trial and during the trial itself. The Court ordered the Defendant to verify its list of documents on affidavit. Notwithstanding an affidavit sworn by him, Mr. Dickens' cross-examination revealed that there were still further documents which might have assisted in revealing the accident profiles. The need for such a profile was emphasised by the Defendant's experts Mills and Lambert. Both expressed themselves as reassured by the accident

profile in concluding the feature was not unsafe. In cross-examination both accepted that such reassurance was not based on an analysis of accident records but probably on some verbal assurance from the Defendant's employees. The value of those witnesses' evidence must be severely undermined by this unsatisfactory approach. It is not even suggested that they *asked* for relevant information. In contrast the Plaintiff took every reasonable step to obtain documents. Junior Counsel produced a Schedule for the Court's assistance. Mr. Sanders produced a Schedule and gave evidence about it when recalled at the conclusion of the trial. The only evidence about the accident from the Defendant was from Mr. Dickens, whose approach to Discovery and whose attitude towards this case renders the value of his evidence doubtful. Nevertheless he attempted to produce a chart based on the Plaintiff's experts' own schedules to show that there were not in fact many accidents in the area where Mr. Davies had his, but rather many took place at the deep end near the steps where there was a high free board. This was inherently unlikely having regard to the difficulty in getting out of the pool via a high free board and the relative ease of (a) the steps and (b) the recessed step in allowing ingress and egress. Furthermore some of the accidents appeared to involve small boys whose strength would have been insufficient. Nor was Mr. Dickens' hypothesis supported by the description of the deep end provided in Mr. Davies' own accident report or in others produced by the Defendant. The Court is asked to look with considerable scepticism on Mr. Dickens' evidence and to prefer the analysis produced by Mr. Sanders as clearly indicating that the accident profile showed the feature to be dangerous. His schedule did not purport to be exhaustive and some accidents on Junior Counsel's Schedule would have been included in a more thorough study. The Defendant's advisers provided no evidence to contradict Mr. Sanders' analysis. The Court is invited to conclude on the evidence available that (a) the step was inherently dangerous and (b) the accident profile (acknowledged by all experts to be important) necessitated intervention before the Plaintiff's accident.

11. What should have been done? Either the step should have been filled in or barriers erected? Barriers had already been erected at the deep end of the pool after the initial opening to respond to a perceived danger. It would not have been difficult or expensive to erect barriers by the sides of the pool. Even if the ledge had been retained, the existence of barriers, coupled with a proper culture at the pool encouraging swimmers to leave via the steps or the beach end would have prevented swimmers like Mr. Davies trying to get out via the sides. It is submitted that on the balance of probabilities a proper response to the danger would have made it highly unlikely that Mr. Davies would have tried to get out via the side. Thus the Plaintiff can establish that

the accident would not have happened had the Defendant taken appropriate precautions.

12. It is the Plaintiff's case that the life guards response to the emergency was inadequate. Either this was the result of their own incompetence, for which the Defendant is vicariously liable. Or it was the result of inadequate training and supervision of life guards for which the Defendant itself were responsible. It could be a combination of the two. In any event, it is submitted that proper systems and competent life guards would have resulted in a far better conducted rescue.

13. What difference would this have made? The medical evidence accepts that with an incomplete lesion there is a chance of recovery or alternatively, bad handling can aggravate the problem. Dr. Frankel accepted that with better handling there was a chance of improvement. Dr. Silver considered that there would probably have been improvement. Dr. Frankel's paper (not a complete equivalent) shows the levels of improvement resulting from postural reduction in hospital. Was the Plaintiff initially an A or a B? We submit probably B as Dr. Silver says. Dr. Frankel considers he was either an A or a B initially. At Oswestry he may well have been categorised as an A but this was probably the result of the swelling following the initial lesion and still does not make it less likely that he was initially a B. It is clear that he can be categorised as a B now. The majority of Bs improve two grades. In fact Dr. Silver suggested a rather more modest improvement (although any improvement would be highly welcome to the Plaintiff) had there been proper handling. At the very least the inadequate response of the life guards lost the Plaintiff a chance of recovery to a significant extent.

14. At what point was the damage done? The Court cannot isolate a particular moment; it may have been the handling of the Plaintiff by his friends, or the removal of him from the pool or the placing of him in the recovery position. The latter would plainly have been wholly contrary to accepted practice if the Plaintiff was conscious and suffering from a suspected spinal injury. The Court is invited to conclude that there was probably an aggravation of the Plaintiff's condition at some stage in the rescue which would probably have been avoided with appropriate handling. Further it is probable that with such appropriate handling there would have been a greater degree of recovery. The Plaintiff would then be entitled to damages to reflect this. The Court is asked to accept Dr. Silver's evidence as to the likely degree of recovery.

15. If the Court prefers Dr. Frankel's evidence there remains the loss of a chance of recovery for which the Plaintiff is entitled to be compensated. The Plaintiff's claim is both in contract and tort. In tort causation must be established on a 51% basis (*Wilsher; Hotson*). In contract, once the breach of contract is established the Court can assess damages to reflect the loss of a chance.

GOOD PRACTICE SUGGESTION

- Do not overstate your position
- As a general rule you should discriminate between your points, unless all are equally bad.[9]

---

[9] See also Example F

EXAMPLE I

Queen's Bench Trial – Clinical Negligence – Claimant's closing submissions by Edward Faulks QC and Dr David Thomson in March, 2005 – 19pp.

Brown v Birmingham and The Black Country Strategic Health Authority and Others concerned the failure by doctors to diagnose meningitis in a child and provide proper treatment. The issues concerned liability and its apportionment, causation, contributory negligence and quantum.

The introduction takes in the background facts even though they are certainly in the opening skeleton or written submission and the judge will by now be well aware of them. Why do so, then? Because (a) of the primacy of the facts and (b) the writers hope the judge will draw upon the description of the facts in this document for his judgment.

The narrative style mixes references to the evidence and submissions easily, and contains a chronological assessment of each Defendant's position. It is very readable with the language used being non-legal and non-technical wherever possible.

The use of interspersed accusatory questions is very effective.

It is a relatively long document; however its length is necessary to provide a comprehensive and detailed analysis of the evidence in the case. It includes references to key passages in the transcript of cross-examination.

It is interesting to note there are no formal conclusions pressed, and no legal analysis - the submissions are entirely fact driven.

The Claimant lost. Permission to appeal was refused by the trial judge and not renewed to the Court of Appeal.

FINAL SUBMISSIONS ON BEHALF OF THE CLAIMANT

[Reference to the trial bundles e.g. "G.1.6" is Bundle G. 1 page 6]

INTRODUCTION

1. Mr and Mrs. Brown are the parents of 3 children (pictured when young @ H.742). Two of them are happy and successful members of society and a credit to their family. Rachel has the misfortune to be severely damaged as a consequence of meningitis. She lives at home with her parents who have found her sheltered employment in their bookbinding company. She is unemployable elsewhere. She has

sufficient self-awareness to realise her limitations and is much cast down by them. Her future, once her parents are too old to look after her or die, is very uncertain.

2. Before her illness Rachel was a pretty, happy little girl (see the photographs @ H.740-745). The Court is asked to accept her parents' evidence that she was a normal little girl and mischievous only in the best sense of that word. Second hand reports from a nursery teacher (G.1.121) should not be preferred to their assessment of her personality. Although it is not without significance that in Dr. Davies' letter Rachel is reported *"to have changed dramatically 'overnight' since the onset of an acute illness in December 1985"*. Indeed it has always been the parents' case that this change in 'personality' was a real source of worry to them and one of the main reasons for their frequent consultations with doctors.

3. Where a child is in low mood or "depressed" or "emotionally blunt" it is natural for parents to question their own responsibility for the child's condition. Similarly when, with the benefit of hindsight, earlier referral of Rachel to a hospital by the parents might have saved her from the consequences of her illness, it is acutely painful to the parents who will tend to blame themselves.

4. It is submitted that the Browns are sensible and good parents. They were neither neurotic about their child's health nor did they ignore worrying signs and symptoms. Some questions in particular will haunt them. It was suggested by the Court to Mrs Brown that she was too incurious about the dermal sinus. And at various junctures in the trial it was also suggested that following the second discharge from hospital they should have gone straight to hospital rather than to their GP. It will be submitted that their actions were those of caring parents. If they deferred too much to doctors then it must be remembered that this was 20 years ago and the Browns are the type of people who respect professional opinion. They can and should not be blamed for their actions in relation to their consultation with doctors. Also they followed medical advice and encouraged Rachel to get back to normal by playing with her friends and going to school, when she was suffering meningitis.

THE DISEASE PROCESS

5. At trial there was a large measure of agreement about this. Rachel was born with a dermal sinus. It was the portal of entry for infection. The presentation in December 1985 and January 1986 was confused by antibiotics. She probably had meningitis in December 1985 and almost certainly did by January 1986 when admitted for the second time. A lumbar puncture during the second admission would on the balance of probability have led to the discovery of meningitis.

6. Hydrocephalus was probably not present until May 1986. But in March and certainly by April 1986 Rachel was showing signs/symptoms of meningitis. A lumbar puncture then would clearly have revealed this. Unfortunately by the time Rachel was sent back to New Cross Hospital in May 1986 it was impossible to save her from some of the consequences of meningitis, despite the efforts of neurosurgeons at the Midland Centre for Neurosurgery and Neurology, where she was transferred on 23rd May. Mr. Hamilton, the senior consultant neurosurgeon there, described her disease as "recurrent meningitis" (G.2. 343). In evidence, he confirmed the parents' evidence that he said to them that he wished he could have seen Rachel sooner.

7. This analysis is supported by the neurosurgical experts [D 373-379] and the microbiologists [D680-684]. Mr Macfarlane's unchallenged evidence at trial confirmed it. The views of Professor J and Dr. G, given in evidence, were to the same effect. The final position of the Health Authority is rather unclear. In its "reasoned response" it was denied that Rachel had meningitis on either of the first two admissions [A17]. In evidence at trial Dr. C refused to accept that Rachel had meningitis during the second admission. The Court is asked to find that Rachel had meningitis in January 1986 and that it could have been detected by lumbar puncture (LP). If this had happened, by one route or another Rachel would have survived unscathed.

8. The presentation was not of classic acute meningitis i.e. very severe headache, fast progressing illness, photophobia, etc. Rather it was the more unusual chronic meningitis. No criticism is offered of the failure to carry out an L.P. on the first admission. The criticism relates to the second admission where the case against the health authority is that they failed to carry out a lumbar puncture so as to *exclude* cranial pathology, [see D 431 paragraph 4.23 - 4.26 (1st 2 lines)] It is accepted that the signs and symptoms were equivocal. The question is whether or not taken as a whole the picture presented was such that a lumbar puncture should have been performed.
The allegations against both Defendants will be discussed chronologically

THE FAILURE BY DR. S TO REFER THE DERMAL SINUS IN INFANCY

9. Dr. S was clearly a competent practitioner who had a good relationship with his patients. The Browns held him in high regard. From the evidence of Mrs S it appears that this was mutual. His surgery was in walking distance. The Browns' evidence was that they consulted him whenever concerned about any of their children. Rachael was born on 25.5.81. The surviving notes show that certainly in the second year of Rachel's life (entry dated 24.5.82) she visited the surgery reasonably

regularly, in wholly typical circumstances, on the evidence of the GP experts.

10.   There are no notes that support visits with Rachel to Dr. S in the first year. Although it is clear that she went to the surgery for vaccinations [G. 1.24], and in accordance with the normal pattern it is likely that there would have been visits to Dr. S in her first year of life for the usual early illnesses or with one or both of the older children. The GP experts thought it likely that there would have been visits with Rachel in the first year [D 670-671]. It is submitted that it is likely that there were and the relevant page(s) have gone missing, as have other pages of her now microfiched medical records. What they would have recorded is a matter of speculation.

11.   The Browns' firm evidence was that they, principally Mrs. Brown, had pointed out the sinus to Dr. S on more than one occasion. There were inconsistencies in their evidence as to how many times. It is not surprising that there are. It does not follow that the evidence is unreliable on the question of pointing out the sinus; let alone that they are lying. The Browns were, it is submitted, patently honest witnesses doing their best to help the Court.

12.   Have they convinced themselves now about the matter? It will no doubt be pointed out that this part of the case was not an aspect pursued by the Browns' previous solicitors in 1986. It is only when they consulted Challinors that it emerged. The handwritten notes added to the Browns' initial summary by a solicitor at Challinors [C.290 A - C] are inconsistent in part viz: *"Dr S said nothing to worry about. Not pointed out to Dr S .... He said he would get it sorted out when she was about 7"*. How reliable a scribbled note is may be a matter of debate. The Browns' evidence was to the effect that they could not comment on what had been written down but they said that their position has always been that they pointed out the sinus to Dr. S and were told that he would refer Rachael when she was 6 or 7 years old for this to be sorted out.

13.   They did not in fact initially blame Dr S for failing to refer. Mr Brown regarded him as their only real ally in the face of a bewildering diagnosis of depression from New Cross Hospital. He came and saw them after Rachel's discharge and explained the hospital's view of Rachel.

14.   When this action was commenced they did not know about the neurosurgeons' BMJ "Lesson of the Week" article [F 717], which was accepted for printing by the BMJ on 29.4.87. In fact it provides considerable support for the Browns' evidence. Although not accurate in every respect (e.g. the expression of sebaceous material), there is specific reference to a consultation: *"on seeking medical advice, however, they had been reassured"; "Unfortunately, as with our patient, even if the lesion is noted the potential danger may not be appreciated by a medical attendant"; "Should a sinus be noted in the neonate or older child the family doctor or paediatrician (our emphasis) should refer*

the patient for surgical exploration before complications occur". Mr. Hamilton said in evidence that he understood the relevant consultation was when Rachel was "a baby".

15. It is therefore submitted that the sinus was pointed out in infancy. Was this to Dr S or to someone else? The Browns were not in doubt about this. They did attend the local clinic, principally for baby weight checks, in the first year. They saw a health visitor and sometimes saw a doctor. If Mrs Brown was concerned about the sinus (the mother's instinct on this was right) is it likely that she would have mentioned it to a 'strange' doctor/health visitor rather than the trusted family GP? Is it is likely that a developmental clinic doctor would have dismissed Rachel's abnormality? The Browns would not accept that they were mistaken. Are they lying? Or have they convinced themselves of something that didn't happen? We invite the Court to find that the sinus was pointed out to Dr. S.

16. Why did Dr S not refer Rachel? On the Browns' account he did not regard the sinus as anything other than a stork mark or other mark without significance. It was small and not very obvious. The hospital failed to notice it. It is not alleged that there was negligence in their failure to do so. Furthermore, the sinus was in a less common place; they are normally much lower down the spine. The Court might not have been surprised if there had been a defence to the effect that it was not negligent of the GP not to refer. But in fact the GP experts agreed that if the sinus was pointed out to Dr S he should have referred. [D 639]

17. It is submitted that this was a mistake by an otherwise good GP, the sort of mistake that all professionals make in the course of their career. If breach of duty is established then causation (it is agreed) must follow.

THE HOSPITAL'S APPROACH DURING THE SECOND ADMISSION

18. There was general agreement that Rachel's illness should be seen as a whole. So the first admission is an important part of the history and presentation. There are certain important matters that arise from that first admission:

   a) Rachel's condition was sufficiently of concern to warrant a GP referring to hospital and for the hospital to keep her for 3 days (quite a long period for a child (per Professor J).

   b) Unusually she was discharged without diagnosis. The discharge letter (G.1.26) omits reference to photophobia (G.1.29). It wrongly says that Rachel did not spike a fever (cf G.1.84).

   c) Dr S (G.1.82) thought she either had a viral infection or a partially treated bacterial infection. The last two words are missing.

Her plan was to leave for 24 hours and then if Rachel was not clearly better to do a full screen with lumbar puncture. Dr. A had a rather different recollection. She thought that chronic meningitis had been one of the diagnoses under consideration by the team at New Cross Hospital.

19. Rachel was "slightly better" after discharge on 19.12.85 [G.1.28] but did not really enjoy Christmas and was not her usual self. Dr. S re-referred on 6.1.86 [G.1.85]. By this time *"Parents are very worried and obviously this is something which appears at regular intervals".* She was reported by him to have a high temperature, anorexia and lethargy.

20. The admission note is a full one [G.1.87]. Amongst other observations she was described as *"emotionally blunt and flat."* There was a history of fever, nausea, headache and general malaise for 6 weeks leading up to admission; the last 4 days had seen a deterioration.

21. The Court is well aware of what is recorded in the medical and nursing notes about this admission. The two aspects of Rachel's condition upon which Dr G places particular emphasis are the fever and her change of personality/mood.

22. Rachel's fever was intermittent but it persisted and had done so for some time. There was no obvious cause. The TPR chart is no longer available but the parties have attempted to extrapolate from the notes what the chart might have looked like. The actual temperatures are likely to have been higher in the absence of the frequent doses of paracetamol [G.1.151]. Fever and malaise were the clinical details usually noted on the Microbiological report forms and the other investigation request forms [G.1.161/D + ff]. The microbiologist expert witnesses considered that Rachel had F.U.O. (fever of unknown origin). The evidence at trial suggested that this was not a precise term but it was accurate in the sense that Rachel did have a persisting fever, the origin of which was not known.

23. Other signs and symptoms included headache leading up to admission, some vomiting (G.1.143) and malaise.

24. The more significant evidence was of abnormal behaviour. The change in personality was a consistent feature of the parents' account at the time to doctors and in their evidence to the Court. Rachel's mood/personality was much recorded in the notes: For example:

> *"emotionally blunt and flat"* – [G.1.89]
> *"shrinking violet"* [G.1.92]
> *"remains miserable"* [G.1.93]
> *"behaviour still withdrawn"* [G.1.94]
> *"remains lethargic and listless, appears much the same behaviourally with or without mother"* [G.1.143]
> *"lolls about. Acts depressed"* [G.1.95] – Dr. C

"avoids eye contact – very passive – no physical abnormality apparent" [G.1.96] – Dr R

"father totally rejects depression ..sullen with me no focus of infection found" – Dr R [G.1.96]

"odd parenting pattern" – Dr C [G.1.96]

"remains lethargic and miserable" [G.1.139]

"...found no abnormality other than behaviour" – Discharge letter [G.1.29]

"behaviour this morning weepy and withdrawn" [G.1.140]

25. Dr C stated that he asked Dr R to explore the question of depression with the parents over the weekend when Dr R was on-call. This was a step neither of the expert paediatric witnesses had taken or heard of in their considerable experience.

26. A "diagnosis" of depression, even if not recorded in the discharge letter, seems to have been reached not only the Browns but also Dr. S. Even if Dr. C did not formally diagnose depression he clearly thought there was a strong functional or behavioural element in Rachel's illness. Unless Dr S lied to the M.D.U. Dr C seems to have told him this. The diagnosis of "indigenous (sic) depression" which impressed itself on the Browns must have come from somewhere.

27. The relevance of Dr C's views of Rachel's behaviour is that it caused him to ignore the possibility of intracranial pathology. In retrospect it was meningitis that caused her to behave in such an odd manner. It would not be surprising if an ill child in hospital was a bit withdrawn but Rachel's behaviour went much further and persisted, as was generally agreed by the experts at trial.

28. Dr A thought there might be an organic underlying illness [G.1. 140]. There was a raised white blood cell count, an excess of neutrophils (a neutrophilia) and a high temperature on 18th January 1986. Dr C said in evidence that there were no focal signs indicating intracranial pathology. Nor were there more focal signs indicating anything wrong with the stomach. He nevertheless carried out an ultrasound on 20th January 1986 and collect urine for 3 whole days so as to exclude neuroblastoma or similar tumours.

29. Why did he not perform a lumbar puncture? It is not a pleasant procedure and in certain circumstances can be dangerous (with non-communicating hydrocephalus). But the frequent references in the health authority's witness statements to the dangers are disingenuous. Dr C accepted that the reason that he did not do a lumbar puncture was nothing to do with the dangers involved in the procedure.

30. In evidence at trial Dr. C said the necessity for an LP *"did not cross my mind"*. In the First Defendant's "reasoned response" [A 16] it is said:

"It is admitted that Dr C and his team did not perform a lumbar puncture. The performance of a lumbar puncture was considered on numerous occasions, but was ruled out."
The evidence from Dr S was to the effect that one thinks of a lumbar puncture straightaway with a sick child with no obvious diagnosis but the possibility of infection, as her note suggests. Why if it was discussed and considered on the first admission did Dr C explain that it was not considered on the second? Dr A's oral evidence was that the team were aware that there was the possibility of partially treated meningitis.

31. Dr C in oral evidence held onto his explanation advanced in his witness statement [C.341 paragraph 41] that Rachel's symptoms during and around her admissions were due to raised intracranial pressure not infection producing meningitis. This is not an analysis shared by the medical experts and is very probably wrong. Rachel was progressively more unwell, culminating in deterioration in April and May [set out in Dr D letter at G.1.121] to her final coma in late May.

32. Dr G's views, expressed with thoughtful moderation, were that it was not acceptable not to perform an LP. He conceded that other views were worthy of respect and no doubt it will be submitted that he conceded that there was some form of *Bolam* defence here. But in fact he never departed from the views he gave in his report and in evidence that a lumbar puncture should have been performed.

33. If an expert says that there are "two schools of thought" as to how, say, an operation should be done then this can be a *Bolam* defence provided the alternative view can withstand logical analysis. But simply to accept that other views are worthy of respect is not without more accepting a *Bolam* defence, unless in so doing the expert is effectively saying that his opinion has now modified or altered having heard the evidence or seen a report. Dr G's concession was little more than politeness. It did not undermine his views in a material sense.

34. Dr C told the Court that as many as 90% of lumbar punctures he performed would be clear. So that it is apparent that an LP is/was used to *exclude* intracranial pathology. In fact intracranial pathology was not excluded nor could it have been in Rachel's case in the absence of an LP.

35. Professor J's initial view in his report was that "she did not have the classic signs of meningitis, for example neck stiffness, which would have alerted doctors to the risk of meningitis and justified consideration of a lumbar puncture". [D 488]. At the joint experts' meeting his position had altered a little. He thought there were borderline indications for performing a brain CT scan to exclude a brain abscess. He also said: "the vague clinical picture, lack of classical signs of meningitis despite reported examination and spontaneous improvement during the in-patient period without antibiotics provided acceptable

grounds for not performing a lumbar puncture." [D 686] This was a less enthusiastic endorsement of the hospital.

36. During his oral evidence his position seemed to move again. This is not to suggest there was anything inappropriate about the modification of his views. He had been in Court. An expert trying to help the Court may reflect further in the light of additional evidence and qualify his views. Professor J appeared to accept that it was a fundamental part of his point of view that Rachel was simply reacting to hospital in the way that children do. Whereas if the evidence was that Rachel's behaviour was "abnormal" and warranted a quasi-psychiatric investigation, his views must be seen as considerably less secure. Particularly if Dr S is right and there was actually a diagnosis of depression made in hospital.

37. When asked questions by the Court, Professor J's answers revealed a considerable shift from his original held view. The following is a summary but the Court will have the benefit of the transcript ordered at the close of Professor J's evidence.

Key:
J – Mr Justice Turner
EF – Edward Faulks QC
PR – Paul Rees QC
PrfJ – Professor J

[earlier in Professor J's oral evidence]

Cross examination by EF – The number of entries regarding her personality was exceptional?

PrfJ - I accept that

…

[later in Professor J's oral evidence]

EF - Have you ever asked a fellow consultant to discuss with the parents a diagnosis of depression?

PrfJ -I do not recall doing so.

EF - That would be an unusual course.

PrfJ - Yes. Going to lengths to ask a weekend on call consultant to focus on depression would be exceptional.

…

[at the end of Professor J's oral evidence]

J - to 24ᵗʰ January 86 – You say there were absent indications, symptoms or signs, of intracranial pathology. You say not proceed to an LP.

PrfJ - Correct

J - If equivocal symptoms and signs of intracranial pathology, what then?

PrfJ - Equivocal?

J - Equivocal.

PrfJ - In terms of neck stiff, more pronounced headache, then swayed to CT scan and progressing.

J - The decision that was made in that situation, where there were equivocal indications, is it within the range of acceptable or non-acceptable [practice]?

PrfJ - [unclear answer] response of clinicians, reasonable examinations, expect them to find neck stiffness in a 4 year old.

J- Going back before that. If equivocal, was it outwith the range of reasonable practice not to proceed to LP?

PrfJ-If equivocal signs, then good practice required a lumbar puncture.

J - So outwith the range of good clinical practice not to have performed it?

PrfJ - Yes.

J - So if equivocal physical signs, it was mandatory. He should have performed a lumbar puncture?

PrfJ - Yes.

Re-examination by PR – I wish to clarify "equivocal" physical signs, in terms of appropriate practice to go to lumbar puncture. What signs require lumbar puncture?

PrfJ - Fever, headache, signs meningism - neck stiffness, neck rigidity, other localising physical signs. For equivocal, in my clinical practice, working around neck stiffness.

J - "Equivocal" just like if I see an elephant, but have difficulty explaining it. Set out what makes any sensible paediatrician...[PR continues]

PR - What equivocal signs are required before any reasonable paediatrician performs a lumbar puncture?

PrfJ - Fever - intermittent persisting, disturbed sleep pattern, not eating.

PR - Signs of meningism?

PrfJ - Yes

Further cross examination by EF - You say what equivocal signs are required? Do you require all those or some of them?

PrfJ - Some of them.

38. Dr C gave evidence to the effect that on discharge there was a very low threshold of referral and he would have liked to have seen Rachel within 48 hours of her attendance on Dr S in March or April 1986. This was even had her symptoms and signs remained the same and because of his continued concern for her and the absence of a diagnosis. And yet he seemed very reluctant to accept that even then a lumbar puncture would have been performed. On this he was not consistent with either Dr. G or Professor J who, whilst not dogmatic on the point, thought that a lumbar puncture would probably have been performed in April. It is submitted that Dr C's reluctance to countenance a lumbar puncture was not reflective of what would have been good practice.

39. Dr. C emphatically refuted the accuracy of Dr S's account of their conversation given to the MDU on 1.8.86 [C.314cJ. He even denied that there had been a telephone conversation. He said that a diagnosis of depression would have been negligent. If the case for Dr S is accepted then it follows that Dr C was pursuing a highly improbable diagnosis and his recollection is deficient. Even if Dr S is not accepted, Rachel's behaviour was of a type that should have caused Dr C to think about the possibility of intracranial pathology.

40. It was a very long hospitalisation and there were some puzzling signs. The microbiologists all agreed that a lumbar puncture should have been performed [D 682]. It was not incumbent upon Dr C as a paediatrician to consult a microbiologist although it was just the sort of case in which he probably should have done (evidence of Professor C). But if he failed to do so there is an onus on him to justify his decision not to perform an L.P. There was nothing about the methodology adopted by the microbiologists that was in any way criticised by the experts. Their views provide support for the opinion of Dr. G.

AFTER THE SECOND ADMISSION

41. Dr C was clear that he would have expected Dr S to refer in March and April and that he would have seen Rachel within 48 hours.
The Browns were worried but had been told by Dr. S of the diagnosis/explanation of depression. This coloured their entire approach to Rachel including their sending her back to school and trying to jolly her on when she was in fact was seriously ill. Mr Brown in particular feels terrible about this; hence his collapse in the witness box.

42. What in fact had transpired between Dr C and Dr S? Had the former been rather abrupt as he was wont to be (as confirmed by Dr R in his oral evidence)? The Browns do not know the extent to which Dr S accepted any diagnosis of depression. In fact the MDU note suggests that he was reluctant to do so. All that they, as parents, could do was try and look after Rachel as best they could and seek such medical advice as was available. Dr S told them of the problems of getting a second opinion. They went to see him twice on 18.3.86 and 19.3.86 and again on 4.4.86.

43. Dr S effectively told them that a second opinion was not a feasible option. It is accepted that a second opinion was not easy in terms of the availability of alternatives or in the light of a future relationship between Dr S and Dr C. Why did the Browns want one? The answer must be that they felt that the hospital had misinterpreted her behaviour as having a 'functional' explanation rather than, as they correctly interpreted the situation, as an indication that Rachel was seriously unwell. Despite the discouragement from Dr S, the Browns did eventually seek a second opinion from Dr. D on 12.5.86; an indication of how desperate they were.

44. Once Dr S had steered them away from a second opinion his choice was between treating Rachel himself or referring her back to New Cross. He had two opportunities to do so in March and in April.

45. Here Dr C's evidence at trial is of importance: When asked what if the position on 20.3.86 was no better and no worse, he said he would want to see Rachel again, within 48 hours. He said he would get her back into hospital. By April, particularly in the light of new symptoms, Dr. C explained again that he would have wanted to see her and agreed that he would have "searched hard for a cause" of her illness. As to Rachael's hyperacusis, whilst Dr C said there could have been a local cause it was more likely to involve the central nervous system. He agreed that he would have been anxious not to send her home until he had got to the bottom of her illness.

46. When Professor J was asked about the position in April 1986, he said that with the passage of time and symptomatology, intracranial pathology would rise much higher in any diagnostic agenda. He said that the possibility of raised intracranial pressure and meningitis would have been considered in April 1986 and that the only way to

exclude meningitis was by lumbar puncture. Dr G, of course, considered that a lumbar puncture should have been performed during the second admission. It follows that, a fortiori, (in his view) one should have been performed on admission March or April.

47. It is therefore submitted that a referral to Dr C in March or April would have resulted in admission and, on balance, the performance of a lumbar puncture. He would have taken steps to get to the bottom of her illness. A lumbar puncture would have revealed meningitis and Rachel would have survived intact.

48. Was it reasonable for Dr S not to refer? To some extent this depends on what transpired between Dr C and Dr S. If depression was not mentioned to Dr S (as Dr C says) then it is the clear view of Dr I that there should have been a referral. His recorded views were based on the assumption that Dr S had been reassured by Dr C by telephone on or about 20.3.86. Similarly Dr W assumed that the disputed telephone call had taken place and that reassurance had been provided by Dr. C. If no such reassurance had been forthcoming from Dr C he effectively conceded that the choice for the doctor was between admission to hospital and close observation, saying to the parents "see you in a few days". He accepted that he would have been "puzzled" by the presentation.

49. The combination of Dr C's evidence and that of the GP experts should, it is submitted, lead the Court to conclude as follows:
(i) Absent "reassurance", Dr S should have referred earlier than he did.
(ii) If there *was* reassurance, the failure to refer in April 1986 taken with the presentation in March, was only acceptable if there was *no* neck stiffness, signs of meningitis, proven irritability, or drowsiness. If none of these were present and if there had been discovered an apparent cause for her (high) fever then admission was not mandatory. But the issue is dependent upon what was found on examination.

50. On causation, Dr. T's evidence stood alone. He did not have a very firm grasp of the history of Rachel's illness. His views seemed to be that if an experienced GP diagnosed tonsillitis (had he?) then it is probable that so would the hospital. On previous occasions Dr S diagnosed "tonsillitis" and gave her treatment with antibiotics and Codeine painkillers, but on 4.4.86 he gave her just antibiotics. Dr G and Professor J would have been less accepting of a diagnosis of tonsillitis followed by administration of antibiotics. [D 690]. It is of significance that the hospital had not given her antibiotics on the previous admission. Dr C's evidence suggests that he would not have either diagnosed tonsillitis or given antibiotics.

51. By April, Rachel was clearly suffering from meningitis. There were some signs and symptoms in an illness which were of continuing concern to Rachel's parents and (on his evidence) to Dr C. In the absence of "reassurance" and a diagnosis of depression emanating from the hospital it was incumbent upon Dr S to refer. Even if there had been

"reassurance", the signs and symptoms were such that on a careful examination, they warranted referral. In retrospect, Rachel had meningitis. Prospectively there was enough here, in the light of the history, to indicate to Dr S that she should be seen by the hospital. If she had been, the story would have been different.

WHAT SHOULD HAVE BEEN DONE?

52. There were a number of missed opportunities to treat Rachel. At any one of those opportunities there was time to intervene. Rachel's "striking" (per Dr C in evidence) behaviour diverted entirely Dr C's attention from the possibility of intracranial pathology to behavioural or personality disorder or depression.

53. Although lumbar puncture was a regular procedure with Dr C (he had a low threshold, on his evidence), he did not perform one. It was considered on the first admission but he stated not apparently thereafter. The explanation appears to be that this was not classic acute meningitis and that her atypical behaviour was never considered to have any possible connection with the C.N.S. Dr G considered the investigations to be "scanty". This was a very long hospitalisation and Rachel's behaviour was sufficiently strange for Dr C to take the unprecedented step of asking a fellow consultant to explore a psychiatric explanation. On Dr C's case this was excluded although no full record of discussion with the parent or grandparents or her pre-illness behaviour or personality was recorded nor was any mention of any possibility of review by a child psychiatrist. If so, then C.N.S. involvement was (at the very least) a possibility. Only an L.P. could exclude intracranial pathology. There was even an assumption that "encephalopathic illness has been excluded..." in Dr D letter [G.1.121]. It could and should have been.

54. The Court will not avoid the fundamental factual issue between Dr C and Dr S. If the latter is right then on his own evidence, Dr C came to a diagnosis which no reasonably competent paediatrician could have reached. This would explain his reluctance even to consider a lumbar puncture.

55. If, on the other hand, no such conversation (as recorded by Dr S) took place or it was not to the same effect, Dr S's position becomes untenable. Even if there was a communication along the lines recorded by the M.D.U., Dr. S does not seem to have accepted the diagnosis. He should, in either event, have referred Rachel back to hospital or to a different specialist earlier than he did.

GOOD PRACTICE SUGGESTION

- Formulate questions that are appealing to the judge by making them look neutral and independent.
- Stand back and ask yourself whether the result you are arguing for is just. If you don't think so it is likely the judge won't either.
- Do not comment on your opponent's skeleton of itself – this is tiresome for the court.
- On appeal you must deal with the other side's position, though this must depend upon how readily it may be answered. If there is an easy answer, provide it. But never answer a point not previously advanced; never try to anticipate. It is much more productive to set out own your own stall than to knock your neighbour's offering.
- If there is no authority to support your argument reason from first principles, use common sense and appeal to obvious logic. Assert that there is no authority because you are 'obviously right' – find a case which demonstrates that your argument cannot be obviously wrong.[10]

---

[10] See also Example A.

EXAMPLE J

Court of Appeal – Appellant Defendant's skeleton opening by Edward Faulks QC and Andrew Warnock in October, 1998 – 14pp together with two appendices of 8pp and a chronology of 2pp.

Phelps v London Borough of Hillingdon was an education claim brought against a local authority for failing to identify the Claimant's dyslexia and educate her according to her needs. The Defendant here appeals against the trial judge's findings as to the nature of the damage suffered by the Claimant, duty, breach, causation and the level of general damages awarded.

The skeleton is of sufficient length to require a small list of contents. Note the use of a key to guide the court to references to the core bundle, judgment below and transcript of oral evidence.

The writers adopt a narrative style to conduct a structured analysis of defects in the judgment for each assertion dealing with the nature of the damage, duty, breach and causation. In addition to the law cited within the text – there are no footnotes – in support of their submissions, two separate appendices are provided. The first contains the relevant statutory framework and deals with three statutes and two pieces of delegated legislation. This self-contained discussion of this area of law is useful for a bench likely to be composed of at least one member (and probably two) who is unfamiliar with it. Appendix 2 contains the remedies available under the statutory scheme. This serves to emphasise the novelty of the form of action brought and therefore supports the Appellant's wider case.

A chronology of the 16 relevant years is reduced to two pages. The events are cross-referenced to the core bundle.

The Appellant succeeded in the Court of Appeal, reported at [1999] 1 WLR 500. However it subsequently lost in the House of Lords, reported at [2001] 2 AC 619.

SKELETON ARGUMENT OF THE DEFENDANTS/APPELLANTS

Contents	*page number*
Introduction	2-3
Nature of the damage	3-5
Duty	5-9
Breach	10-12
Causation	12-14
Damages	14
Appendix 1 (statutory framework)	15-20
Appendix 2 (alternative remedies)	21-22
Appendix 3 (chronology)	23-24

key: cb= core bundle, j = judgment.

References to oral evidence are given by way of date and page number (eg 24.7.98 p3).

INTRODUCTION

1.1   This appeal involves a comparatively novel form of action in which the plaintiff claimed damages against her local education authority ("LEA") for failing to identify that she was dyslexic (sometimes referred to as having specific learning difficulties) and failing to educate her appropriately according to her needs.

1.2   In appeals heard under the name of *X v Bedfordshire County Council* [1995] 2 AC 633 the House of Lords considered 3 such actions in the context of striking out applications. The House of Lords held that education authorities did not owe a direct common law duty of care in relation to the exercise of their powers and discretions relating to children with special educational needs conferred on them by the Education Act 1981 (P762). They declined to strike out a claim based on an allegation that a LEA provided a psychological service to the public, although Lord Browne-Wilkinson, (with whom the other lords agreed), considered that if on the evidence at trial it emerged the psychology service was simply part and parcel of the system established by the local educational authority for the discharge of its statutory duties the existence and scope of any such duty might have to be excluded or limited (P763). Their lordships also declined to strike out as unarguable allegations that individual educational psychologists and teachers owed duties of care for which their LEA employers might be vicariously liable.

1.3   The fact that the House of Lords declined to strike out particular claims as not disclosing a reasonable cause of action does not involve a converse finding that those claims *did* disclose a cause of action (see *Morgan v Odhams Press Ltd* [1971] 1 WLR 1239). In *X*, the House of Lords did not have the benefit of hearing evidence and going into the facts at trial - a matter emphasised by Lord Browne-Wilkinson at 741 C-D and 763 G-H. The tone of his judgment generally was far from encouraging to this sort of claim.

1.4   The case which is the subject matter of this appeal is believed to be the first in which a court has found a local education authority liable (in another recent first instance case, *Christmas v Hampshire County Council* [1998] ELR 1, the Plaintiffs claim failed on the facts). In his judgment, the learned judge held that an educational psychologist employed by the Defendant, a Miss Melling (now known as Mrs. Loffler) owed a duty of care to the Plaintiff, that she was in breach of that duty and that the Defendant local authority was vicariously liable in respect of that breach. The learned judge dismissed claims made against the Plaintiff's teachers on the facts, although he held they could have been held liable as a matter of law.

1.5 In this Appeal the Defendants appeal against the learned judge's findings as to the nature of the damage suffered by the Plaintiff, duty, breach, causation and the level of general damages awarded (see the Notice of Appeal at cb 1-3).

NATURE OF THE DAMAGE

2.1 The learned judge made the following findings in relation to the nature of the damage claimed:

(a) That the Plaintiff's claim to have suffered a positive psychiatric injury was not made out (j, p43 A-E);

(b) That claims in respect of loss of confidence, low self-esteem, embarrassment and social unease were not matters that sounded in damages (j,p44G);

(c) That a failure to mitigate the adverse consequences of a congenital defect sounded in damages and that if necessary he was prepared to regard this as an "injury" (j47);

(d) That the damage claimed was not too remote (j47).

2.2 It is submitted that the learned judge erred in the following respects in making the finding set out at (c) above:

i) The learned judge adopted the dicta of Lord Bingham in the CA in X at p703 and cited with approval the dicta of Evans LJ at 705H-706F (j,45), but he gave insufficient weight to the fact that those observations, which were obiter, were made in the context of an application to strike out and in the absence of evidence;

ii) The learned judge ought to have made a definitive finding as to the nature of the damage claimed by the Plaintiff. The nature of damage has a bearing on whether or not a duty of care is owed in respect of that damage. It also has important practical consequences in this type of litigation, for instance with respect to limitation (3 years with the possibility of a discretionary extension if the action is one for a personal injury -ss 11 and 33 of the Limitation Act 1980) and pre-action discovery and discovery from non-parties which are only available in actions for personal injuries (Supreme Court Act 1981 ss33(2) and 34(2), RSC O24r7(A));

iii) On his own findings as to the nature of dyslexia, which were consistent with the expert evidence, the learned judge held:

> "It (dyslexia) is an inborn condition. It has been described as
> the result of a neurological dysfunction or cognitive defect but
> the actual cause is unknown. It is not curable but with appro-
> priate teaching and support those with SpLD can be helped to
> achieve higher levels of literacy than would otherwise have
> been the case and, by understanding their condition, to de-
> velop techniques for mitigating its effects. However, the degree
> to which people with SpLD can be helped varies widely: some,
> sadly, make little progress at all." (j, 3-4).

In the premises the learned judge ought to have concluded that
dyslexia was a constitutional condition which did not amount to
a "personal injury." Alternatively the learned judge ought to
have held that dyslexia had not been proved to amount to a personal injury.

iv) The learned judge ought to have concluded (a) that the claim was
a purely economic one and (b) that it was in the nature of a claim
for the loss of a potential gain (namely better employment
prospects) rather than a claim in respect of damage to existing
economic rights. The difficulty the judge had in arriving at the
proper measure of damages (j38-40,48) is an indication of the
uncertainty he had as to the basis in law of the claim. In fact, it
is submitted that there was no finding by the judge as to how the
Plaintiff would have been had the Defendants not been negligent.

DUTY

3.1 The learned judge erred in holding that the educational psychologist
("EP") owed a duty of care to the Plaintiff:

(a) Judged by reference to the nature of the damage, his finding
amounted to the imposition of a duty in tort to confer an economic benefit upon the Plaintiff. Although a duty in tort in
respect of a lost gain was imposed in *White v Jones* [1995] 2AC
207, the imposition of the duty in that case was exceptional and
influenced by the fact that no other remedies were available to
the plaintiff. There is no need for such a duty to be imposed in
this case where a variety of administrative and statutory remedies
are available (see appendix 2).

(b) In *Van Oppen v Clerk to the Bedford Charity Trustees* [1990]
1 WLR 235 it was held that a school does not owe a general duty
to promote the economic welfare of the children who attend it
(see 260E to 263F, 267C and see also the judgment of Evans
LJ in the CA in *X* [1995] 2AC 633 at 717A-C). That being the

case, it is submitted that an EP who advises the school cannot be said to owe such a duty;

(c) In the absence of an assumption of personal responsibility for economic loss an employee does not owe a duty in respect of such loss (*Williams v Natural Life* [1998] 1 WLR 830. There was no evidence of such an assumption in this case;

(d) There was no relationship of proximity between the Plaintiff and the EP. On the evidence the Plaintiff's referral to the educational psychologist by Mellow Lane, and the EP's assessment, were part and parcel of the LEA's statutory duty to identify children with special educational needs (eg evidence of Mr. Stafford, cb 128 par 15). On the facts, the role of the EP was in fact similar to that of the psychiatrist in *M v London Borough of Newham* (part of *X*) where the HL held no duty was owed (see [1995] 2 AC 633 at 752D-754B). Although some of the advice may have been shared with the parents it was primarily directed at the teachers and other LEA employees responsible for educating the Plaintiff. Miss Melling's report was stamped *"This report is confidential to the Authority. Contents should not be disclosed to the child or the parents without the permission of the Educational Psychologist responsible"* (unfortunately the stamp is not legible on the copy of the report at cb243). Further, much of the EP's input did not involve the Plaintiff or her parents at all - for instance the Care Committee (see for example cb p 248). For a recent application of the proximity concept see *Capital & Counties v Hampshire County Council* [1997] QB 1004 where the Court of Appeal held that a fire brigade does not have a sufficiently proximate relationship with a householder when it answers a call and actually turns up and fights the fire. There will only be sufficient proximity if the fire brigade creates new danger or adds to the risk by their activities (see also *Alexandrou v Oxford* [1993] 4 All ER 328).

(e) The relationship between the parents and the EP and school was one of potential and actual conflict. The Education Act 1981 itself recognised the possibility of such conflict in that it made it a criminal offence for a parent not to comply with a notice requiring an examination for the purposes of a section 5 assessment (Schedule 1 paragraph 2(4)). The potential for conflict is highlighted by the fact that family relationships are a matter an EP should consider (see Dr. Conn, 23.7.97 page 143/144, Dr. Gardner 24.7.98 pages 137/138). Further, on the evidence the parents were constantly dissatisfied with the provision made for Pamela Phelps and, for instance, insisted she should be sent to a special school (see cb p250, 297, 355, 122 par4, 126 par 6,) although that allegation did not form part of the Plaintiff's case at trial.

(f) On the evidence the assessment of the Plaintiff's needs was an on-going multi-disciplinary process which involved a large number of individuals and agencies (see the narrative at pages 5 to 13 of the judgment). They included:

  i   Miss Meyerhof, an LEA educational psychologist to whom the Plaintiff was referred by her primary school, Hayes Park Infants School in 1980 (report at cb 329-330);
  ii the staff at the Child Guidance Clinic to which the Plaintiff was then referred, including Mrs. Jones, a psychiatric social worker and a Dr. Urquhart (psychiatrist);
  iii the Plaintiff's general practitioner, with whom Dr. Urquhart was in correspondence;
  iv Mrs. Kerbekian, a psychotherapist who saw the Plaintiff for a number of sessions (unfortunately interrupted by bereavements and illnesses);
  v   the staff at Hayes Park Infants School;
  vi the staff at Hayes Park Junior School;
  vii Mrs. Roberts, an Advisory Remedial Teacher, who tested the Plaintiff's reading and spelling on 4th May 1984 (j9F);
  viii Mellow Lane Special Needs Department, the existence of which was in accordance with the overall scheme of the Education Act 1981 (j10D), and in particular Mrs. Murphy, Mrs. Taylor and a Miss Isherwood;
  ix the Plaintiff's other teachers at Mellow Lane, and her year heads and the headmaster;
  x   Miss Melling, the educational psychologist;
  xi Mellow Lane's care committee, chaired by Mr. Pelligrini, and attended at various times by the education welfare officer, the educational psychologist (Miss Melling), the special needs co-ordinater (Mrs Taylor or Mrs Murphy), the advisory remedial teacher (Mrs. Roberts), any relevant Head of Year or teacher involved, a social worker (eg cb 248, 264);
  xii the Plaintiff's parents, who also owed a statutory duty to ensure she received an education suitable for her aptitude (section 36 of the Education Acl 1944 as amended by the Education Act 1981)

In his evidence Dr. Conn identified a number of other professionals who might also be involved in an assessment of a child's needs, including occupational and speech therapists (23.7.97 p172). it is submitted that it is unfair and inappropriate to isolate any one of the individuals involved in the process and decision making (much of which was made by committee). If the educational psychologist or teachers owe duties, then what of other members of the Care Committee, or even the Plaintiff's parents?

(g) The Plaintiff's claims derived from the Defendants' duties under the 1944 and 1981 Education Acts (for a summary of the statutory framework see Appendix 1). It is clear that there can be no claim for breach of statutory duty under those Acts. The courts will generally be reluctant to superimpose a common law duty in such circumstances (see *Yuen Ken Yeu v Attorney General of Hong Kong* [1988] AC 175 at 195D). As Lord Hoffman said in *Stovin v Wise* [1996] AC 293 at page 414H *"the fact that parliament has conferred a discretion must be some indication that the policy of the Act conferring the power was not to create a right to compensation. The need to have regard to the policy of the Act therefore means that exceptions will be rare."* In X it was held that a local authority does not owe a duty of care in relation to decisions made when performing its statutory duties under the Education Acts. That being the case, it is submitted it is not fair just or reasonable that a duty of care should be owed by the EP whose input, on the evidence is just one part of that decision making process.

(h) The imposition of a duty of care in these circumstances will lead to a diversion of scant resources from education to litigation. It is not simply a question of the financial cost of defending actions such as this one, but also of human resources. In this case the head of Special Needs, a deputy head of year, a deputy head-teacher (now a head-teacher elsewhere) and the headmaster of the Plaintiff's school were called as witnesses. The judge was critical of the fact that other members of staff who had taught the Plaintiff were not called, in particular the Plaintiff's form teacher, reading assistant and another special needs teacher (j P11). In any one case a very large number of teachers and members of staff may have had dealings with the child concerned. To require all of them to attend court - which will often be necessary to defend the action properly in the light of the judge's comments - would have a considerable impact on the education system.

(i) An important feature in this case was the nature of the teaching actually provided to the Plaintiff in the classroom. The fact that the school does not keep the old exercise and work books of the child puts a very difficult burden on the school in proving the nature of the teaching provided. It is important to note that these claims may be tried many years after the relevant events because of the extended limitation period where a minor is involved.

BREACH

4.1   In assessing the Plaintiff Miss Melling used a diagnostic test known as the Weschler Intelligence Scale for Children, or WISC test (see her report at cb 243-244). An explanation of the nature of the test, which consists of a number of sub-tests, is given in the evidence of Miss Melling at 22.7.97 p136. Miss Melling found no specific weaknesses (a term of art). Subsequent WISC and WAIS (the adult version of WISC) assessments applied by Mr. Walker (cb 16), Mr. Rabinowitz (cb 140) and Dr. Gardner (cb 214) when the Plaintiff was much older revealed an "ACID" profile, namely specific weaknesses in the arithmetic, coding, information and digit span sub-tests, although the Plaintiff's scores on any one sub-test varied from assessment to assessment.

4.2   The learned judge found as a fact that an ACID profile was not revealed when Miss Melling examined the Plaintiff (j31C).

4.3   However, he went on to hold that not having found an ACID profile, Miss Melling ought to have performed further diagnostic tests, and in particular the Bangor test (j32-33).

4.4   It is respectfully submitted that the learned judge was wrong in so holding:

(a)   It had never formed part of the Plaintiff's pleaded case that the Bangor test or any other further diagnostic test ought to have been performed nor did such an allegation appear in any of the Plaintiff's expert reports;

(b)   In cross-examination, Dr. Conn accepted that the diagnostic test applied by Miss Melling, namely the Weschler test, was appropriate and a "very good choice of instrument" (23.7.97, pp 145-146);

(c)   In cross-examination. Dr. Conn put it no higher than that he "would probably" have gone into a different level of thoroughness (23.7.97 p148);

(d)   Dr. Conn's view that he would probably have performed a further test was one informed with hindsight, namely the knowledge that the Plaintiff is dyslexic;

(e)   Miss Milling had an alternative explanation for the Plaintiff's literacy problems, namely emotional problems as suggested in the Child Guidance files. The experts on both sides accepted that she was entitled to take into account the Child Guidance files (Dr. Conn 23.7.97 page 125-126, Dr. Gardner 24.7.97 p138);

(f)   The learned judge (j p32) placed undue emphasis on Dr. Gardner's evidence (given in response to a question from the learned judge) that he would like to feel he would have carried out some more tests. In fact, Dr. Gardner went on to say that he did not know what Miss Melling's thoughts were, but there was a suggestion that at least part of what Miss Melling was thinking was that there was an ongoing emotional component to the Plaintiff's difficulties (25.7.98, p22). At no time did he state that good practice dictated the carrying out of further tests or that Miss Melling was wrong to conclude that emotional problems were an explanation. On the contrary he stated that there was evidence of an emotional impact on Pamela (25.7.97, p28).

4.5   The learned judge further erred in holding that Miss Melling ought to have re-tested the Plaintiff on a later date:

(a)   It was unfair to isolate Miss Melling and hold that she ought to have taken a decision to re-assess, when her continued involvement with Pamela was as part of a care committee where other individuals were present and did not make a further referral;

(b)   It was a view informed by hindsight. There were other reasons available for the Plaintiff's continued inability to progress, in particular her absenteeism (for instance 31½ days in her 1st year, 11 in her 2nd, 54 half-days out of a possible 174 between September and February in her 3rd year - see Schedule of Absences at cb 437 to 440 and also cb 292-294), behavioural problems (see for instance cb 264, 284, 449-455) and illnesses.

CAUSATION

5.1   At page 35C of his judgment the learned judge stated:
"There was a considerable volume of evidence about the nature and appropriateness of the special needs teaching. I do not consider it necessary to review this evidence. The short point is that the plaintiff was not taught specifically as a dyslexic because she was not diagnosed as such."

5.2   The learned judge erred in so holding. It was necessary for the learned judge to review this evidence in order to make a finding as to whether or not the fact Miss Melling did not diagnose dyslexia had any causative effect.

5.3   It is submitted that the fact that the learned judge did not review the evidence calls into question his later conclusion that had the Plaintiff been diagnosed as dyslexic, she would have been taught differently (J40B-E).

5.4   Further, the learned judge erred in that he failed to consider the nature of the provision which was being made available to dyslexic children in other LEAs at the relevant time. The picture elsewhere was relevant to the question of whether or not the Plaintiff in fact received an education appropriate for a dyslexic child as judged by the standards of the time.

5.5   On a consideration of the above matters, the learned judge ought to
have concluded that the nature of the provision made for the Plaintiff
would not have been materially different had dyslexia been identified:

(a)   In his report Dr. Conn stated a diagnosis of dyslexia would have
resulted in "a rich panoply" of appropriate teaching schemes,
strategies and materials being made available to the Plaintiff.
When pressed to elaborate on this in examination in chief, he
stated that it would have resulted in an individualised programme centred on multi-sensory techniques with over-learning
(23.7.97 pages 110-114);

(b)   The Plaintiff in fact received in the order of 20-25% withdrawal
from mainstream classes for small group or one to one tuition.
In his report (cb 221), Dr. Gardner, stated that even by todays
standards this would be considered substantial;

(c)   It was the evidence of Rhian Taylor, the head of Special Needs
Department at Mellow Lane, that the basis of all teaching within
the Special Needs Department was the multi-sensory and over-
learning approach advocated in "Alpha to Omega", a book
which the experts on both sides agreed was one of the best texts
available for teaching dyslexics (23.7.97 pages 38-39, 53);

(d)   The exercise books disclosed by the Plaintiff evidenced application of multi-sensory techniques and the use of Alpha to Omega
(see cb 359 to 366). It is important to remember that the exercise
books still available demonstrate only a small part of the work
which would have been done by the Plaintiff (see the evidence of
Rhian Taylor, 23.7.97 at 45-46);

(e)   The mathematics teaching provided relied little on the written
word;

(f)   Drama teaching was used as was a computer (Plaintiff's evidence
21.7.98 p65; Dr. Gardner 24.7.97 p155/6)

(g)   The Plaintiff was enrolled on a foundation course in her 4th year
which Dr. Gardner (whom the learned judge regarded as particularly well qualified, careful and fair (j32F, 56C)) considered
appropriate for a child with learning difficulties (24.7.97 p157).

(h)   It was Dr. Gardner's opinion that the remedial tuition provided
to the Plaintiff was reasonable by the standards of the time
(24,7.97 p156)

(i)   The evidence of Dr. Gardner that the tuition provided to the
Plaintiff compared favourably with that provided in other local
education authorities at the relevant time (see 24.7.97 p149-160
and cb235-237 and see also the Survey of Pupils with Special
Educational Needs in Ordinary Schools at cb 412-423). The
court is here considering an LEA (and its employees) discharging
statutory duties with limited resources. It is not appropriate to

transpose standards from the private sector (see *Knight v Home Office* [1990] 3 All ER 23).

DAMAGES

6.1 It is uncertain what the basis of the award for general damages was. No damages can lie for loss of confidence, hurt feelings etc. As submitted above, the difficulty the judge had in arriving at an appropriate figure both for general and special damages is reflective of the insecure basis of the claim generally. The onus is on the Plaintiff to establish a quantifiable loss. She failed to do so.

APPENDIX I

THE STATUTORY FRAMEWORK

1. The statutory provisions which governed Pamela Phelps case were the Education Act 1944, Education Act 1981, and the Education (Special Educational Needs) Regulations 1983. Both Acts have now been repealed, but the relevant law has been re-enacted in substantially the same form in the consolidating Education Act 1996 ("the 1996 Act"). (There was also an intervening consolidating Act, now also repealed, the Education Act 1993). The Regulations have also been repealed and replaced (again in substantially the same form as far as is relevant to this case) by the Education (Special Educational Needs) Regulations 1994.

EDUCATION ACT 1944

2. Section 8(1) established the duty of local education authorities ("LEAs") to ensure that sufficient schools were available in their area for providing primary education and secondary education. The schools available in an area would not be deemed sufficient unless, in the words of the section, they were sufficient in "number, character and equipment to afford for all pupils opportunities for education offering such variety of instruction and training as may be desirable in view of their different ages, abilities and aptitudes .."

3. Section 8(2), as amended by the Education Act 1981 section 2(1), required LEAs to have regard in particular to, inter alia "(c)... the need for securing that provision is made for pupils who have special educational needs." Section 36 of the 1944 Act as amended by section 17 of the 1981 Act placed a duty on parents to cause every child of

compulsory school age to receive "efficient full-time education suitable to his age, ability, and aptitude and to any special educational needs he may have, either by way of regular attendance at school at school or otherwise."

EDUCATION ACT 1981

4. The Education Act 1981 was "an Act to make provision for children with special educational needs."

5. Section 1(1) defined a child as having special educational needs if "he has a learning difficulty which calls for special educational provision to be made for him" (the same definition now appears in s312 of the 1996 Act).

6. By section 1(2)(a), a child who had "a significantly greater difficulty in learning than the majority of children his age" had a learning difficulty (re-enacted in s312(2)(a) of the 1996 Act).

7. In relation to a child aged 2 years or over, "special educational provision" meant "educational provision which is additional to or otherwise different from the educational provision made generally for children of his age in schools maintained by the local education authority" (s1(3)(a) - re-enacted in s312((4)(a) of the 1996 Act).

8. By section 4 the LEA had a duty to identify children with special educational needs (now s321 of 1996 Act).

9. By section 5 (now s323 of the 1996 Act), where the LEA was "of the opinion" that a child for whom they were responsible had special educational needs which called for special educational provision or that he probably had such needs, they had a duty to make an assessment of those needs. Before making an assessment they were required to notify the child's parents of the proposal to make an assessment, the procedure, the name of an officer from whom further information can be obtained, and their right to make special representations.

10. By Schedule 1 to the Act the Secretary of State was required to make regulations as to the nature of the advice which had to be sought on a section 5 assessment. The advice had to include medical, psychological and educational advice (paragraph 1(2) of part 1 of the Schedule). By Schedule 1 Part 1 paragraph 2, the LEA could secure the attendance of a child for examination by service of a notice on his parent. A parent who failed to comply was liable to summary conviction. The position is now governed by Schedule 26 of the 1996 Act.

11. By the Education (Special Educational Needs) Regulations 1983 the LEA was required to seek medical, psychological and educational advice and "any other advice which the authority consider desirable in the case in question .." -Reg 4(1). (See now reg 6 of the 1994 Regulations, which also requires advice to be sought from the parents and social services).

12. A person from whom advice was sought by the LEA could consult such persons as it appeared to him expedient to consult and he was required to consult any persons specified by the LEA as a person having relevant knowledge or information relating to the child - Reg 4(3). (Now reg 6(3) of the 1994 Regulations).

13. By regulation 5, the educational advice was to be sought from the head-teacher of a school which the child had attended at some time within the preceding 18 months or, if that was not possible, from a person whom the LEA were satisfied had experience of teaching children with special educational needs or knowledge of the different provisions which might be called for in different cases to meet those needs. Where the head-teacher had not himself taught the child within the preceding 18 months, his advice was to be given after consultation with a teacher who had so taught the child (reg 5(2)). The current position is governed by reg 7 of the 1994 Regulations and is slightly, although not materially different.

14. By reg 6 the medical advice was to be sought from a registered practitioner who was either designated for the purposes of the regulation by the district health authority or was nominated by them in the case in question. (See now reg 8 of the 1994 Regs, which now requires the advice to he sought from the district health authority, who in turn will obtain the advice from a fully registered medical practitioner).

15. The psychological advice which was to be sought was governed by regulation 7. It had to be from either a person regularly employed by the LEA as an educational psychologist or from a person, in the case in question, engaged by the LEA as an educational psychologist. If the educational psychologist had reason to believe that another psychologist had relevant knowledge of or information relating to the child, his advice was to be given after consultation with that other psychologist. The same requirements are now set out in reg 9 of the 1994 Regulations.

16. In making an assessment, the LEA had also to take into account representations made by the child's parents and evidence submitted by them and any information furnished by or on behalf of any district health authority or social services authority (reg 8, now reg 10 of the 1994 Regulations).

17. If the LEA concluded that they were not required to determine the special educational provision that should be made for a child after a section 5 assessment, his parents could appeal in writing to the Secretary of State (section 5(6)). The LEA had to notify the parents in writing of that right to appeal (section 5(7). On an appeal, the Secretary of State could, if he thought fit, direct the LEA to reconsider their decision. (Under the 1996 Act the parent's appeal is now to the Special Educational Needs Tribunal (s325). An appeal from that Tribunal to the High Court lies on a point of law under the Tribunal and Inquiries Act 1992 s 11).

18. If, on the other hand, the LEA were of the opinion after a section 5 assessment that they should determine the educational provision that should be made for a child, they had to make and maintain a statement of his special educational needs (section 7 of the 1981 Act). The position is now governed by s324 of the 1996 Act,

19. The parents of a child for whom the LEA were responsible but for whom no statement was being maintained could also request an assessment of their child's educational needs and the LEA had to comply with that request unless in their opinion it was unreasonable (section 9(1)). Section 9(1) did not give the parents the right to dictate the form of the assessment, however, and it was a matter for the local authority whether or not upon receiving such a request the assessment they made was a section 5 one. (*R v Surrey County Council, ex p G* (1994) Times, 24 May.) The parents' right to request an assessment is now governed by s329 of the 1994 Act, which provides the parents can request an assessment under section 323 and that the LEA must comply with that request if it is "necessary".

20. Section 7 set out the procedure for making a statement, including the fact that a draft had to be served on the parent, who could make representations on it and require a meeting with an LEA officer to discuss it. A parent who still disagreed with a statement after such a meeting could request further meetings, and the LEA upon receipt of such a request had to arrange such meetings as they considered would enable the parent to discuss the relevant advice with the appropriate person (the person who gave the advice, or any other person who, in the opinion of the local authority, is the appropriate person to discuss it with the parent). Once a statement was finalised the local authority had to serve it on the parent and notify him in writing (section 7(9)(b)) that he had a right of appeal against the special educational provision specified in the statement under section 8 of the Act.

21. By section 8 of the Act the LEA had to make arrangements enabling the parent of a child for whom they maintained a statement to appeal against the contents of the statement. The appeal committee could confirm the statement or remit the matter to the LEA for reconsideration. If the appeal committee confirmed the decision, or the LEA gave a decision after a case had been remitted to them, the parent could then appeal in writing to the Secretary of State. The current right of appeal is to the SENT and is set out in section 326 of the 1996 Act.

APPENDIX 2

REMEDIES

STATUTORY PROCEDURES/JUDICIAL REVIEW

1. If the LEA was not maintaining a statement, the parents could have requested an assessment of their child's educational needs (section 9(1) of the Education Act 1981). The LEA could only refuse that request if it was unreasonable. Unreasonableness could be determined by judicial review. It was for the LEA to decide the form of the assessment (*R v Surrey County Council, ex p G* (1994) Times, 24 May. (The current position under the 1996 Act is that the parents can request a statutory assessment, which the LEA must carry out if (i) no such assessment has been made in the 6 months prior to the request and (ii) it is necessary for the authority to make an assessment. If the LEA decides not to accede to the request, the parents can appeal to the Special Educational Needs Tribunal ("SENT"). SENT is a tribunal within the terms of the Tribunal and Inquiries Act 1992 and an appeal from SENT on a point of law will therefore lie to the High Court (s11 of the 1992 Act)).

2. If the LEA did carry out an assessment under section 5 of the 1981 Act but decided not to statement, the parents could appeal to Secretary of State (s5(6)). Decisions of the Secretary of State were subject to judicial review in the normal way. Under the 1996 Act the Appeal now lies to SENT (section 325 of that Act).

3. If the LEA decided to issue a statement but the parents disagreed with its contents, they could appeal to an LEA appeals committee. If the appeals committee found against them, they could then appeal to Secretary of State. If on the other hand the appeals committee remitted the case to the LEA and the parents disagreed with the new decision then made by the LEA, they could appeal to Secretary of State (s8). The Appeal is now to SENT - section 326 of the 1996 Act).

4. If the LEA were maintaining a statement, the parent could ask for a new, section 5 statutory assessment if one had not been made within the previous 6 months. The LEA had to comply with such a request unless it was "inappropriate." (s9(2)). Inappropriateness would again have been a matter for judicial review. Under the 1996 Act, the parents can appeal to SENT is such a request is refused (s 328).

OMBUDSMAN

5. The Local Commissioners for Administration have jurisdiction to investigate maladministration (Local Government Act 1974 sections 25, 26). "Maladministration" includes bias, neglect, inattention, delay, incompetence, ineptitude, perversity, turpitude, arbitrariness. It relates to the manner in which a decision has been taken rather than the merits of the decision itself (*R v Local Commissioner for Administration for the North and East area of England, ex p Bradford Metropolitan City Council* [1979] QB 287).

6. The Ombudsman should not normally investigate an action in respect of which a person has a right of appeal, reference or review to or before a tribunal constituted under any enactment, or to a Minister of the Crown, or where the person has an action at law.

GOOD PRACTICE SUGGESTION

- The Law[11]
  Provide the judge with a reasonable grasp of the relevant law, dealing with any recent on-point binding authorities, except where the principles are clear.

---

[11] See also Example C

EXAMPLE K

Court of Appeal – Respondent's skeleton argument by Jonathan Sumption QC, David Anderson QC and Jemima Stratford in November 1999 – 18pp.

R v Secretary of State for Health ex parte Imperial Tobacco Ltd and Others concerned injunction proceedings brought by tobacco companies to prevent the Secretary of State from introducing immediate legislation to ban tobacco advertising by statutory instrument. At first instance Turner J. granted relief in order to maintain the status quo.

Since this document is required to be produced considerably in advance of the hearing it contains a time estimate and list of essential pre-reading. Unlike first instance trials and applications the court is much more likely to read the skeleton in advance.

The writer opens with the key issue and a summary of his points. The prose style has directness. There is no element of lawyer's obfuscation or the use of legal language in a technical way, which respondents often resort to. The language is business-like. There is great intellectual force in the argument but readability is maintained in the text by the extensive use of footnotes to raise citations, quote from and comment upon the authorities, refer to the Appellant's skeleton and core bundle, and provide secondary strands of argument.

The appeal was allowed. The case is reported at [2000] 2 WLR 834.

RESPONDENTS' SKELETON ARGUMENT

Time Estimate: 2 days.

Pre-Reading:

- Core Bundle 1 tabs 1, 2, 2A, 4, 5, 6, 7, 8, 9 10
- Core Bundle 2 tabs 4D (Arts 100a, 7a), 4E (Art 129), 5
- Core Bundle 3 (evidence on interim relief)
- Core Bundle 4 tabs 3 (Meltzer) and 5 (Waterson)
- Core Bundle 7 tab 16 (Written Observations of tobacco companies in ECJ, paras 2.1-2.8, 2.49-2.51, 3.13-3.17, 3.28-3.32, 3.40-3.46.)

Chronology: A chronology of events is supplied herewith.

INTRODUCTION

1. The issue before the Judge was not whether there should be immediate legislation to ban tobacco advertising. It was whether such legislation should be introduced forthwith by statutory instrument under the European Communities Act 1972 on the basis of a Directive which (i) under the existing jurisprudence of the ECJ is likely to be void, (ii) does not, even if valid, have to be brought into effect in English law before July 2001, and (iii) is currently the subject of six challenges before the ECJ, including one by Germany, which will almost certainly be resolved well before July 2001. If the Directive is void, any statutory instrument will fail, and any steps purportedly taken under it will have been unlawful.[1]

2. The Respondents will make four points on the appeal:

   (1) The challenge to the validity of the Directive is not just arguable but strong.

   (2) The test of a case strong enough to justify a stay of actual or prospective legislation is whether there is a serious case to be tried. But although this threshold is relatively low, the stronger the merits of the applicant's case for final relief, the stronger will be his case on the balance of convenience. More than that it is neither possible nor desirable to say.

   (3) The balance of convenience in this case strongly favours the grant of an injunction. The risk of injustice flowing from the enforcement of a void piece of criminal legislation substantially exceeds the risk of injustice flowing from the continued advertising of tobacco products for the relatively short period required to obtain the authoritative ruling of the ECJ.

   (4) Turner J.'s approach to the law and his assessment of the competing factors were impeccable, and there are no grounds for setting aside his discretion.

THE CHALLENGE TO THE DIRECTIVE

3. The challenge to the validity of the Directive arises mainly from the fact that the competence of EC institutions in the field of public health outside the workplace is extremely limited. Article 129 of the EC Treaty empowers the Community to encourage co-operation between Member States and others, to promote research and health information and education, and to make non-binding recommendations. But there is no power to legislate, and by Article 129.4 the power of EC

---

[1] *R v Minister of Agriculture Fisheries and Food ex parte Fédération Européenne de la Santé Animale* [1988] 2 CMLR 661, 665.

institutions to harmonise the law of Member States in the field of health is expressly excluded.[1]

4. Under the jurisprudence of the ECJ, EC legislation must identify the source of the power under which it is made and state the facts which bring the measure within that.[2]

5. Whether the measure is properly made under that power depends on the 'main objective' test. This test is fundamental to the whole of the ECJ's jurisprudence governing the judicial control of the exercise of legislative powers by EC institutions. The relevant features of the test are as follows:

(1) Whether a community measure is property founded on a power conferred by the treaty depends on whether the *main objective* of that measure is one to which the relevant power is directed. The essential point is that the measure cannot be brought within the scope of the power simply on account of some secondary objective or incidental consequence which the measure may achieve but which is not part of its main objective.[3]

(2) This test applies in particular to measures purportedly based on Article 100a, which empowers the Council by a qualified majority to adopt harmonisation measures 'which have as their object the establishment and functioning of the internal market'.[1] The article might otherwise be taken to authorise on the basis of qualified majority voting any harmonisation measure whatever. It is, however, clear law that the fact that a measure provides common rules in a matter which significantly affects the costs or business opportunities of competing enterprises is not enough to bring it within Article 100a. The establishment and functioning of the internal market must be its main objective, not simply an incidental benefit of legislation directed mainly at some other objective.[2]

---

[1] Core Bundle 2, tab 4E.

[2] Case C-45/86 *Commission v Council* (Generalised tariff preferences) [1987] ECR 3-1493, 1519 (para. 5).

[3] Case C-70/88 *Parliament* v *Council* (Post-Chernobyl) [1991] ECR 1- 4529,4566-7 (para. 17); Case C-l 55/91 *Commission v Council* (Waste) [1993] ECR 1 - 939, 968-9 (paras. 16-21); Case C-426/93 *Germany v Council* (Business registers) [1995] ECR 1-3723, 3753-4 (para. 33); Case C84/94 *United Kingdom v Council* (Working Time) [1996] ECR 1-5755, 5802, 5808 (paras. 21-2, 45); Case C-271/94 *Parliament v Council* (Edicom) [1996] ECR 1-1689, 1711-7 (paras. 17-33).

[1] Core Bundle 2, tab 4D.

[2] All the cases cited in the preceding note concerned measures purportedly founded on Article 100a. The clearest statement of principle appears in *Commission v Council* (Waste) [1993] ECR 1-939, 968 (paras. 18-9), where after reciting the substantial impact of the waste directive on the functioning of the internal market arising from the establishment of a basis for disposing of waste common to competing enterprises, the Court observed: 'Admittedly, it must be acknowledged that some provisions of the directive... affect the functioning of the internal market. However, contrary to the Commission's contention, the mere fact that the establishment or functioning of the internal market is affected is not sufficient for Article 100a of the Treaty to apply. It appears from the Court's case-law that recourse to Article 100a is not justified where the measure to be adopted has only the incidental effect of harmonising market conditions within the Community.'

    (3) Where a measure can be shown to have two objectives governed by different articles of the Treaty, both of which are essential to its operation and neither of which can be described as secondary or incidental then, subject to a significant proviso, it may be justified under both. The proviso is that the two articles of the Treaty should deal with legislative measures in a manner which is mutually consistent so that it is possible to apply both concurrently. If the provisions of the two empowering articles deal with legislative measures in different and inconsistent ways, a primary objective must be selected and the measure justified under the article directed to that objective.[3]

    (4) The main objective of a Community instrument does not depend on what the EC institution propounding it thinks but on what the Court, construing the instrument objectively, regards as its main objective.[1] In this process, the most significant factor is the examination of its terms, but in accordance with the ordinary principles for construing Community measures, it is also relevant to examine the legislative history of the instrument and any 'mischief' (or 'occasio legis') apparent from the surrounding circumstances.

6. The Tobacco Advertising Directive purports to be an internal market measure based on legislative powers conferred by Article 100a.[2] According to the recitals, the object is to harmonise the laws of member states relating to a particular class of services, namely the advertising and sponsorship of tobacco products, with a view to eliminating barriers to the movement of these services between member states and factors distorting competition in these services.[3]

7. This suggested basis for a harmonisation measure is wholly indefensible. The Directive is primarily if not exclusively a health protection measure. If it has any effect on the functioning of the internal market, the effect is incidental to its primary objective of improving public health. The following points are made:

    (1) With extremely limited exceptions, the Directive purports to impose a total ban on all forms of advertising and sponsorship throughout the Community.[1] A total ban on the provision of the relevant class of services is incapable of being regarded as a mode

---

[3] Case C-300/89 *Commission v Council* (Titanium Dioxide) [1991] ECR 1-2867. The clearest statement of the ratio of this case is in Joined Cases C-164/97 and C-165/97 *Parliament v Council* (Forests) [unreported. 25.2.99], at para. 14, in which it was held to have been concerned with cases in which a measure has two 'equally essential' objectives. 'The institution is required to adopt the measure on the basis of both of the provisions from which its competence derives... However, no such dual basis is possible where the procedures laid down for each legal basis are incompatible with each other'. The inconsistencies dealt with in the case law are procedural inconsistencies, e.g. relating to the decision-making procedure required for the adoption of measures under different provisions of the treaty. But there is no logical reason for limiting the principle to that situation.

of regulating the free movement of those services within the Community or of eliminating factors distorting competition in the provision of those services.

(2) National laws relating to tobacco advertising and sponsorship apply uniformly within each national territory. There is no question of differences between national laws operating as barriers to trade between Member States or as factors distorting competition, save possibly in cases where advertising and sponsorship in one Member State has an impact in another. Yet the Directive purports to apply not only to advertising with an impact across national borders (e.g. some sponsorship agreements and advertisements in publications which are traded on a material scale between Member States), but also to advertising and sponsorship whose impact is in the nature of things purely local (e.g. poster advertising and the sponsorship of local events). If Article 100a really were the justification for the measure, it would fail for want of proportionality. The reality is that the measure can be justified as proportionate to the mischief only if the mischief is the perceived impact of tobacco consumption on health, to which the local nature of much advertising and sponsorship would be irrelevant.

(3) There is a strong presumption in the jurisprudence of the ECJ that EC measures are to be construed in a manner which is consistent with fundamental human rights and in particular with the ECHR.[2] A total ban on advertising and sponsorship relating to tobacco products is on the face of it a significant infringement on the freedom of expression guaranteed by Article 10 of the ECHR, and in particular on the right to impart and receive information. It can be justified only on the footing that it falls within the reservation in Article 10 for measures necessary for the protection of health. There is no reservation in Article 10 for measures intended to improve the functioning of the internal market.

(4) For these reasons, and indeed as a matter of simple common sense, it is impossible to accept that the main objective of the

---

[1] Case C-45/86 *Commission v Council* (Generalised tariff preferences) [1987] ECR 3-1493, 1520 (para. 11): 'It must be observed that in the context of the organisation of the powers of the Community the choice of the legal basis for a measure may not depend simply on an institution's conviction as to the objective pursued but must be based on objective factors which are amenable to judicial review'. In Case C-300/89 *Commission v Council* (Titanium Dioxide) [1991] ECR 1-2867, 2898 (para. 10), the Court added to this formulation: 'Those factors include in particular the aim and content of the measure'.The proposition is restated in all the later eases.

[2] Core Bundle 1. tab 9. The Directive recites **Articles** 57(2) and 66 also. It was common ground below that Articles 57(2) and 66 (which deal with the free movement of self-employed persons and freedom to provide services) add nothing, and that the validity of the Directive **turns** on the applicability of Article 100a.

[3] Recitals (1) and (2).

[1] Article 3.1.

[2] Case C-260/89 *Elleniki Radiophonia Tileorassi AE* [1991] ECR 1 -2925, 2963-4 (paras. 41-2).

Directive is to improve the functioning of the internal market, and that the promotion of public health is merely secondary or incidental.

(5) It is equally difficult to accept the argument advanced by the Appellants below that the Directive is a measure with two 'equally essential' objectives, namely the protection of health and the functioning of the internal market. It is obvious that any intended impact on the functioning of the internal market must be incidental and not 'essential'. But even if this were a true dual purpose measure, it is incapable of being treated as such in a dispute about the validity of the Directive, because Article 100a (which deals with the internal market) and Article 129 (which deals with health) are incapable of being applied together. The harmonisation of national laws relating to health is expressly excluded from the legislative competence of the EC whereas measures for the harmonisation of national laws impeding the functioning of the internal market are expressly included. A choice would therefore have to be made.

(6) Article 129.1 of the Treaty provides that 'health protection requirements shall form a constituent part of the Community's other policies' and Article 100a(3) provides that the Commission, when making proposals for internal market measures which concern (inter alia) health, 'will take as a base a high level of protection'. This means that where measures properly classified as internal measures have an impact on health, EC institutions are required to ensure a high level of health protection. They do not confer on EC institutions legislative competence in matters of health protection which they would not otherwise have.

(7) Most of the above points were forcefully made to the Council of Ministers by its own legal service in its opinion of 3 December 1993, which concluded that there was no power to make the proposed Directive.[1] The same view has been expressed by the Legal Affairs Committee of the European Parliament, which has rejected Articles 57(2), 66 and 100a as a proper basis for the Directive,[2] and by a substantial body of eminent opinion, including two former advocates-general of the ECJ.[3] There has never been any adequate answer to the points made by the legal service, either in these proceedings or elsewhere.

---

[1] Core Bundle 2, tab 5. The legal service had previously advised in 1989 on a draft Directive which restricted only certain forms of advertising, which it considered could be brought within Article 100a on the basis that it regulated the provision of advertising services relating to tobacco. The extension of the draft directive so that it became a total ban, however, took the measure outside the powers of the Council, because a total ban could not be justified as the regulation of the mode of providing the service, and because any such ban was not proportional to the internal market interests engaged.

[2] Meltzer Affidavit, para. 65 [Core Bundle 4, tab 3].

[3] Core Bundle 2, tab 6.

(8) It appears that the only reason why the UK government denies that the Directive is primarily a public health measure is to try to escape the limitations on the legislative competence of the EC in the field of health and to legislate in the UK without direct Parliamentary authority.

8. The points made in the preceding paragraph are based on the text of the Directive. But they are borne out by the legislative history of the Directive, which shows that it was devised and promoted at every stage by the organs of the relevant institutions concerned with public health and was promoted as a health protection measure, part of a concerted European campaign to reduce the incidence of cancer which was inaugurated by the Council in 1985. It was presented as such in the recitals of every draft until shortly before it was adopted, when references to health were deliberately removed.[4] In the United Kingdom, the government has sought to justify the Directive before the courts as an internal market measure, but it has consistently presented it to every one else as a health protection measure.[1] This convenient inconsistency is disingenuous and unattractive.

PRINCIPLE GOVERNING INTERLOCUTORY STAY OF LEGISLATION

9. The only aspect of the legal test which is disputed concerns the strength of the case on the merits which must be shown by an applicant for interlocutory relief. Since the Respondents' case is strong enough to justify interlocutory relief on any of the various tests proposed, this may not be a critical question on this particular appeal.

10. It is submitted that the law can fairly be summarised as follows:

---

[4] The history of the Directive, which is illuminating, is set out in the affidavit of John Lawrence Meltzer [Core Bundle 4, tab 3]. The recitals to the draft directive originally referred to the European Council's action programme against cancer of June 1985, and continued:
'WHEREAS the Council and the representatives of the governments, meeting within the Council, in their resolution of 7 July 1986 on a programme of action of the European Communities against cancer set for this programme the; objective of contributing to an improvement in the health and quality of life of citizens within the Community by reducing the number of illnesses due to cancer and, accordingly, regarded measures to counter the use of tobacco as their prime objective.'
See Meltzen paras. 42, 62 [Core Bundle 4, tab 3].

[1] Meltzer Affidavit, paras. 66-71 [Core Bundle 4, tab 3], The application of the Directive has been handled throughout by the Department of Health, whose minister issued a press release after the adoption of the Directive describing it as 'the most important step the European Union has taken towards reducing smoking since tobacco advertising was banned from television. Most importantly, it is a giant leap forward in the fight to reduce smoking, save lives and protect children from the pernicious effects of tobacco advertising and promotion.' (Para. 66). The Draft Regulations by which the government proposes to give effect to the Directive are expressly presented as giving effect to the white paper 'Smoking Kills': Core bundle 1, tab 7, page 80],

(1) The jurisprudence of the ECJ recognises that persons have a legal right to protection against purported but void EC legislation and national measures giving effect to void EC legislation. This may in appropriate cases require national courts to grant them interim relief pending a decision of the ECJ.[2]

(2) The right to obtain interim relief from a national court depends, like all other matters of remedy and procedure, on national law. In England:

(i) The principles derived from *American Cycmamid Co. v Ethicon Ltd* [1975] AC 396 arc applicable to the exercise of discretion in cases concerning the grant or refusal of interim relief against the Crown pending the outcome of a reference to the ECJ.[1]

(ii) The first question to be asked, therefore, is whether there is a serious question to be tried.[2] The mere fact of a reference having been made will normally be enough to ensure that this requirement is satisfied.[3]

(iii) The second question to be asked is whether damages would be an adequate remedy for the disadvantaged party in the event that it transpires at the trial that an injunction was 'wrongly' granted or refused. In cases involving the public interest, this question is rarely determinative of the issue of interim relief. A public authority normally suffers no loss by being unable to enforce the law. An applicant's loss will not normally give rise to a claim in damages against the public authority even if the legislative act is held to be void.[4]

(iv) The third question to be asked is whether the balance of convenience favours the grant of the relief sought.[1] The most helpful formulation of this test is that of Hoffmann J in *Films Rover International Ltd. v Cannon Film Sales Ltd.* [1987] 1 WLR 670, which involves asking which course appears to

---

[2] Joined Cases C-143/88 and C-92/89 *Zuekerfabrik* [1991] ECR 1-415, 540-1 (paras. 16-21); *R v Secretary of Stale for Transport ex parte Factortame Ltd* [1991] 1 AC 603 (ECJ).

[1] *R v Secretary of State for Transport ex p Factortame Ltd* [1991] 1 AC 603, 671F-674D (Lord Goff); *R v H.M. Treasury, ex p British Telecommunications plc* [1994] 1 CMLR 621, 648.

[2] *Factortame*, at 671H (Lord Goff).

[3] *R v S/S Health ex p Scotia Pharmaceuticals Ltd. (No.2)* [1997] EuLR 650, 652D (Mann LJ); *Primecrown Ltd. v M4CA/R v MCA ex p Smith and Nephew Pharmaceuticals Ltd.* [1997] EuLR 657, 661E (Latham J).

[4] *Ibid.*, 672G-673B (Lord Goff). Damages are not normally recoverable for invalid administrative action, although in *Factortame* they would have been (and have subsequently been held to be) recoverable for a 'grave and manifest' disregard by a public authority of its Community obligations. This possibility probably does not arise in the present case, because an attempt by the Crown to give effect to void EC legislation as if it were valid is not a breach of the UK's community obligations. It is merely an act which EC law does not justify.

[1] *Factortame*, 672D (Lord Goff).

carry the lower risk of injustice if it should turn out to have been 'wrong'.[2]

(v) In assessing the balance of convenience, the strength of the underlying case of the party applying for an injunction may be one of the relevant factors. There will be cases (*Factortame*, for example) in which even though a reference has been made to the ECJ, it is possible to predict with a fair degree of confidence what the ultimate result will be. In other cases, no such prediction is possible, and the strength of the underlying case is likely therefore to assume a lesser role in the balance of convenience.[3]

(3) The operation of these principles is subject to special guidelines laid down by the ECJ for cases in which the grant of interim relief would suspend the operation in a Member State of what would (if the measure is valid) be a community obligation.[1] The guidelines require that in such cases the national court should be satisfied (i) that there are 'serious doubts' about the validity of the measure, and (ii) that the applicant would suffer 'serious and irreparable damage' by the refusal of interim relief. In both respects, the guidelines represent substantially the test which an English court would apply under its own law. It must also (iii) have due regard to community interests in weighing the competing considerations involved. Point (i) is sufficiently reflected in

---

[2] Hoffmann J.'s test is echoed in *Factortame*, at 660D-E (Lord Bridge) and 683 A-C (Lord Jauncey), and is approved by Laws J in *R v MCA ex p Rhone Poulenc Rorer Ltd.* [1998] EuLR 127, 145A-D.

[3] *R v H.M. Treasury, ex p British Telecommunications plc* [1994] 1 CMLR 621, 647. The application for relief failed in this case on the facts, which were extreme: the applicant was seeking an interlocutory mandatory injunction requiring the Crown, some six months after the relevant statutory instrument had come into force, to lay before Parliament an instrument amending it in the sense required (according to their case) by the true construction of the underlying Directive. The importance of the case for present purposes lies in the Court of Appeal's treatment of the principle. It heard argument from the Crown, based upon the passages from *Factortame* cited above, to the effect that in considering an application for interim relief of this nature, 'decisive or predominant weight should be given to a prediction of the likely outcome of the question submitted to the European Court of Justice' (p. 643). That approach was rejected as 'mechanistic' and 'formulaic' (p. 647). Cf. *R v MCA ex p. Rhone Poulenc Rorer Ltd* [1998] EuLR 127 at 134 F-G, where Laws J. looked at the merits of the case which had been referred but only for the purposes of verifying that there was a serious issue to be tried (135D-139B); and *R v S/S Health ex p Scotia Pharmaceuticals Ltd. (No.2)* [1997] EuLR 650 and *Primecrown Ltd. v MCA/R v MCA ex p Smith and Nephew Pharmaceuticals Ltd.* [1997] EuLR 657, where the balance of convenience was held to justify the maintenance in force of injunctive relief against the Secretary of State or Medicines Control Agency, without any reference to the underlying merits of the claim.

[1] Joined Cases C-143/88 and C-92/89 *Zuckerfabrik* [1991] ECR 1-415, 542 (paras 22-33); Case C-465/93 *Atlanta Fruchthandelsgesellschaft* [1995] ECR 1- 3761, 3791-2 (para 32-7); Case C-68/95 *T. Port* [1996] ECR 1-6065, para 48. Contrary to the Appellants' suggestion at para. 2.24 of their Skeleton Argument, all three cases concerned the suspension of German administrative measures based on directly applicable Community measures, which already imposed obligations on Member States. Suspension of the national measures therefore involved an effective suspension of the Community obligations imposed by those Regulations.

the requirement of English law that there should be a serious question to be tried.[2] Point (ii) is substantially the same as the requirement of English law that damages should not be an adequate remedy.[3] Point (iii) would have a prominent place in any English court's analysis of the balance of convenience.

11. The Appellants' case about the legal test for interim relief is based, essentially, on two propositions. The first is that where interim relief would suspend the application of legislation already in force, the law requires the Court to be satisfied *either* that the consequences for the Applicants of refusing relief will be terminal (or at any rate catastrophic), *or* that the challenge to the validity of the Directive is likely to succeed and not just 'strongly arguable'. The Appellants' second proposition is that there is no material difference between interim relief which suspends the enforcement of existing legislation, and interim relief which delays the introduction of proposed legislation.

12. It is submitted that this is not a tenable position:

(1) There is an obvious difference between staying the introduction of prospective secondary legislation and staying the enforcement of existing legislation. There is a public interest in recognising the enforceability of enacted law which is entirely absent where the law is only in the contemplation of the legislator. Moreover the public interest in legal certainty will normally favour preserving the status quo. Where legislation has not yet been introduced, legal certainty militates in favour of a stay because if it is refused and the legislation is introduced and then found to be void, everything done under it will have to be treated retrospectively as unlawful. In the latter case legal certainty militates against a stay, because if the measure is enacted, stayed and then found to be valid, the stay will be lifted with uncertain and

---

[2] The Appellants suggest in their Skeleton Argument (para, 2.14) that para. 36 of the Judgment in Case 465/93 *Atlanta Fruchthandelsgesellschaft* [1995] ECR 1-3761, 3791 requires the national court in such cases to satisfy itself 'to a high degree' that the challenge to the validity of the measure is likely to succeed. This is not correct. Para. 35 of the Judgment requires the national court to satisfy itself that there are 'serious doubts' about the validity of the measure. Para. 36 concerns only the procedural consequences of para. 35: i.e. the national court must say why it is satisfied of that. The conclusive statement of the test is contained in the formal declaration, which expresses it in terms of 'serious doubts' but requires the national court to take account of community interests: p. 3797, esp. paras. 2(1) and (3). The same test was formulated by the ECJ both in the earlier decision in *Zuckerfabrik* and in the later decision in *T. Port*

[3] The Appellants argue (Skeleton Argument, para. 2.13(3)) that this test requires an applicant to show that 'in the absence of interim relief it would be exposed to a situation liable to endanger its very existence or to restrict its market share irreversibly'. No authority is cited for this proposition, which is wrong. The test in EC law simply reflects in this domain the principle of proportionality, and is based on considerations of policy almost indistinguishable from those adopted in England in *American Cyanamid:* see, in particular, Case T-155/96R *City of Mainz v Commission* [1996] ECR 11-1655, para 19. The modern practice of the Community courts is to 'weigh the interests involved in order to determine whether the condition regarding urgency is satisfied': Case T-41/96R *Bayer v Commission* [1996] ECR D-3S1, para 58

possibly unsatisfactory consequences for those who have infringed it in the meantime.

(2) As has been pointed out above, the Appellants' argument is not warranted as a matter of English law by anything in the decision of the House of Lords in *Factortame*, and is directly contrary to the Court of Appeal's decision in *BT*, although both of those were cases in which it was sought to interfere with the operation of enacted law. In *Factortame* the legislation challenged was primary legislation which had been in force for some 15 months at the time when the case was argued before the House of Lords. The House was very conscious of this.[1] Yet even against that background, Lord Goff stopped short of suggesting that a strong *prima facie* case was always required before an injunction could be granted. In particular, he pointed out that such a strong case might not be required where serious and irreparable harm had been suffered, and stressed that the matter was one for the discretion of the court, taking into account all the circumstances of the case.[2]

(3) As a matter of EC law:

(i) The starting point is that EC law does not purport to harmonise national rules of law governing matters of legal procedure or the availability of judicial remedies. It intervenes only to ensure that national law is not applied so as to displace community obligations.

(ii) There is no present community obligation on the UK to implement the Directive. On the footing the Directive is valid, its terms require the UK to implement it in its national law by July 2001. The ECJ has held that where a period is allowed for the implementation of an EC measure, Member States 'cannot be faulted' for failing to act before the end of that period.[3] The 'threat to Community law' which the Appellants suggest would follow from the grant of interim relief is therefore illusory. For these reasons, the *Zuckerfabrik/Atlanta* guidelines referred to above[4] have no application to this case.

(iii) Even if they did, they would not require a national court to apply any more stringent test than 'serious doubts' about the validity of the measure, accompanied by a proper regard for community interests.[1]

---

[1] *Factortame.* 673B-674A (Lord Goff).
[2] *Ibid.*, 674B-D.
[3] Case C-129/96 *Inter-Environnement Wallonie ASBL v Région Wallonne* [1997] ECR 1-7411, paras 41-45. The Court pointed out that a Member State could even enact inconsistent national legislation during the period allowed for implementation, provided that the effect was not to 'compromise the result prescribed' afterwards.
[4] Para. 10(3).
[1] See notes to para. 10(3) above.

THE BALANCE OF CONVENIENCE

13. In the concluding section of his Judgment, Turner J. fairly summarised all the factors for and against the granting of interim relief.[2] His conclusion was that 'the balance of convenience comes down firmly in favour of the maintenance of the present position.' There are no grounds for interfering with this assessment.

14. For convenience, the evidence on these points is summarised in the Annex to this document. The following are the salient points:

(1) The most important single point is probably the public interest.

(i) Legal certainty is a significant public interest in English law. It is also a recognised public interest in community law, which requires Member States to implement EC measures in a way which gives persons a clear and precise understanding of their rights and obligations, and does not cause confusion.[3]

(ii) It is very much against the public interest that secondary legislation should purportedly be made by the Government at a time when there is no obligation on its part to do so and the validity of that legislation is seriously in issue even on the government's own view of the matter. If the Directive is held to be invalid, the Respondents will have been prevented for the duration of the ECJ proceedings from doing things which were at the relevant time entirely lawful, without any prospect of compensation. Persons such as tobacconists and newsagents who display advertising material will have been exposed to criminal conviction for acts which were lawful when they did them, unless the courts are prepared to paralyse the criminal enforcement of the Regulations by making yet further references to the ECJ. The extensive rights of entry, search and seizure conferred by the Regulations will have been exercised without a shadow of legal right. A significant infringement of freedom of expression will have occurred without any justification of the kind envisaged in Article 10 of the ECHR, and without even a proper statutory justification.

(2) As against these consequences, the only public interest to which the Appellants can point is the public interest in reducing tobacco consumption, which the Appellants claim would be assisted by an advertising ban and a simultaneous health education campaign.[1] This might have to be delayed by a mere 9-15 months. As to that:

---

[2] Judgment, pp. 64-5.
[3] Case C-119/92 *Commission v Italy* [1994] ECR 1-393 (para. 17).
[1] Appellants' Skeleton Argument, paras. 3.17-3.19.

(i) The Judge did not overlook the point, as the Appellants have alleged.[2] He assumed, because the government had taken that view, that an early end to tobacco advertising was in the public interest and he gave full weight to the fact.[3]

(ii) He did not treat it as conclusive, and with reason. The Appellants themselves arc exceedingly modest in their assessment of the impact of an advertising and sponsorship ban on tobacco consumption. Their Regulatory Impact Assessment, which accompanied the draft Regulations, stated (on the basis of a report by Clive Smee, the Chief Economic Adviser to the Department of Health) that any reduction in consumption would be 'fairly small'. It suggested that the actual figure 'might be around the 2.5% mark, in the long run.' It acknowledges that there could be *no reduction whatsoever* in tobacco consumption as a result of banning advertising, and certainly none in the short term.[4]

(iii) A simultaneous health education campaign can be mounted to coincide with the introduction of a tobacco advertising ban whenever that happens. It was accepted below, and recorded by Turner J that the campaign could "as well be done at another time of the Government's choosing".[1] There is no evidence of any expenditure on this campaign that would be wasted in consequence of a postponement.

(3) The impact on the Respondents is considerable. Turner J acknowledged that 'the applicants would suffer significant losses if the regulations come into force on the intended date'.[2] He also accepted also that the 'significant financial losses of the Applicants would be 'difficult to quantify' and that there would be 'interruption to trades and resultant loss of employment'.[3] It is not clear what he meant by saying that this damage 'probably' fell short of irreparable harm. It was not terminal, but it clearly could not have been repaired by an award of damages because there is not ordinarily a right to damages arising from complying with void legislation.

(4) In addition to the impact on the Respondents, the proposed regulations will clearly have a substantial impact on ancillary trades

---

[2] Appellants' Skeleton Argument, para. 3.23.
[3] Judgment, p. 58.
[4] Core Bundle 1, tab 7, page 96 (including footnote).
[1] Core Bundle 1/1/64. The Government further seeks in its skeleton argument (3.19) to rely upon the special significance of the Millennium. The unimportance of that point is evident from the fact that it was not even mentioned in the White Paper [Core Bundle 5/3/138-141], the RIA [Core Bundle 1/7], or the Government's evidence dealing specifically with its education programme [Core Bundle 3/6/87-88, paras 11-14].
[2] Judgment, p. 63. The Appellant is wrong to suggest (Skeleton, para. 3.27) that the Judge found the damage suffered by the Respondents and others fell short of serious harm.
[3] Judgment, p. 65.

concerned with advertising, such as poster printers and hoarding contractors, as well as on the promoters of artistic and sporting events presently sponsored by tobacco manufacturers which will not necessarily find alternative sources of funding.

DISCRETION

15. The principles to be applied by the Court of Appeal in reviewing a decision of the High Court whether or not to grant an interlocutory injunction were set out by the House of Lords in *Hadmor Productions v Hamilton* [1983] 1 AC 191, per Lord Diplock at 220A-E:

> [T]he function of an appellate court ... is not to exercise an independent discretion of its own. It must defer to the judge's exercise of his discretion and must not interfere with it merely upon the ground that the members of the appellate court would have exercised the discretion differently.

    This means that the exercise of the judge's discretion may be set aside only (i) if 'based upon a misunderstanding of the law or of the evidence before him'; or (ii) on the basis of further evidence or a change in circumstances since the order appealed from; or (iii) where 'the judge's decision to grant or refuse the injunction is so aberrant that it must be set aside upon the ground that no reasonable judge regardful of his duty to act judicially could have reached it.'

16. The Appellants appear to be proceeding on the basis that it is open to the Court of Appeal to re-examine the weight placed by Turner J on each of the factors raised by either side. In relation to the balance of convenience, not one of the allegations made in the Respondent's Skeleton Argument falls within the categories identified by Lord Diplock .

COSTS

17. The Respondents suggest that Turner J 'erred in law' in certifying that the case was fit for three counsel.[1] This was a matter for his discretion, which involved no question of legal principle and is quite unsuitable for decision in the Court of Appeal.

---

[1] Skeleton, para 5.1.

GOOD PRACTICE SUGGESTION

- Pre-reading
  Make sure the judge is told what he absolutely *must* pre-read, if nothing else. Assume that for this purpose his time commands a high premium. Give an accurate time estimate for the material you want him to read.
- Visual Impression
  Overall visual impression is important to most judges, and indeed most readers. The task of reading a document should be made easy. This means you need to consider both how the reader will come to a particular document and what use he is going to make of it. By that I mean will the judge read it once and put it aside? Or will he wish to mark it up with annotations and make greater use of it than just one reading? Will he use it as a Baedeker to guide him through the case, and have it sitting on his desktop within his line of sight but perhaps out of reading distance? You should be aware of such matters since you want to create a document which is not going to be beyond arm's length from the judge from the time the case is opened, to the time he comes to write his judgment.
- Using white space well is a balancing exercise between the visual presentation of the document, the need for the reader to annotate it, and the effect white space will have on the overall length of the text. Margins need to be wide enough for notes to be written, say 1.5". There should be gaps between numbered paragraphs. The typeface should be large enough, usually 12 point, which is normally clear enough to read at a distance of two to three feet away. You should consider what references to remove from the text and place into footnotes.
- Leave enough room to trail tangential propositions. Touch upon them just enough to avoid it being said they were not dealt with in the skeleton. If necessary you can put any tangential propositions into footnotes. Keep them out of the text, which you should reserve for the main thrust of argument.

EXAMPLE L

Court of Appeal – Respondent's skeleton argument by Spike Charlwood in June 2003-11pp.

Polley v Warner Goodman & Street was an allegation that litigation solicitors failed to serve a claim form prior to the expiry of its validity, so causing a claim for personal injuries to become time-barred. At first instance the claim itself failed for limitation. The issue concerned the date of accrual of the cause of action.

There is a chronological narrative of events. The writer's style emphasises detail, both in the text and in the extensive use of footnotes to refer to the evidence, passages of the judgment below, offer secondary points or comments on the authorities. Commentary on the key authorities is kept in the main text (see paragraphs 17-20). The language used is business-like rather than formal.

The appeal was dismissed. The case is reported at [2004] PNLR 40.

SKELETON ARGUMENT on behalf of the Respondents

INTRODUCTION

1. This is the Defendants' skeleton argument in opposition to the Claimant's appeal from the judgment of HHJ Anthony Thompson QC dated 23 October 2002. [33-45][1] That judgment followed the trial of a preliminary issue on limitation and dismissed the Claimant's action on the basis that his cause of action had accrued more than 6 years before the issue of the claim form.

BACKGROUND

2. The Defendants are a firm of solicitors. On 9 August 1990 the Claimant consulted them in relation to an injury he sustained in an accident at work in June 1990. On 13 January 1993 he was granted legal aid to sue Hydro Polymers Limited ("HPL"), his employers at the time of his accident. On 25 May 1993 County Court proceedings were issued against HPL. Under CCR O.7, r.20[2] those proceedings ought, unless the period was extended by the court, to have been served by no later than 24 September 1993. On 16 September 1993, i.e. a little more than a week before the proceedings were otherwise

---

[1] References in square brackets are to the pages of the bundle filed with the Appellant's Notice.
[2] See p.180 of the 1993 Green Book. There was no material alteration of the rule prior to the coming into force of the CPR.

required to be served, the Defendants applied, without evidence, to extend the validity of those proceedings. On 29 September 1993, i.e. 5 days after it had expired, District Judge Naylor extended the validity of the proceedings for 4 months.

3. The proceedings were served on 30 November 1993. On 16 December 1993 HPL's solicitors applied to set aside the order extending the period for service of the proceedings.[3] On 18 April 1994 that application was granted by District Judge Bailey-Cox[4] and there was no appeal from that order. The present proceedings were issued on 14 April 2000, i.e. more than 6 years after the period for service provided for by the County Court Rules expired, but (just) less than 6 years after the order of 18 April 1994.

4. Recognising the limitation difficulties which this potentially created, the Claimant sought in his Particulars of Claim[5] to rely if necessary on s.32(1)(b) of the Limitation Act 1980 ("the Act") (the provision relating to deliberate concealment). The Defendants denied that the Claimant was able to rely on s.32(1)(b) and averred that the claim was barred by the Act.[6] Accordingly, on 19 September 2000 District Judge Sparrow ordered that there should be a trial of a preliminary issue on limitation.

5. That trial was listed to be heard on 23 October 2002 and, following the House of Lords' decision in *Cave v Robinson Jarvis & Rolf* [2002] 2 WLR 1107,[7] it was conceded by the Claimant that reliance on s.32(1)(b) of the Act was unsustainable.[8] Accordingly, the Claimant – who has never sought to rely on s.14A of the Act[9] – had to fall back on the argument that his cause of action had not accrued until 18 April 1994 (i.e. the date on which HPL's application to set aside the order extending the period for service of the proceedings was heard and granted).[10]

6. HHJ Anthony Thompson QC rejected this argument, it is submitted rightly, and agreed with the Defendants that the Claimant's cause of action against the Defendants had accrued on 24 September 1993 (i.e. the date on which the period for service of the proceedings limited by the CCR expired). He therefore held that the Claimant's case had been brought out of time and dismissed it.

---

[3] Further detail as to the background to this matter appears from the affidavits filed in relation to this application. Copies of these affidavits, paginated sequentially to the documents filed with the Appellant's Notice, accompany this skeleton argument.

[4] His reasons are set out in the judgment of HHJ Anthony Thompson QC at p.3, line 20 – p.4, line 17. [35-36]

[5] See paragraph 13. [50-55]

[6] See paragraphs 2 and 4 of the Defence. [57-58]

[7] For the avoidance of doubt, the Defendants do not presently intend to refer to the substance of this decision.

[8] See paragraph 6 of his skeleton argument for use at the preliminary issue. [62]

[9] Presumably because he was clearly advised by letter dated 20 April 1994 that he might have a claim against the Defendants. See paragraph 2 of the Defence [57] and p.4, lines 20-26 of HHJ Anthony Thompson QC's judgment. [36]

[10] The witness statements filed in relation to the preliminary issue went in substance to the s.32(1)(b) issue and are therefore not relevant to this appeal.

THE ISSUE FOR THE COURT OF APPEAL

7. It is this finding relating to the date on which the Claimant's cause of action accrued that the Claimant has appealed. Accordingly, the issue for the Court of Appeal is this: when, in the circumstances of this case, did the Claimant's cause of action against the Defendants accrue?[11]

THE DEFENDANTS' CASE IN SUMMARY

8. It is the Defendants' case that HHJ Anthony Thompson QC was right and right for the right reasons. Thus:

    8.1. damage was sustained by the Claimant, and his cause of action therefore accrued, on 24 September 1993 when the Defendants failed to serve the proceedings against HPL within the time provided for by the CCR;[12]

    8.2. the order extending time did not alter that fact because:[13]

        8.2.1. of the period of 5 days between the expiry of the time provided for by the rules and the making of the order; and

        8.2.2. "more compelling[ly]" it was "inevitable, or almost inevitable" that the application to set aside would be made and the order ought not to have been made; and

    8.3. there is no public policy reason to reach a different conclusion.[14]

9. Further or alternatively, his judgment can be upheld on the following additional grounds:

    9.1. even if not all of the relevant damage was done on or before 24 September 1993, sufficient damage was done to start the limitation period running; and

    9.2. *Hopkins* is inapplicable to and/or distinguishable from the present case.

---

[11] In outline, therefore, there seems to be a measure of agreement between the parties as to the issue for the Court of Appeal. The Defendants do not, however, accept that the summary facts set out in paragraph 3 of the Claimant's skeleton argument are sufficient to define the issue. The reasons for this are set out below, but include in particular the facts that: (i) the extension of time granted on 29 September 1993 was obtained on an unsustainable basis and was always liable to be set aside; and (ii) that extension was not granted until 5 days after the time for service of the proceedings against HPL had expired. Further, the Defendants do not accept that the issue is to be answered by reference to, or depends on the answers to, the questions posed in paragraph 4 of the Claimant's skeleton argument.

[12] Transcript, p.9, lines 24-7. [41]

[13] See, respectively: transcript, p.10, lines 8-14; and transcript, p.10, line 15 – p.11, line 17. [42-43]

[14] Transcript, p.12, lines 7-16. [44]

PRELIMINARY MATTERS

10. The Defendants will rely on the following preliminary matters:

10.1. the burden of proof is on the Claimant to plead and prove an accrual of his cause of action (if any) within the limitation period: *London Congregational Union Inc v Harriss & Harriss (a firm)* [1988] 1 All ER 15 at 30d-g *per* Ralph Gibson LJ;[15]

10.2. the Claimant's cause of action (if any) in tort[16] accrued when he first suffered damage as a result of the Defendant's (assumed) negligence: *Nykredit Mortgage Bank plc v Edward Erdman Group Ltd (No 2)* [1997] 1 WLR 1627 at 1630, *per* Lord Nicholls (approving *Forster v Outred & Co (a firm)* [1982] 1 WLR 86);

10.3. "Actual damage is any detriment, liability or loss capable of assessment in money terms and includes liability which may arise on a contingency": *Hatton v Chafes* [2003] EWCA Civ 341, para.12(iii);

10.4. damage often occurs before it can be crystallized and difficulties of quantification do not prevent damage from being said to have occurred: *Nykredit* (above) at 1632; and

10.5. "... within the bounds of sense and reasonableness the policy of the law should be to advance, rather than retard, the accrual of a cause of action. This is especially so if the law provides parallel causes of action in contract and in tort in respect of the same conduct. The disparity between the time when these parallel causes of action arise should be smaller, rather than greater." *Nykredit* (above) at 1633.[17]

11. Following on from this last point, the existence of, and the protection provided by, s.14A of the Act[18] should not be forgotten. That section provides as an alternative to the usual 6 year limitation period a period of 3 years from the date on which, in summary, a claimant knew or ought to have known of his claim. Any claimant in a case such as the present seeking to rely on the usual 6 year period is therefore someone who has allowed the 3 year alternative to pass without taking action.

---

[15] With whom (on this point) both Sir Denys Buckley and O'Connor LJ agreed. See 34f and 37f.

[16] The Claimant accepts that his claim in contract adds nothing to the claim in tort. See paragraph 8 of his skeleton argument. [16]

[17] Thus, the courts have on numerous occasions rejected arguments that damage did not occur until long after the breach in question. See, for example, the cases referred to in *Nykredit* itself. More recent examples include *Khan v Falvey* (below) and, in April this year, *McCarroll v Statham Gill Davies* [2003] EWCA Civ 425.

[18] Described, for example, by Sir Murray Stuart-Smith at para.11 of *Khan* as mitigating the harshness of the common law rule.

THE ACCRUAL OF THE CAUSE OF ACTION: THE DEFENDANTS' CASE

12. It is the Defendants' case that, as a matter of common sense, damage was suffered by the Claimant as soon as the original period of its validity had expired, i.e. on 24 September 1993.

13. It is the Defendants' primary case that at that time the Claimant's case became valueless, i.e. that all of the relevant damage flowing from the admitted negligence of the Defendants was done then.

   13.1. Alternatively, the Defendants' secondary case is that, even if all of that damage was not done then, sufficient damage did then occur to start the limitation period running.

(i) **The Defendants' primary case**

14. The Defendants rely on the following matters in support of their contention that all of the relevant damage was done on 24 September 1993:

   14.1. the limitation period against HPL had expired and the action against them therefore could not be rescued by re-issue;

   14.2. service was no longer possible without an extension of time and no such extension had been granted;

   14.3. the application for an extension of time in fact made should not have resulted in an order favourable to the Claimant and had no prospect of resulting in an order which would survive an application to set it aside;

   14.4. there was no good reason for obtaining an extension and therefore no prospect of ever saving the claim against HPL once the original validity of the proceedings had expired;

   14.5. points 3 and 4 above made an application to set aside the extension granted inevitable; and

   14.6. the order made was set aside.

15. In summary, therefore, the Defendants submit that the HPL claim was doomed as soon as the proceedings were not served within the original period of their validity and that all that happened on 18 April 1994 was that that fact was confirmed, alternatively that the loss was crystallized.

16. For the avoidance of doubt, insofar as the above submission requires the Court to look at the matter in the light of all the information available at the date of the hearing and/or with the benefit of hindsight, it is the Defendants' submission that that is the correct approach. See *Hatton v Chafes* [2003] EWCA Civ 341 (where this was the approach in fact adopted by the Court of Appeal in a case raising similar issues to the present case) and *DnB Mortgages Ltd v*

Bullock & Lees [2000] Lloyd's Rep PN 290 at 295, col.1 – 296, col.1 (where the Court expressly approved such an approach in when conducting the *Nykredit* basic comparison).

(ii)   The Defendants' secondary case

17.   Even if the Court does not accept that all of the relevant damage was done by 24 September 1993, the Defendants submit that: (i) at the very least, some damage was done; and (ii) that damage was sufficient to start the limitation period running. This is because:

   17.1.   the extant application to extend time did not mean that damage had not occurred. See, by analogy, *Nykredit*, one consequence of which is that fluctuations in the property market may mean that, at a time after the comparison required by that case has first shown a loss, that comparison shows no loss, but that does not start the limitation period running again;[19]

   17.2.   it is irrelevant that further damage, by way of further diminution in the value of the action, might occur in the future. See *Khan* at para.s 11 and 56; and

   17.3.   even if an application to set aside the extension of time was not inevitable, the proceedings were at least vulnerable to being set aside.[20]

THE ACCRUAL OF THE CAUSE OF ACTION: RESPONSE TO THE CLAIMANT'S CASE

18.   The Claimant seeks to rely on: (i) *Hopkins v MacKenzie* [1995] PIQR P43; and (ii) a public policy argument, in support of his appeal.[21] Neither, the Defendants submit, assist him.

(i)   *Hopkins v MacKenzie*

a.   *Preamble*

19.   *Hopkins* has found little favour with the appellate courts in recent years. Thus:

---

[19]   See *The Mortgage Corporation v Lambert* [1999] Lloyd's Rep PN 947 at 950-951 *per* David Oliver QC (sitting as a deputy judge of the Chancery Division). The Court of Appeal (whose judgment is reported at [2000] Lloyd's Rep PN 624) did not need to deal with this issue.

[20]   For confirmation that such vulnerability is sufficient to amount to a loss, see the reference to contingent loss set out in paragraph 10.3 above. See also paragraphs 9-13 of the Defendants' skeleton argument before the trial judge.

[21]   NB that the Claimant has not sought to save his claim by reference to the claim for costs in paragraph 14(2) of the Particulars of Claim. [55] This is clearly correct, if for no other reason than that the Claimant has suffered no such loss. The order to pay costs provided that, "There be no enforcement without leave" and, as more than 6 years has passed since it was made, it is no longer enforceable. See *Parr v Smith* [1995] 2 All ER 1031 and reg.130 of the Civil Legal Aid (General) Regulations 1989.

19.1. despite the comprehensive review of the law undertaken in *Nykredit* and the express approval of many authorities in that case, *Hopkins* was not even referred to in *Nykredit*;

19.2. the Court of Appeal on 3 occasions prior to *Khan* noted that *Hopkins* is a case which turns on its own facts. See *Gordon v JB Wheatley & Co* [2000] Lloyd's Rep PN 605 at 610, col.1; *Knapp v Ecclesiastical Insurance Group plc* [1998] PNLR 172 at 187B-G;[22] and *Havenledge v Graeme John* [2001] Lloyd's Rep PN 223, para.s 16, 40 and 52-53;

19.3. in *Khan* itself:

19.3.1. Sir Murray Stuart-Smith (at paras 22-33) in reality[23] left no room for any continued application of *Hopkins*;

19.3.2. although he sought to reconcile *Hopkins* with other authority, Chadwick LJ (at paras 48-57) confined it to a very narrow basis and noted (at para.57) that:

"... the circumstances in which a claim can be advanced on that limited basis are likely to be rare."; and

19.3.3. so far as is material, Schiemann LJ agreed with the other members of the court (at para.63); and

19.4. *Khan* was recently followed in preference to *Hopkins* by the Court of Appeal in *Hatton v Chafes* [2003] EWCA Civ 341.

20. Accordingly, it is submitted that the Claimant's attempted reliance on *Hopkins* is misconceived. In particular, Hobhouse LJ in *Knapp* observed (at p.187G) that:

"[he did] not consider that *Hopkins v MacKenzie* can be taken as qualifying the earlier decisions of the Court of Appeal or the principles to be derived from them."

The Court should therefore apply those earlier decisions and principles and accept the Defendants' case as set out above.

b. *Specific answers to* Hopkins *in this case*

---

[22] *Per* Hobhouse LJ. Buxton LJ gave a concurring speech which did not mention *Hopkins*. ButlerSloss LJ agreed.

[23] The Defendants accept that he prefaced his conclusion (at para.33) with the words "if and in so far as", but submit that taken as a whole the passage referred to has this effect.

21. In addition to the point made in the preamble above, the Defendants rely on the following specific answers to *Hopkins* in this case:

   21.1. it does not deal with the Defendants' primary case. As in *Khan* (especially at paras 25-29) and *Hatton* (especially at paras 17-18), the Claimant's case was doomed to failure from 24 September 1993 onwards and had no residual value;

   21.2. in this case there was a failure to comply with a rule which required a step to be taken on or before a given time (c.f. cases of delay over a period of time). It is therefore an example of the type of case referred to by Chadwick LJ in *Khan*, paras 54-55[24] in which there is no residual value following the default;

   21.3. the Claimant seeks damages for the loss of the chance of prosecuting his claim against HPL[25] and so it is not even potentially the sort of limited claim for loss consequential on a strike out which Chadwick LJ contemplates (in *Khan*, para.57) might be permissible;

   21.4. as some damage (at least) occurred on 24 September 1993, the Claimant cannot escape the limitation period by pleading other damage. See *Khan* (especially at paras 23[26] and 33);

   21.5. the argument at paragraph 14 of the Claimant's skeleton argument[27] [18] is inconsistent with the decision in *Khan* (e.g. at paras 25-29) that an action can be valueless before it is struck out; and

   21.6. the Claimant's attempt to apply *Hopkins* in this case is an attempt to extend it and should not be permitted in the light of the authorities referred to in the preamble above.

(ii) **Public policy**[28]

22. The Claimant's public policy argument should be rejected for each of the following reasons:

   22.1. the mere existence of an application, and then an order, for an extension of time cannot give the HPL action any value when: (i) a recognised procedure for setting it aside exists; and (ii) the order ought not to have been made;

---

[24] Cited by HHJ Anthony Thompson QC at p.9 of his judgment. [41]

[25] See paragraph 14(1) of the Particulars of Claim. [55]

[26] *Per* Sir Murray Stuart-Smith. He said: "A Claimant cannot defeat the statute of limitations by claiming only in respect of damage which occurs within the limitation period, if he has suffered actual damage from the same wrongful acts outside that period." (emphasis added)

[27] In effect, that the action was still proceeding and had not been struck out and therefore must have had some value.

[28] For the avoidance of doubt, the Defendants do not accept the premise behind the Claimant's third ground of appeal. [3] HHJ Anthony Thompson QC did not hold that the extension of time was of no effect, but that it added no value to the HPL action.

22.2.   to take advantage of the procedure for setting aside such orders does not involve any undermining of the court and neither does a recognition that that procedure could be invoked;

22.3.   post-*Hall v Simons* [2002] 1 AC 615 there is, broadly, no bar on collateral challenges to decisions made in civil proceedings and none which would be relevant here; and

22.4.   in any event, the argument elides economic value and jurisdiction. Until set aside (or appealed) the order for an extension was a valid order of the court, but it does not follow from that, and is not a necessary corollary of the validity of the order, that that order was economically valuable to the Claimant. Indeed, given that: (i) it was liable to be set aside; and (ii) the setting aside of the order lead to an adverse costs order, in some senses the order had a negative economic value to the Claimant (in that he would have been better off without it).

CONCLUSION

23.   For all these reasons, the Claimant's appeal should be dismissed.

GOOD PRACTICE SUGGESTION

- Preliminary matters[12]
  When preparing an opening note or skeleton submissions for trial, create a checklist to cover preliminary matters, such as amendments to the statements of case, the admissibility of evidence, admissions and final pre-hearing applications. Use this to ascertain what the court needs to be told and put the information within a self-contained section near the beginning of the note or submissions.

- Summary[13]
  A headline or executive summary of the contents of the skeleton is often useful to the judge. If you choose to provide one it should be at the beginning of the document, and you will need to consider how much it will expand your creation. It can be part of the background introduction and, if there, judges will give some leeway in receiving matters which you afterwards repeat in more detail.

     A summary at the beginning is distinct from a concluding paragraph at the end, which should be used only where it helps to draw together the strands of a complicated picture.

     Substantive argument should be given once only. If either a summary is introduced, or a conclusion provided, it is wise to use different words if possible, rather than say exactly the same thing.

---

[12] See also Examples D and G.
[13] See also Example K.

EXAMPLE M

House of Lords – Case for the Appellant by Jonathan Sumption QC and Guy Philipps QC in April, 2003 – 10pp.

Lloyds TSB General Insurance Holdings Ltd and Others v Lloyds Bank Group Insurance Co. Ltd. concerned the construction of wording in a Bankers Composite Policy of insurance. This would determine whether 22,000 claims of pensions misselling by the bank's financial services consultants could be brought within the aggregation clause in the policy for the purpose of limiting the deductibles, which would otherwise exclude liability for covering small claims.

For the jurisdiction, the writers use a strikingly conversational style. Although relaxed, it deals with the technicalities of the case. The opening paragraphs are subtitled 'Introduction' but in fact counsel plunge straight in and the writing has considerable pace.

The findings of the lower courts are given as a narrative (see paragraph 7) but the argument section retains its narrative style - there is no formality and counsel choose not to use legal language.

The law is removed to footnotes so as not to interrupt the flow of the main text. However discussion of the law and the citation of authority is minimised. There are no substantial quotations.

The strength of the document is in the purity of argument. It assumes (rightly) what the recipient has no need to be told, which is an indication of the seniority and confidence of counsel and the level of judiciary.

The appeal was allowed and is reported at [2003] UKHL 48, [2003] 4 All ER 43 and [2003] 2 All ER (Comm) 665 HL.

CASE FOR THE APPELLANT

INTRODUCTION

1. On the face of it, this is a dispute about a particular form of words in a Bankers Composite Policy, a type of insurance policy which is of relatively recent origin and has been more carefully drafted than most documents of its kind that come before Your Lordships. Its commercial implications, however, are wider than that summary might suggest.
2. The Policy is written in four sections covering different heads of liability. Sections 1, 2 and 3 insure all the main operating companies of

the TSB group as it existed in 1993-4, before that group merged with Lloyds Bank. The companies of the group are identified at the end of the Policy. They included TSB Bank, a major national branch bank, the Hill Samuel Group, comprising the well-known merchant bank together with its associated leasing and asset management companies, a number of hire purchase companies formerly belonging to the United Dominion Trust group and a significant insurance company, Independence Insurance Co. Ltd. Section 1 insures against loss arising from the fraudulent acts of employees. Section 2 insures against loss arising from electronic and computer crime. Section 3 insures against legal liability for third party claims made during the period of insurance and arising from widely defined categories of breaches of duty by officers or employees of an assured, including breaches of the Financial Services Act 1986 or rules made under it. Section 4 can be ignored: it directly insured the legal liabilities incurred by directors and officers in their own right.

3. It is a common feature of Sections 1, 2 and 3 that they insure their different subject-matters subject to high deductibles and limits. In each case losses are insured only in excess of £1 million (or, in the case of certain assureds, £2 million), up to a limit of £100 million (in round figures). The deductibles have been designed to exclude small claims, notwithstanding the retail nature of most of the businesses carried on by financial services groups such as TSB. The commercial logic of this will be obvious. In any such organisation there is a level of claims which must be regarded as the unfortunate but inevitable consequence of carrying on a complex business on a large scale through geographically dispersed agents. These are for practical purposes part of the ordinary costs of the business. Without a high deductible, insurance against them would be prohibitively expensive. The deductibles and limits reflect the fact that this policy is designed to insure against catastrophic losses outside the day-to-day experience of such a group.

4. The TSB group has dealt with more than 22,000 small claims based on allegations that they mis-sold personal pensions to persons considering transferring out of an occupational pension scheme. They have paid out more than £125 million in compensation, but no single claim has exceeded about £35,000 and most have been for much less than that. In the ordinary course, a mass of claims of this kind could be expected to be made over a considerable period of time, spread over successive periods of insurance. However, the Securities and Investments Board and the various self-regulating organisations performing similar functions directed financial services providers in 1994 actively to seek out potential claimants and compensate them, a practice which not only resulted in a very considerable increase in the volume of claims but also ensured that they would be concentrated within a comparatively short period of time. This can give a spurious impression of unity to what is in reality a large body of distinct and variegated

claims. Each of the 22,000 claims dealt with by the TSB group concerns a different client. Each of them was occasioned by the failure of one of a large sales force of 'Financial Services Consultants' (or 'FSCs') to give 'Best Advice', as required by the regulations of the Life Assurance and Unit Trust Regulatory Organisation ('LAUTRO') to which TSB belonged.[1] In other words, he failed to ascertain the particular financial needs of the particular client and/or failed to tailor the product to those needs.

5. There is no provision for the aggregation of claims in Sections 1 or 2 of the policy, but Section 3 provides that for the purpose of applying the deductible, a series of third party claims shall be aggregated and treated as one if they 'result from any single act or omission (or related series of acts or omissions)'. The insured have sought to bring themselves within the aggregation clause and to treat all 22,000 claims as one, by pleading in para. 6 of their Particulars of Claim that they all resulted not just from the failure of sales representatives to give Best Advice, but from an antecedent act or omission, namely (i) TSB's decision to engage in the pension transfer business at all, (ii) their failure properly to train and supervise their FSCs. In these proceedings, the insured have not in practice sought to support their right to aggregate on the basis of (i). They rely on (ii).

6. The deductible and the aggregation clauses are fundamental to the nature of the insurance and to the fixing of the premium, because the risk associated with catastrophic liabilities is quite different from the risk associated with an accumulation of small claims, however similar in kind. The concern of the insurers is that the insured's case elides the two in a way which significantly alters the nature of the bargain. It is almost always possible where an insured has committed different breaches of duty on different occasions, to point to some common antecedent state of affairs without which they would not have happened. It may be something as fundamental as the decision to engage in the relevant business at all. Or it may be some intermediate feature of the insured's business operations, such as a lack of talent or perspicacity on the board of directors, poor recruitment policies in the personnel department, or weak supervision by middle management.

---

[1] The legal basis of the duty is the Financial Services Act 1986, Part I, Chapter V ('Conduct of Investment Business'). By Section 48, the Secretary of State, whose functions were delegated to the Securities and Investments Board, was empowered to make rules governing the conduct of investment business. These were not to be directly binding on members of a recognised self-regulating organisation, save insofar as the rules said so in terms; Sections 48(1), 63A. By Section 10 and Schedule 2, para. 3 a self-regulatory organisation is required to have rules governing the conduct of investment business which afford investors protection at least equivalent to those made by the SIB under Section 48. These rules were binding as a matter of contract, as between a self-regulatory organisation and its members. The combined effect of Section 62(1) and (2) was that breach of them was also a breach of duty actionable at the suit of any person suffering loss. TSB was a member of LAUTRO, whose Conduct of Business Rules (called the 'Code of Conduct') are at Schedule 2 of its rule-book. Paragraphs 1, 6-8 and 12 impose upon members of LAUTRO an obligation to procure that its representatives ascertain the circumstances of each investor and give that investor 'Best Advice'.

If the application of the aggregation clause is to depend on considerations such as these, it will potentially apply in most cases, depending
on what the insured chooses to identify as the underlying cause of any
particular claim. Whenever this happens, the Court will be required
to answer the practically unanswerable question whether a given
breach of duty can be said to have resulted from (i) a culture in the
company which was conducive to such breaches, or (ii) the personal
default of those whose conduct has directly caused the loss.

7. The judge (Moore-Bick J.) held (i) that on the pleaded facts, the absence of proper training and supervision was a 'single act or omission'
from which all the claims resulted, and also (ii) that the claims arose
from a 'series of acts or omissions' which were 'related' by virtue of
being 'directly attributable to a single underlying cause', namely the
absence of proper training and supervision. The Court of Appeal rejected his conclusion on the first point, but agreed with his conclusion
on the second. Potter LJ agreed with it on the ground that all the acts
and omissions giving rise to liability had a 'single underlying cause or
common origin'. Longmore LJ agreed with it on the ground that they
were similar in nature. Hale LJ appears to have agreed with Potter LJ,
although this is not entirely clear from her judgment.

8. It is submitted that when the nature of TSB's liability to the various
claimants is examined, it is apparent that the claims resulted neither
from a 'single act or omission', nor from a 'related series of acts or
omissions'.

'SINGLE ACT OR OMISSION'

9. The starting point is that the 'act or omission' in the aggregation clause
refers to the particular breach of duty which justifies the third party
claim.[1] The phrase and its context themselves suggest this, but the
matter is put beyond doubt by the endorsement to Section 3 of the
Policy, paragraph 2 of which defines 'act or omission'. It means the
several breaches of duty specified in the Insuring Clause at paragraphs
(iii)(a)-(j). These paragraphs of the Insuring Clause identify breaches
of duty one or more of which must be the basis of the third party
claimant's claim if liability in respect of it is to be insured.

10. It follows that when the deductible clause uses the phrase 'act or
omission' and requires that the series of claims to be aggregated must
'result from' that 'act or omission', it necessarily refers to the basis of
the third party's claim. The use of the phrase 'result from' does not
mean that the aggregation clause is concerned with the causes of the

---

[1] This is not necessarily the same thing as the breach of duty which the third party claimant has alleged, for
once the facts alleged are ascertained (in this case the absence of Best Advice) the third party claimant's
legal classification of those facts cannot affect the scope of the aggregation clause.

assured's breach of duty. The required causal nexus is between the claim and the breach of duty, not between the breach of duty and some antecedent state of affairs.

11. This reflects the commercial function of aggregation clauses in liability insurance. Their object is to give effect to the principle that the insurance is to protect against the financial consequences of a breach of duty giving rise to a claim, by allowing the aggregation of multiple claims flowing from one breach of duty. This is quite different from the commercial function of most aggregation clauses in excess of loss reinsurance, the usual commercial context in which such clauses have come before the courts. Widely framed aggregation clauses, such as those which aggregate all losses arising from one 'originating cause', are commonly used in excess of loss reinsurance because their object is to enable the reinsured to deal with the problem of the accumulation in his book of multiple risks generated by the same underlying problem and therefore liable to occur concurrently.[1]

12. In any pension mis-selling claim, the basis of the third party's claim is the way that the sales representative of the provider dealt with the client. In other words, he gave no, or no sufficient advice, or inappropriate advice. That is the relevant 'act or omission' because it is what justifies the third party claimant's claim if anything does.

13. TSB's failure properly to train or supervise their sales staff was not the basis of the third party claims. The following points are made:

   (1) The duty to give Best Advice is derived from Clauses 6-8 and 12 the Code of Conduct, which is annexed as a Schedule to the Rules of LAUTRO. Best Advice comprises a number of obligations, some of which are absolute, and some of which are obligations to exercise best endeavours to some specified end.

   (2) While parts of the duty to give Best Advice are qualified, TSB's obligation to procure that Best Advice is given, is absolute. This is so, because the duty to give Best Advice is, like the rest of the rules of LAUTRO, a duty binding on TSB itself as a member of LAUTRO and as the 'authorised person' under the Act: see Rule 3.4(4)(a) and section 62 of the Act. It follows that this duty would be broken by TSB if Best Advice was not given by the sales representative to the third party claimant, regardless of the reason why it was not given, and in particular regardless of the steps which TSB took or failed to take to equip the FSC for his task or detect his defaults.

   (3) A number of rules of LAUTRO, in particular Rules 3.4(1), (2), (3) and (4)(b) and 3.4A, do require members to have proper

---

[1] See, in the context of XL reinsurance, Lord Mustill's comparison between 'event' clauses and 'originating cause' clauses, in *Axa Reinsurance (UK) Plc. v Field* [1996] 1 WLR 1026, 1-32, 1035. The form of aggregation clause in the present policy is, if anything, even narrower in its scope than the 'event' clauses which Lord Mustill was considering.

procedures for selecting, training and monitoring representatives who deal with clients. However, where TSB owes an absolute duty to the client to procure a particular result (the giving of Best Advice), it cannot concurrently owe an independent duty to the same client to tabs appropriate steps to bring about that result. The position as between the TSB and the client may be tested by supposing that the client pleaded against TSB a failure properly to train or supervise its sales staff. If Best Advice was nevertheless given, the absence of proper training and supervision would be immaterial. If it was not, the client's claim would succeed without more, and the absence of training and supervision would still be immaterial. Proper steps are simply a precaution which TSB is required to take in order to avoid being in breach of the duty to give Best Advice. The relevant breach is still the absence of Best Advice.

(4) For the same reason, even if (contrary to this submission) there was a concurrent duty owed to the client properly to train and supervise staff, breach of that duty was not the 'act or omission' from which liability resulted. It was simply part of the historical explanation for the 'act or omission' giving rise to liability. The historical explanation of a breach of duly within the insuring clause is irrelevant in a liability policy, even if it discloses other breaches of duty: see *Goddard & Smith v Frew* [1939] 4 All ER 358, *West Wake Price & Co. v Ching* [1957] 1 WLR 45, 48, 57, and (in a different context) *Caudle v Sharp* [1995] LRLR 433, 440 (Evans LJ), 443 (Nourse LJ).

14. It is accepted that cases will not often arise in which one and the same failure to give Best Advice will give rise to a 'series of third party claims', although this can happen when advice is given to a husband and wife together and they have (or later acquire) distinct interests in the subject-matter. But while Best Advice is the context of the present dispute, the aggregation clause must not be read as if it was designed with that specific context in mind. It was intended to operate in conjunction with an Insuring Clause which covers widely defined categories of civil liability. Examples in other contexts of cases in which a 'single act or omission' may give rise to a 'series of third party claims' include claims against a fund manager for a decision adversely affecting a number of funds, or a unit trust with a number of unit-holders; or concurrent claims for defamation arising from statements published on the same occasion to several claimants.

'RELATED SERIES OF ACTS OR OMISSIONS'

15. This phrase appears in brackets, as a qualification of the phrase 'single act or omission'. Coherence of exposition makes it necessary to examine it separately, but it is not in fact separate. It is an integral part of a sentence which must be construed as a whole. It is submitted that the main reason why the Court of Appeal fell into error is that they did not do this.

16. The phrase in brackets follows words which, read with their associated definitions elsewhere in the policy, were deliberately designed to limit aggregation to cases of multiple claims arising from one and the same breach of duty. It slightly enlarges what would otherwise be the scope of the aggregation clause by applying it to cases where the loss the subject of the third party's claim (or series of claims) was produced by the combined effect of more than one act or omission.

17. The main point made on behalf of TSB is that the bracketed phrase was intended to permit the aggregation of distinct claims with a common origin. It is submitted that this cannot be correct, for the following reasons:

    (1) If it is enough to justify aggregating claims that the acts or omissions have a common origin in some antecedent state of affairs, then the effect of the bracketed words is so wide as to make the preceding words ('result from any single act or omission') redundant. It must be most unlikely that the parties intended by the bracketed phrase to let in the problematical analysis of the cause or causes which they had carefully excluded in drafting the rest of the provision.

    (2) It seems indisputable that a 'related series' of acts or omissions is being contrasted with a 'single' act or omission. The object of the bracketed words is not to transform the effect of the clause but to ensure that its limitation to claims resulting from a 'single' act or omission did not have the unwanted effect of excluding cases where no single act or omission sufficed to produce the loss or justify the claim.

    (3) The reference to a 'related' series of acts or omissions raises the question: related to what? As a matter of language, the only sensible answer to that question is that a 'related series of acts or omissions' is a series of acts or omissions which are related *to each other*. If it had been intended to refer to a relationship between each individual act or omission and something else, then as a matter of grammar and intelligent legal drafting, the parties would surely have said what the several acts or omissions were to be related to (e.g. a common 'originating cause' or 'event', as in the common forms of XL wording). The draftsman plainly believed that he had answered the question what claims could be

aggregated. He cannot have intended a test which permitted aggregation on the basis of a common link at some earlier point in the chain of causation, without any definition of how far back it was permissible to go.

18. TSB's alternative argument accepts that the various 'acts and omissions' must be related to each other rather than to some antecedent state of affairs. It seeks to find that relationship in the fact that they are of a similar nature. It is submitted that this is difficult to defend for all the reasons suggested in the preceding paragraph, as well as for at least two other reasons. In the first place, the mere 'similarity' of distinct acts and omissions does not imply any relationship between them at all. Secondly, it is completely unclear, if 'similarity' be the test, in what respects the acts or omissions must be similar. The only respect in which these acts or omissions were similar is that they were all breaches, on different facts, of one or other aspect of the duty to give Best Advice.

CONCLUSION

19. As the authorities show, the Courts have not shied away from analysis in this field. But there is in fact no difference between the analytical and the 'common sense' answer to the questions now before Your Lordships. The substance of all the third party claimants' claims against TSB was that each of them had been badly advised by an FSC. There was no link between the separate pieces of advice or the occasions on which they was given. The 'common sense' view of the matter is that the assumed absence of proper training and supervision was simply a fact which made the relevant breaches of duty more likely to occur. The artificial reclassification of these claims in order to alter the impact of the deductible is without commercial merit as well as being unsound in law.

20. The insurers do not dispute that the Respondents might, had they anticipated this kind of problem, have wished to protect themselves by insurance against a 'systemic failure' leading to an unusually large number of individually small claims with a considerable aggregate value. But that would have been a different kind of risk, warranting a different premium. It would have been achieved as a matter of drafting either (i) by making the relevant connecting link something other than the breach of duty which founded the third party claimant's claim or, more probably, (ii) by making the deductible applicable to the assured's aggregate claims bill. As Lord Mustill observed of the XL market in *Axa Reinsurance (UK) Ltd v Field* [1996] 1 WLR 1026, 1035, keen interest is shown in the 'techniques of limits layers and aggregations'. They are central to the scale of the risks assumed. The

Respondents are substantial organisations with experienced insurance departments and access to the best legal advice, who employed professional brokers to obtain this insurance. They are as much aware of all this as the insurers are.

21. The Appellants respectfully submit (i) that this appeal should be allowed, (ii) that it should be declared in answer to the Preliminary Issue that the claims did not result from a single act or omission or from a related series of acts or omissions within the meaning of the deductible clause of Section 3 of the Policy, (iii) that this action should be dismissed, and (iv) that the Respondents should be ordered to pay the Appellants' costs of the action, including those incurred in respect of the appeals to the Court of Appeal and to Your Lordships' House.

GOOD PRACTICE SUGGESTION

- Footnotes[14]
  Almost all of the advocates who contributed to my research use footnotes in the presentation of written argument, and employ these for two main reasons. First, they de-clutter the text. This means that citation references can be removed from prose passages where they might otherwise interrupt the reader's flow. Second, they provide a home for supporting material and relevant, but extraneous, information. Therefore they can be used for detailed legal argument, or argument on a secondary level to the principal contentions, or to deal with tangential propositions. Footnotes provide the reader with a choice of continuing with the main text or diverting his attention to supporting material.

  The use of footnotes should be as sparing as possible, since it transpires that judges are not very keen on having them. Except in the preparation of articles they should normally be at the foot of the relevant page, not at the end of the whole text.

- Remember that judges are almost always informed by the legal consequences of finding particular facts. They are likely to revisit their findings of fact until they get the solution they want. Therefore look for an acceptable legal consequence and use the facts to usher the judge in that direction.

- Try to be candid. Generally deal with any obvious defects in your case, where the point is pleaded against you or you are otherwise convinced that the other side will be taking it, putting it in the best light possible. The court will give you credit for proper confession and avoidance. Your candour will add weight if you are making appropriate concessions.

---

[14] See also Examples C,D,E,G,K,L,O.

EXAMPLE N

House of Lords - Respondent's Case by David Pannick QC and Dinah Rose in March 2005 - 26pp.

R. v Human Fertilisation and Embryology Authority ex parte Quintavalle concerned the ability of the Respondent authority to licence a clinic to conduct tissue typing for a stem cell transplant under the Human Fertilisation and Embryology Act 1990.

Here highly technical material is dealt with in a narrative form. The language is necessarily measured and formal but still readable. The length of sentences is mixed, but generally they are fairly short. References to the evidence and findings of the courts below are dealt with in the main text.

Citation references and quotations are all in the main body of the case: there are no footnotes.

The argument is internally coherent and has a chronological progression. The conclusion is simple and direct.

The Appeal was dismissed. The case is reported at [2005] UKHL 28, [2005] 2 WLR 1061.

CASE FOR THE RESPONDENT

INTRODUCTION

1   Mr and Mrs Hashmi have a son, Zain, born on 26 December 1998. Zain suffers from beta thalassaemia major, a serious and potentially fatal genetic disorder, with the effect that he produces an inadequate number of red blood cells. Because of his medical condition, Zain needs to take a daily cocktail of drugs and he requires regular blood transfusions in hospital in order to keep him alive. His quality of life is poor, and his life expectancy is low. If Mrs Hashmi were assisted to conceive and give birth to a baby with compatible tissue, Zain could be treated with a stem cell transplant from the umbilical cord blood. If successful, this treatment would radically change his future prospects. (See the Witness Statement of Dr Simon Fishel at paragraph 36, Appendix Part II, p.373). A successful stem cell transplant could achieve a relatively normal life for Zain.

2   Pre-implantation genetic diagnosis ("PGD") is a well-established practice used in the course of *in vitro* fertilisation treatment when it is known that parents are at risk of bearing a child suffering from a serious genetic disorder. About three days after *in vitro* fertilisation, one

or two individual cells are removed from a six or eight cell embryo by biopsy, and tested in order to select embryos for implantation that are free from disease, or (in the case of diseases such as haemophilia that are sex-linked) embryos of a particular sex. The Authority licenses PGD and it is not alleged by the Appellant in these proceedings that it is unlawful for the Authority to do so.

3 Tissue typing (or Human Leukocyte Antigen typing) is an additional step whereby the same embryonic cells are tested for their compatibility with a sibling who already suffers from a serious or life-threatening disease. If a baby with compatible tissue is born, blood from its umbilical cord can be used to save the life of the affected sibling, with no adverse effect for the baby (indeed no invasive procedure relating to the baby).

4 Prior to the grant of the impugned licence in this case, Mrs Hashmi had tried to give birth to a matching sibling on two occasions. One pregnancy was terminated because of the presence of beta thalassaemia major. The other pregnancy led to the birth of Mr and Mrs Hashmi's son, Harris, who is not a tissue match for Zain. See the Witness Statement of Dr Fishel at paragraph 9 (Appendix Part II, p.367).

5 Tissue typing therefore:

(1) Offers the real prospect of saving the life of a child such as Zain.

(2) Involves no detriment (indeed, no invasive procedure) to the child born as a result of tissue typing.

(3) Avoids imposing the appalling dilemma for a mother such as Mrs Hashmi of whether she should try to have another child without knowing whether that child is a tissue match for Zain (involving repeated preganancies, with either abortions or the continued increase in the size of the family). Tissue typing is designed to avoid what Dr Fishel described (Appendix Part II, p.374, paragraph 41) as "reproductive roulette".

6 The Authority submits, and the Court of Appeal agreed, that it has power under the Human Fertilisation and Embryology Act 1990 ("the 1990 Act") to license a clinic to conduct tissue typing in the course of *in vitro* fertilisation treatment, since:

(1) Save where a practice is expressly prohibited, the 1990 Act was intended to confer a discretion on the Authority to decide whether treatment falls within the scope of paragraph 1(1) of Schedule 2 in the light of its benefits and detriments.

(2) The meaning of "treatment services" defined as services "for the purpose of assisting women to carry children" - in section 2(1) and "whether embryos are suitable" for implantation under paragraph 1(1)(d) of Schedule 2 should first be assessed by

reference to PGD: a technique that was foreseen (though not actually practised) at the time when the legislation was enacted.

(3) Consideration of PGD shows that "assisting women to carry children" is not confined to services that physically assist a woman to carry a child successfully to term. The content of the 1990 Act, and the pre-legislative material, demonstrate that an activity may be one "assisting a woman to carry children" if it provides information which is vital to her decision whether or not to have an embryo implanted into her body. PGD is a process "assisting a woman to carry" a child because it informs her about a gene or chromosome defect in the embryo by reason of which she is (or may be) unwilling to bear the child.

(4) Moreover, PGD helps "to determine whether embryos are suitable for [the] purpose" of implantation. In this context, "suitable" allows for consideration of the genetic or chromosome characteristics of the embryo relevant to "assisting" women in the sense identified in (3) above.

(5) If treatment services were to be confined to those necessary or desirable to enable the woman to carry the foetus to full term (as Maurice Kay J held at first instance), or if the "suitability" of embryos for implantation does not cover genetic or chromosome characteristics affecting the child in the post-natal period, that would prohibit PGD (despite the fact that PGD has been carried out for many years without objection), it would conflict with the content of the 1990 Act, and it would conflict with the purposes of the 1990 Act as shown by pre-legislative materials.

(6) If the Authority may license PGD, then it may license tissue typing:

    (a) Tissue typing is also a process "assisting a woman to carry" a child. Like PGD, it assists a woman in Mrs Hashmi's position to carry a child by providing her with vital information, for her willingness to carry the child depends, or may depend, on knowing that the birth of the child would be capable of improving the health of her other child.

    (b) And it is a practice which helps to determine whether "embryos are suitable for [the] purpose" of implantation by reference to their gene or chromosome characteristics.

    (c) Tissue typing assesses the genetic characteristics of the embryo for a medical reason: to identify whether the stem cells can save the life of the embryo's sibling, a relevant factor under section 13(5) of the 1990 Act. That medical assistance would involve no harm to the embryo in either the ante-natal or post-natal period.

(7) As Parliament intended, it is therefore for the Authority to decide whether to license tissue typing, and on what conditions.

(7) Under the impugned decision, the Authority permitted a clinic, the Centre for Assisted Reproduction at The Park Hospital, Nottingham, to undertake tissue typing in conjunction with PGD, for the purpose of treating the Hashmi family, subject to defined conditions.

(8) Following the grant of the licence by the Authority, it is a matter already in the public domain (in accordance with the wishes of the Hashmi family) that treatment was carried out for but, sadly, Mrs Hashmi miscarried. It has been reported that a further treatment cycle is to be carried out in 2005.

(9) The decision of the Authority which is challenged in this appeal did not permit the biopsy of an embryo solely in order for tissue typing to be conducted. The Authority decided that only when a biopsy is in any event to be conducted for the purpose of PGD may tissue typing also be performed. Your Lordships' House may wish to note, however, that after the judgment of the Court of Appeal in this case, the Authority decided in July 2004 that it was prepared, in appropriate cases, to license applications for tissue typing to select embryos so that stem cells from the umbilical cord of the resulting child could save the life of a seriously ill sibling, even if the embryo was not itself being tested for a serious genetic disease.

THE COURTS BELOW

10 Mr Justice Maurice Kay held that the Authority does not have the power to grant a licence permitting tissue typing, since tissue typing cannot be said to be necessary or desirable for the purpose of providing treatment services as defined in the 1990 Act. He decided that treatment services are confined to those which assist the woman to carry the foetus to full term.

11 The Court of Appeal (Lord Phillips of Worth Matravers MR, Lord Justice Schiemann and Lord Justice Mance) allowed an appeal by the Authority, agreeing with the principles summarised in paragraph 6 above.

THE DECISION OF THE AUTHORITY

12 The Authority's Ethics Committee began to consider the ethics of tissue typing in November 2000, following reports of a case in the USA: see paragraph 22 of the Witness Statement of Dr Maureen Dalziel (Appendix Part II, p. 170).

13 In November 2001, the Ethics Committee produced an opinion (Appendix Part II, p.78) concluding that tissue typing was ethically acceptable in specified circumstances.

14 The Ethics Committee's opinion was considered by the Authority at its meeting on 29 November 2001. The considerations debated by the Authority, and its conclusions, are described by Dr Dalziel at paragraphs 23-27 of her Witness Statement (Appendix Part II, pp.170-174).

15 The Authority concluded that tissue typing would only be acceptable where, in particular:

(a) The condition of the affected child was severe or life-threatening, of a sufficient seriousness to justify the use of PGD;

(b) the embryos were themselves at risk of the genetic condition suffered by the affected child;

(c) all other possibilities of treatment and sources of tissue for the affected child had been explored;

(d) the intention was to take only cord blood for treatment, and not other tissues or organs;

(e) the couple undergoing the treatment had undergone counselling as to the implications.

Moreover, tissue typing was not to be permitted where the intended tissue recipient was a parent, and embryos were not to be genetically modified to provide a tissue match. Families were to be encouraged to participate in follow-up studies.

16 These considerations are reflected in the conditions of the licence granted by the Authority to the CARE clinic on 22 February 2002: see paragraphs 28-31 of the Witness Statement of Dr Dalziel (Appendix Part II, pp.174-175) and see the Licence (Appendix Part II, p.223).

ANALYSIS OF THE ISSUES

17 The Authority suggests that the most efficient way to address the issues is as follows :

(1) First, to address whether PGD screening is within the scope of paragraph 1(1)(d) read with paragraph 1(3) of Schedule 2 as a "treatment service" - that is a service "for the purpose of assisting women to carry children" - which determines whether embryos are "suitable" for the purpose of implantation. With the assistance of the pre-legislative material, that will enable Your Lordships to identify the meaning of the relevant statutory provisions. The Appellant suggests at paragraph 36 of her Printed Case that

it is "arguable" that the Act allows the Authority to licence PGD screening. The Respondent submits that it is appropriate to consider the application of the Act to PGD in order to identify the true meaning and effect of the relevant statutory provisions, so that the issue in the present appeal can be resolved.

(2)   If so, then to address whether tissue typing is within the scope of those provisions.

18   At paragraph 17 of his Judgment, Mr Justice Maurice Kay interpreted paragraph 1(3) of Schedule 2, read with section 2(1), as only permitting the licensing of services arising out of

"an impaired ability to conceive or to carry a child through pregnancy to full term and birth".

Mr Justice Maurice Kay considered that treatment services were confined to services that would physically assist a woman to carry a child successfully to term. Therefore tissue typing could not be licensed under the 1990 Act.

19   The Authority points out that if the narrow approach adopted by Mr Justice Maurice Kay were correct, the 1990 Act would not allow the Authority to license any PGD testing for adverse medical conditions (however serious) which do not affect the viability of the foetus, but which affect the child after birth.

20   The Authority submits, by reference to the content of the 1990 Act and by reference to its purposes (as explained in the pre-legislative materials), that analysis of PGD shows that

(1)   An activity may be one "assisting a woman to carry children" for the purposes of section 2(1) and paragraph 1(3) of Schedule 2 if it provides information which is vital to her decision whether or not to have an embryo implanted into her body.

(2)   The Authority further submits that the phrase "suitable" for the purpose of implantation in paragraph 1(1)(d) of Schedule 2 allows for consideration of gene or chromosome characteristics of the embryo relevant to the decision of the woman whether to have the embryo implanted in her. Whether an embryo is "suitable" depends on all the factors made relevant by the statutory context.

21   As observed by Lord Justice Mance at paragraph 128 of his Judgment,

"To see the legislation as interested only in women's ability successfully to experience the physical process of pregnancy and birth would seem to me to invert the significance of the human wish to reproduce. Just as placing an embryo in a woman is only a first step towards a successful pregnancy, so pregnancy and the experience of birth are steps towards an expanded family life, not an end in themselves".

THE CONTENTS OF THE 1990 ACT RELEVANT TO THE LEGALITY OF PGD

22 The 1990 Act contains some express prohibitions on practices which Parliament considered to be ethically objectionable. For example,

   (1) Section 3(2) prohibits the placing in a woman of a live embryo other than a human embryo.
   (2) Section 3(3) prohibits a number of practices, including placing an embryo in any animal.
   (3) Paragraph 1(4) of Schedule 2 states that a licence cannot authorise altering the genetic structure of any cell while it forms part of an embryo.

23 Save where such express prohibitions apply, Schedule 2 is intended to confer a broad discretion on the Authority to decide when it is appropriate to license ethically controversial treatment services and research activities relating to embryos. The Appellant has to show that the words used by Parliament authorising the grant of licences are not capable of applying to PGD and tissue typing. Your Lordships' House will recognise a substantial degree of latitude for a specialist body in relation to such a question and ask, in relation to general words such as "assisting" and "suitable", which call for the exercise of a judgment, whether the Authority has adopted an approach reasonably open to it: see, for example, *R v Monopolies and Mergers Commission ex parte South Yorkshire Transport Ltd* [1993] 1 WLR 23, 29 and 32F-33A (Lord Mustill for Your Lordships' House) and *R v Broadcasting Complaints Commission ex parte BBC* [2001] QB 885, 892-893 at paragraphs 14-16 (Lord Woolf MR for the Court of Appeal). The fact that under paragraph 1(1)(g) of Schedule 2 Regulations may confer a power to license other practices does not justify a narrow construction of what is otherwise the broad scope of Schedule 2, paragraph 1(1).

24 The Authority submits that its interpretation of paragraph 1(3) of Schedule 2, read with section 2(1), as permitting the licensing of PGD to assess the chromosome and genetic characteristics of the embryo which will be manifested in the post-natal medical condition of the child is supported by other provisions of the 1990 Act.

25 Paragraph 3 of Schedule 2 authorises the licensing of research. In particular, paragraph 3(2)(e) states that a research licence may be granted for the purpose of

"developing methods for detecting the presence of gene or chromosome abnormalities in embryos before implantation".

Paragraph 3(3) adds that the additional purposes which may be specified in Regulations made under paragraph 3(2)

"may only be so specified with a view to the authorisation of projects of research which increase knowledge about the creation and development of embryos, or about disease, or enable such knowledge to be applied".

The Authority submits:

(1) There is nothing to suggest that paragraph 3(2)(e) and paragraph 3(3) are confined to abnormalities or disease which will prevent the foetus from developing to full term. They also cover abnormalities and disease which will affect the child after birth.

(2) It would be surprising indeed were the Authority to have power to grant a licence for researching on embryos in relation to abnormalities and disease which will affect a child after birth, but for the 1990 Act then to prohibit the Authority from acting on that research so as to allow the testing of embryonic material for the presence of such abnormalities or disease in order to decide whether to implant a particular embryo in a particular woman. Indeed, paragraph 3(3) specifically refers to enabling the knowledge obtained in research, including knowledge about disease, "to be applied". So paragraph 3(3) confirms that the research into gene or chromosome abnormalities and disease is intended by Parliament to be applied, should the Authority grant an appropriate licence, whether or not it affects the viability of the foetus.

(3) Paragraph 3 of Schedule 2 is therefore inconsistent with any suggestion that the Authority may license the testing of the gene or chromosome characteristics of embryonic material only if the test concerns the viability of the foetus.

(4) Indeed, any legal test based on viability would raise complex questions as to what degree of risk to viability was contemplated by Parliament.

26 If, as explained in paragraph 25 above, Schedule 2 permits the application of research so as to allow (under licence) the testing of embryos for gene and chromosome characteristics which do not affect the viability of the foetus, the phrase "for the purpose of assisting women to carry children" in section 2(1) and in paragraph 1(3) of Schedule 2 must be interpreted accordingly:

(1) Treatment services are not confined to services that would phys-
     ically assist a woman to carry a child successfully to term. An
     activity may be one "assisting a woman to carry children" if it
     provides information which is important to her decision whether
     or not to have an embryo implanted into her body, in the sense
     that in the absence of positive information she will or may not
     proceed to bear the child.
(2) PGD is a process "assisting a woman to carry" a child because
     it gives her the knowledge that the child would not be born suf-
     fering from an adverse condition caused by a gene or chromo-
     some defect. Without such knowledge, a woman who carries (or
     whose husband carries) an hereditary genetic disease would not,
     or may not, be prepared to have children.

27 If, as explained in paragraph 25 above, Schedule 2 permits the appli-
    cation of research so as to allow (under licence) for the testing of
    embryos for gene and chromosome characteristics which do not affect
    the viability of the foetus, the phrase (in paragraph 1(1)(d) of Schedule
    2) "to determine whether embryos are suitable" for the purpose of
    implantation must be interpreted accordingly:

    (1) If, as submitted in paragraph 26 above, PGD is a practice within
         section 2(1) as "assisting women to have children" because of
         the provision of information about the gene or chromosome
         characteristics of the embryo, it would be surprising were PGD
         to fall outside the scope of a service determining whether the
         embryo is "suitable" for implantation. "Suitability" must take
         its meaning from the context, which includes information rele-
         vant to "assisting" women as interpreted in paragraph 26 above.
    (2) Paragraph 1(1)(d) envisages two distinct activities:

        (a) Measures to

             "*secure* that embryos are in a *suitable condition*"

             to be placed in a woman.
        (b) Measures to

             "*determine* whether embryos are *suitable*"

             for that purpose.

(3) The Authority points out:

(a) The term "suitability" is a broad one. Parliament did not express itself either in terms of the viability of the embryo, or of its health or freedom from defect.

(b) The first of the activities referred to at paragraph 1(1)(d) (to "secure" that embryos are in a "suitable condition") is concerned with measures that may be taken to improve and safeguard the condition of the embryo. The second activity (to "determine" whether embryos are "suitable") is specifically concerned with, and intended to permit, the *selection* of suitable embryos.

(c) The phrase "whether embryos are suitable" is wider than "whether embryos are in a suitable condition", and must indicate that when selecting embryos for implantation it is legitimate to have regard to factors other than the pure physical condition of the embryo. Indeed, the antithesis in paragraph 1(1)(d) is made meaningless unless the phrase "whether embryos are suitable" refers to suitability for a reason other than their physical condition. But if (as must be the case) "whether embryos are suitable" refers to suitability for a reason other than their physical condition, it must refer to their genetic qualities. It is for the Authority to decide what factors may properly be taken into account by clinics when deciding whether embryos are "suitable" in this respect: see Lord Justice Mance at paragraphs 115 and 127 of his Judgment.

(d) The Appellant's Printed Case at paragraphs 26-29 and 40 focuses on the phrase "whether embryos are in a suitable condition" and ignores the broader concept of "whether embryos are suitable" for the purpose of being placed in a woman. The Appellant has sought to argue that the narrower language ("suitable condition") used to describe the first activity licensable under paragraph 1(1)(d) ought to be used to read down the second limb of that paragraph. In fact, where Parliament has chosen to use two different phrases ("suitable condition"; "suitable"), each ought to be given its appropriate, different meaning. It is contrary to the clear language of the statute to seek to confine the second limb of paragraph 1(1)(d) to selection on the basis of the physical condition of the embryo.

(e) The question whether a particular embryo is suitable to be placed in a particular woman will depend on all the facts of the case. It does not depend simply and exclusively on the viability or freedom from physical defect of the foetus. Otherwise the contrast between the two parts of paragraph 1(1)(d) would serve no sensible purpose.

(d) Read with regard to paragraph 3(2)(e) and paragraph 3(3) of Schedule 2, and Parliament's approval of the licensing of tests to assess whether an embryo has gene or chromosome abnormalities, "suitable" is a broad enough concept to allow for consideration of the genetic and chromosome characteristics of an embryo.

28 The Authority's submissions are supported by other provisions of the 1990 Act which make it very clear that the viability of the foetus is not the only relevant consideration:

(1) Section 13(5) of the 1990 Act provides that in every case where a woman is to be provided with treatment services under the 1990 Act, it is a condition of the licence authorising the treatment that account must be taken of the welfare of any child who may be born as a result of the treatment, and of any other child who may be affected by the birth. As Lord Justice Mance observed at paragraph 122 of his Judgment, on the Appellant's argument that the concepts of "assisting" and "suitable" in the 1990 Act must be given a narrow construction, the requirement in section 13(5) cannot be fulfilled

> "in one most effective way, by screening to avoid the implantation of an embryo which has or may have a genetic abnormality which would affect the child after birth and, potentially, also affect siblings, in cases where the birth of such a child might impose heavy stress on the family generally. In short, section 13(5) points towards a wider concern for the future child and siblings, which is better served if the legislation is read as permitting such screening".

The Appellant contends at paragraph 45 of her Printed Case that section 13(5) cannot determine what constitutes "treatment services". But the content of section 13(5) helpfully indicates that Parliament intended the provisions of the Act to be understood and applied by reference, amongst other matters, to the welfare of the other children of the family. It is also an indication that, when considering whether an embryo is "suitable" for implantation, the effect of the implantation of that particular embryo on other children in the family is a relevant consideration.

(2) Similarly, in relation to the Authority's duty under section 25(1) to maintain a Code of Practice, section 25(2) states that the Authority is required to give guidance for those providing treatment services about

> "the account to be taken of the welfare of children who may be born as a result of treatment services (including a child's need for

a father), and of other children who may be affected by such births".

Indeed, as Lord Justice Mance observed at paragraph 123 of his Judgment, although the purpose of treatment services must be to assist women to carry children, they may be services provided to others, such as the potential father. His concerns about future health and welfare would be relevant factors and

> "This too tends to point against any conclusion that the legislation focuses solely on the woman's narrow physical ability to become pregnant and give birth".

29 The definition of "treatment services" in the 1990 Act is designed to ensure that, in principle, consideration may be given to all factors that are relevant to the decision of the woman whether to carry the embryo. It is then for the Authority to decide whether, pursuant to paragraph 1(3) of Schedule, the activity is "necessary or desirable".

30 The Appellant suggested in the Court of Appeal that PGD is consistent with the conclusion stated by Mr Justice Maurice Kay because abnormal genetic conditions involve a greater risk that the foetus will not be carried to full term. But that argument cannot succeed (as explained by Lord Phillips of Worth Matravers MR at paragraph 45 and Lord Justice Mance at paragraphs 118-119 of their Judgments):

(1) There are genetic conditions such as beta thalassaemia which do not affect the viability of the foetus but do have an adverse post-natal effect. See the Witness Statement of Professor John Raeburn at paragraphs 5-9 (Appendix Part II, p.419) and the Witness Statement of Dr Fishel at paragraph 45 (Appendix Part II, p.375).

(2) The language of the 1990 Act demonstrates that Parliament was concerned with conditions which adversely affect the health of the child after birth, as well as those which affect the viability of the foetus. See paragraphs 25 and 28 above.

(3) The pre-legislative material (see paragraphs 33-46 below) confirms that the mischief with which the 1990 Act was concerned included conditions which adversely affect the health of the child after birth.

THE PURPOSES OF THE 1990 ACT

31 The submissions based on the content of the 1990 Act set out in paragraphs 22-30 above are supported by the pre-legislative material which shows that the intention was to allow the Authority to licence

tests such as PGD which do not concern the viability of the foetus but assess gene or chromosome characteristics which affect the post-natal condition of the child.

32 In *R (Quintavalle) v Secretary of State for Health* [2003] 2 AC 687, Your Lordships' House decided :

(1) A court should not adopt a narrow, literal interpretation of the 1990 Act, but should seek to give effect to its purpose. See Lord Bingham of Cornhill at p.695, paragraph 8 (for Your Lordships' House); and Lord Steyn (with whom Lord Scott of Foscote agreed) at p.700, paragraph 21.

(2) In doing so, the Court should have regard to the Warnock Report and the White Paper. See Lord Bingham of Cornhill for Your Lordships' House at pp.696-697, paragraph 11. Indeed, it has long been established that courts can identify the mischief at which legislation was aimed by looking at an official report: *Black-Clawson International Ltd v Papierwerke AG* [1975] AC 591, 614B-E per Lord Reid, with the agreement of Viscount Dilhorne at p.622E-F, Lord Wilberforce at p.629C-D, Lord Diplock at p.638F-H, and Lord Simon of Glaisdale at p.646E-G. As Lord Simon stated:

> "A public report to Parliament is an important part of the matrix of a statute founded on it. Where Parliament is legislating in the light of a public report I can see no reason why a court of construction should deny itself any part of that light and insist on groping for a meaning in darkness or half-light".

(3) A court should apply the general principle stated by Lord Wilberforce in *Royal College of Nursing v Department of Health and Social Security* [1981] AC 800, 822 of seeking to apply an Act of Parliament to scientific developments which post-date the legislation where the language and purposes of the Act make it possible to do so.

33 The 1990 Act has its origins in the Report of the Committee of Inquiry into Human Fertilisation and Embryology (1984, Cmnd. 9314) chaired by Dame Mary Warnock (Appendix Part II, pp.125-141). Chapter 9 addressed "the wider use of these techniques", that is techniques for alleviating infertility:

(1) Paragraph 9.1 stated:

> "So far in this report we have been concerned with the alleviation of infertility. The processes we have considered can, however, also

be seen as a facility, a service available to anyone, whether infertile or otherwise, to enable them to have a child in a particular way".

(2) At paragraph 9.2, the Report identified the difficulty faced by families who knew of the possibility that they might pass on an hereditary disease which may severely handicap a child. The Report noted:

> "Couples who know of the possibility of such disorders in either or both families face a difficult choice. For some conditions, prenatal diagnostic screening already provides a means of detecting abnormalities or genetic disorders in the foetus. This may provide parents with an opportunity for termination of pregnancy if they want it. However, there are people for whom a termination is unacceptable. For them, the choice at the moment is a harsh one, between the risk of having handicapped children, and having no children at all".

(3) At 9.3, the Report continued:

> "For such people, the use of a technique involving donated eggs or semen which do not contain the genetic material associated with the hereditary disease offers real hope of giving birth to healthy children".

(4) The Report recommended at the end of paragraph 9.3:

> "it should be accepted practice to offer donated gametes and embryos to those at risk of transmitting hereditary disorders".

34 The Warnock Report then considered the selection of the sex of an embryo for the purpose of avoiding certain sex-linked genetic disorders. This is nothing to do with the viability of the foetus but is concerned with a child's medical condition after birth:

(1) Paragraph 9.4 of the Warnock Report identified the issue:

> "'Sex selection' is a term which covers two different concepts. It may be used to refer to the choice of the gender of an embryo before fertilisation occurs, or to the identification of the gender of an already existing embryo. Either could be of benefit in avoiding certain sexlinked genetic disorders. Knowledge of foetal sex can be crucial where either member of a couple is known to be the carrier of a sex-linked hereditary disorder such as haemophilia or Duchenne muscular dystrophy. The sex of any child to which they may give

birth will determine whether or not the child may have inherited the disorder".

(2) At paragraph 9.8, the Report recognised the possible development of preimplantation gender identification of embryos for this purpose:

"Pre-implantation gender identification would not involve the mother in any abortion procedure, because embryos of the sex associated with the handicapping condition would not be transferred to her uterus".

(3) At paragraph 9.11, the Report approved of the possibility of selecting embryos to ensure they are free from sex-linked genetic disease:

"We see no reason why, if a method of selecting the sex of a child before fertilisation is developed, this should not be offered to couples who have good medical reasons for choosing the sex of their child".

(4) Paragraph 9.11 then expressed disapproval of such sex selection for social reasons. Recognising that this topic was controversial, the Report suggested that it should be kept under review, referring to Chapter 13 - the Chapter which recommended the establishment of a statutory licensing authority.

(5) The recognition that sex selection was acceptable where used for medical reasons (and the proposal that sex selection for social reasons should be a matter for the regulator), is inconsistent with the suggestion that medical procedures in relation to embryos were regarded as capable of being licensed only if carried out to further the ability of the woman to bear the child to full term and that the suitability of the embryo must be considered in isolation from its post-natal characteristics.

35 At paragraph 12.1 the Warnock Report noted that the proposed licensing body would be able to consider other possible techniques and procedures involving the use of human embryos, save where the Committee's proposals precluded certain developments altogether:

(1) One such possible technique and procedure considered by the Report, at paragraphs 12.12-12.13, was

"embryonic biopsy", "to investigate the chromosomal structure of embryos fertilised *in vitro* by a couple who have a high chance of procreating an abnormal child".

The Report noted that such a technique was not scientifically possible in 1984, but might become possible in the future. The Report was considering what is now known as PGD.

(2) By reason of paragraph 12.1, the Report recommended that whether such a procedure would be allowed (and in what circumstances) would be a matter for the proposed licensing body.

(3) Again, that is inconsistent with the suggestion that medical procedures in relation to embryos were regarded as acceptable only if carried out to further the ability of the woman to bear the child to full term.

36 In December 1986, the Government published a consultation document, "Legislation on Human Infertility Services and Embryo Research" (Cm 46), paragraphs 48-56 of which set out the competing arguments for and against allowing research involving embryos (see Appendix Part II, pp.161-162). Paragraph 48(d) recognised that one of the suggested benefits of embryo research was

"detecting gene or chromosome abnormalities before implantation".

Paragraph 49 explained:

"It is argued that the greatest potential benefits of research involving human embryos lies in the prevention of congenital disorders. Studies of eggs, sperm and early embryos may lead to ways of preventing some chromosomal abnormalities developing. Also, in the future, those who support research envisage the development of techniques including embryonic biopsy which might allow the very early detection of embryos which had single gene or chromosome defects which would result in seriously abnormal babies. In the UK some 7000 babies a year (about 1 per cent of all babies) are born with an obvious single gene inherited defect. Pre-implantation 'diagnosis' could ultimately result in some fall in that number".

"Embryonic biopsy" is what is now known as PGD. A footnote to paragraph 49 added:

"The technique of embryo biopsy could extend the use of IVF from treating infertile couples to those at risk of passing on an hereditary handicap. It would involve the removal and culture of one or two cells from an embryo still *in vitro* and need not affect the subsequent development of the embryo. It could, however, give the possibility in some instances of rejecting defective embryos in favour of healthy ones and reducing the number of requests for abortion on grounds of foetal

> abnormality. Attempts are also being made to develop noninvasive techniques for detecting defective embryos".

The consultation document was recognising that the potential benefits were not confined to matters which affect the ability of the mother to bear the child to full term, but also cover whether the child would or might be born with a seriously adverse medical condition.

37   In November 1987 the Government published a White Paper, "Human Fertilisation and Embryology: A Framework for Legislation" (Cm 259) (Appendix Part II, pp.142163). Paragraph 13 (Appendix Part II, p.145) accepted the recommendation of the Warnock Report that a licensing body should be created

> "to regulate and monitor practice in relation to those sensitive areas which raise fundamental ethical questions".

Paragraphs 28-30 of the White Paper (Appendix Part II, pp. 147-148) recognised that there were two competing views in relation to embryo research and that alternative draft clauses should therefore be put before Parliament to enable Parliament to choose between them. But it is important to note that neither of the two competing views recognised in the White Paper drew a distinction between tests on an embryo to ascertain whether the mother could carry the foetus to full term and tests on the embryo to ascertain whether the mother would give birth to a child without a serious disease.

38   Rather, paragraph 29 of the White Paper stated:

> "The key distinction in the debate surrounding embryo research appears to be between the use of an embryo with the intention of achieving (with that embryo) a successful pregnancy leading to a healthy baby; and its use for other reasons (eg improvement of knowledge about disease)....".

So the debate was whether the licensing body should have power to approve research on embryos for general purposes. The White Paper did not doubt the acceptability of tests to assess whether the foetus, if carried to full term, would be healthy. The Appellant's interpretation of "treatment services" in section 2(1) of the 1990 Act would conflict with the White Paper by confining licensed activities to those relevant to assisting the woman to carry the foetus to full term, and would prevent the licensing of any activities relevant to whether the baby (when born) would be healthy.

39   As demonstrated by paragraph 3 of Schedule 2 to the 1990 Act, Parliament decided to approve the wider of the two options identified in the White Paper. Paragraph 3 allows for research on embryos which further general knowledge about infertility and disease etc, whether

or not the use of the embryo assists in a successful pregnancy (and a healthy baby) involving that embryo.

40   The Bill that became the 1990 Act was introduced in Your Lordships' House on 22 November 1989.

41   As promised in the White Paper, the Bill contained alternative draft provisions: to permit the licensing of research, and to prohibit the licensing of research. Both Your Lordships' House and the House of Commons voted in favour of embryo research.

42   By the time of the third reading debate in the House of Commons, it was known that Dr Robert Winston had successfully implanted female embryos after genetically screening out male embryos which were, or might have been, affected by gender linked genetic disorders.

43   The Secretary of State for Health, Mr Kenneth Clarke, made plain the intention of the legislation to allow the Authority to license treatment services designed to identify whether the child would suffer from a handicap after birth, and not only to identify whether the foetus could be carried to full term. See the third reading debate on 23 April 1990 (*Hansard* at column 37) (Appendix Part II, p.450) where Mr Clarke stated :

> "Not all new reproductive technologies are aimed at helping infertile couples to have children. Some are designed to help people to have healthy normal children by allowing a range of congenital diseases and handicaps to be detected prenatally by pre-implantation diagnosis. The possibility of preventing genetic disease is one of the reasons most frequently cited in support of embryo research".

44   At columns 37-38, Mr Clarke was asked by an opponent of embryo research to confirm that a ban on embryo research would not prevent screening of embryos for genetic handicaps, because such testing would continue to be permitted under what is now paragraph 1(1)(d) of Schedule 2. Mr Clarke confirmed that this was so.

45   It is therefore plain that Parliament understood and intended that paragraph 1(1)(d) of Schedule 2 read with paragraph 1(3), and the statutory concepts of "assisting" and "suitable" which they contain, should be given a broad interpretation which allowed for the pre-implantation screening of embryos to identify possible genetic handicaps which would be manifested after the birth of the child. Consistent with the Warnock Report and the White Paper, Parliament did not intend to confine the Authority to the licensing of treatment which would assist the woman to carry the foetus to full term.

46   For these reasons, the pre-legislative material strongly supports the conclusions already derived from the content of the 1990 Act:

(1) Parliament envisaged that embryonic material could be tested for gene or chromosome characteristics whether or nor those characteristics threaten the viability of the foetus;

(2) services "for the purpose of assisting women to carry children" in paragraph 1(3) of Schedule 2 cover the provision of information to the woman about the genetic or chromosome characteristics of the embryo central to the decision of the woman whether to have the embryo implanted in her; and

(3) "whether embryos are suitable" for implantation under paragraph 1(1)(d) of Schedule 2 covers the genetic and chromosome characteristics of the embryo relevant to "assisting women" as explained in (2) above.

TISSUE TYPING

47 If the Authority is correct in its above submissions that it has power to license PGD because

(1) treatment services are "for the purpose of assisting women to carry children" when they provide information about the genetic characteristics of the embryo so as to assist the women to decide whether to proceed with implantation; and

(2) a treatment service is designed to determine "whether embryos are suitable" for the purpose of being implanted in a woman where it provides information about the genetic or chromosome characteristics of the embryo relevant to assisting woman (as explained in (1) above),

it follows (for the reasons set out in paragraphs 48-52 below) that tissue typing may lawfully be licensed by the Authority.

48 As explained by Lord Phillips of Worth Matravers MR at paragraph 48 of his Judgment, the activities licensed by the Authority for tissue typing are the same as those licensed for the purposes of PGD to enable women to bear children free from hereditary diseases :

(1) The creation of embryos *in vitro.*

(2) Biopsies of the embryos.

(3) Analysis of the cells removed by biopsy by the use of a DNA probe in order to identify those embryos likely to produce children with desired characteristics.

(4) Implantation of those embryos into the woman.

49 The fact that tissue typing seeks to identify different characteristics from PGD (producing a child with stem cells matching a sick or dying

sibling, as opposed to producing a child free from genetic defects) is not crucial for the purpose of determining whether the process

(1) is one "for the purpose of assisting women to carry children", since in each case the process provides information which assists the woman to decide whether she wishes to have the embryo implanted in her; and

(2) is one which determines whether the embryo is "suitable" for implantation, since that term covers the genetic or chromosome characteristics of the embryo relevant to the assistance provided to the woman (as interpreted in (1) above).

50 The Authority emphasises :

(1) Consideration of the legality of PGD demonstrates that the concepts of services "for the purpose of assisting women to carry children" and the "suitability" of the foetus extend beyond purely physical problems affecting the viability of the foetus during pregnancy and birth, and cover the provision of information about the medical condition of the child after birth.

(2) Tissue typing is designed to identify the genetic characteristics of the embryo because those characteristics are relevant to the health of the existing child, Zain. Tissue typing is not carried out for social reasons. See Lord Justice Mance at paragraph 135. Section 13(5) contemplates that the welfare of existing children is a relevant factor. That must cover the positive benefits to the existing family of the mother having another child, and not just whether there would be detriments. See Lord Justice Mance at paragraph 133 of his Judgment. The benefits to the health of Zain are very substantial. And the use of the stem cells from the umbilical cord involves no harm to the child and no invasive procedure. By contrast, to prohibit the licensing of tissue typing would inevitably cause substantial detriments to the family: the continuing illness of Zain (and the consequent strains it would inevitably impose on parents and siblings) and the agonising choice for Mr and Mrs Hashmi of whether to try to have another child without knowledge of whether that child's umbilical cord could assist Zain.

(3) The "assistance" given by tissue typing is the provision of information crucial to enable the parents to decide whether the embryo should be implanted in the woman, having regard to the impact on the family as a whole given the medical problems they face. In this context, the information helps to determine whether the embryo is "suitable" for implantation, that is whether it has the genetic characteristics relevant to the medical concerns of the family.

(4) Where Parliament intended to impose absolute prohibitions in relation to potential scientific developments, it did so, for example by section 3(2) and section 3(3). It imposed no prohibition relevant to the present context. Indeed, as noted by Lord Justice Mance at paragraphs 139 and 143 of his Judgment, neither the Warnock Report nor the White Paper recommended an absolute prohibition in relation to embryo testing or in relation to sex selection for reasons unconnected to the medical condition of the child-to-be. By contrast, the White Paper at paragraphs 36-42 (Appendix Part II, pp.149-150) did recommend absolute prohibitions of nucleus substitution and of techniques aimed at modifying the genetic constitution of an embryo. The White Paper stated at paragraph 36 that on those issues the Government took a more restrictive approach than the Warnock Report. As stated by Lord Bingham of Cornhill for Your Lordships' House in *R (Quintavalle) v Secretary of State for Health* [2003] 2 AC 687, 699, paragraph 18, those recommendations were the basis of section 3(3)(d) of the 1990 Act which prohibited replacement of the nucleus of a cell of an embryo. The White Paper did not recommend, and Parliament did not impose, similar prohibitions in relation to embryo testing or in relation to sex selection for reasons unconnected to the medical condition of the child-to-be because it wished the merits of such testing to be determined by the Authority which would assess the medical and ethical considerations. The same principle must apply to tissue typing.

(5) Applying the principle stated by Lord Wilberforce in *Royal College of Nursing v Department of Health and Social Security* [1981] AC 800, 822, and approved by Your Lordships' House in *R (Quintavalle) v Secretary of State for Health* [2003] 2 AC 687, a biopsy for tissue typing falls well within the scope of paragraph 1(1)(d) and paragraph 1(3) of Schedule 2, as explained by Lord Justice Mance at paragraph 144 of his Judgment:

(a) As with PGD, its purpose is to identify the genetic composition of the embryo so as to provide information relevant to whether that embryo should be implanted in the woman.

(b) Whereas PGD is concerned with what the genetic information reveals about the future health of the child which the embryo will become, and tissue typing is concerned with what the genetic information reveals about the ability of the child which the embryo will become to promote the health of a sick sibling, and the impact on the welfare of the family, this is well within the same genus. As demonstrated by the Warnock Report, the White Paper and the 1990 Act, Parliament envisaged the possibility or the likelihood of future scientific developments, even though it did not know precisely what they would be, and decided (other than where absolute prohibitions were imposed) to confer power on the Authority to decide when it would be appropriate to grant a licence for testing an embryo to identify its genetic composition for reasons relevant to the decision of the woman whether to have it implanted in her. There is nothing in the content of the 1990 Act, or in any of the pre-legislative material, which suggested that although licensing may allow for activities broader than the viability of the foetus so as to identify the genetic or chromosome characteristics of the embryo, that could only be for medical reasons relating to the medical condition of the post-natal embryo and not for other medical reasons concerning an existing child.

51 The Appellant seeks to draw a distinction between PGD and tissue typing, on the ground that "at most" the definition of "treatment services" in the 1990 Act is only wide enough to encompass "the process of carrying an embryo *and ensuring that that embryo is healthy, in the sense that it is free from defects*" (Appellant's case, paragraph 17: emphasis added). This distinction is entirely unsupported by the statutory language, which makes no reference to the "health" of an embryo in the definition of treatment services (or licensable embryonic selection under paragraph 1(1)(d)). Further, the distinction the Appellant seeks to make would be unworkable in practice. Once the Appellant accepts that "treatment services" may extend beyond assistance with the purely physical process of carrying a child to full term, so that embryonic testing and selection may go beyond the selection of embryos which are viable from those which are not, no dear distinction can be drawn between embryos that are "defective" and those which are "healthy": for example, is a blind embryo "defective"? Or a short-sighted embryo? Further, the Appellant's argument would prohibit sex selection for the purpose of preventing sex-related inherited diseases, like haemophilia (one of the common uses of PGD). PGD is used to select only female embryos for implantation. However, it cannot be said that all the male embryos are "defective" or "unhealthy". Only 50% of the boys borne to a female carrier of haemophilia suffer from the disease. The question of the purposes for which embryonic selection is acceptable is an ethically sensitive one, and properly falls within the powers of the Authority to regulate through licence conditions and the statutory Code of Practice, and with the assistance of its expert and lay members, and its ethics committee. It is not a question that can be resolved through the construction of the primary legislation.

52 Thus, for example, the Authority carried out a consultation in 1993 into the question of sex selection. The response was unambiguously opposed to sex selection for nonmedical reasons, whilst supporting the use of PGD to select sex for the purpose of avoiding serious disease.

The HFEA's policy on sex selection is contained at paragraph 8.9(i) of the Sixth Edition of the Code of Practice, which provides: "8.9 Treatment centres are expected not to:

(i) select the sex of embryos for social reasons."

In practice, this policy allows appropriately-licensed clinics to select the sex of embryos using PGD only for the avoidance of serious sex-linked disorders. The issue of sex selection was the subject of a further consultation by the Authority in 2002 and 2003, resulting in the publication of a report entitled *Sex Selection: options for regulation.*

53   The Appellant relies on the Parliamentary Debate in Your Lordships' House on 8 February 1990, when the Duke of Norfolk moved an amendment (at column 996) to amend paragraph 1(1)(d) of Schedule 2 because he was concerned that the words "in a suitable condition to be placed in a woman" might allow for the selection of an embryo to comply with the parents' wishes for "a boy or a girl or a blond child or a blue-eyed child". The Parliamentary Under-Secretary of State at the Department of Health, Baroness Hooper, told Your Lordships' House (at column 999) that paragraph 1(1)(d) was designed to ensure that "defective embryos are not unwittingly placed in a woman". The Duke of Norfolk withdrew the amendment (at column 998). The Respondent submits that this exchange does not assist on the issues in the present case, since:

(1)   The Duke of Norfolk's concern was that part of paragraph 1(1)(d) which referred to whether embryos are "in a suitable condition to be placed in a woman". He did not refer to the additional concept in paragraph 1(1)(d) of "whether embryos are suitable" for the purpose of being placed in a woman.

(2)   The Duke of Norfolk's concern was sex selection (or the selection of an embryo to ensure a child with blonde hair or blue eyes) for social purposes. He was not addressing a case where there is a medical reason for the selection of a particular embryo.

(3)   Because of the narrow focus of the concern expressed by the Duke of Norfolk, and because of the state of scientific knowledge in 1990, the Parliamentary Under-Secretary of State was not addressing the question whether paragraph 1(1)(d) allows for the consideration of whether an embryo is suitable for implantation because of medical reasons relevant to tissue typing, that is the genetic ability of the foetus, after birth, to assist in saving the life of a sibling.

(4)   In any event, reliance on the statement by Baroness Hooper is impermissible. She was commenting on the intended scope of a statutory power rather than seeking to interpret the provisions

of the Bill: see *R v Secretary of State for the Environment, Transport, and the Regions ex parte Spath Holme Ltd* [2001] 2 AC 349, 392A-D (Lord Bingham of Cornhill for Your Lordships' House). Lord Hope of Craighead agreed at p.404B-D and expressed similar reasoning on the use of *Hansard* at pp.407E-408F. Lord Hutton agreed with Lord Bingham of Cornhill at p.413H and expressed similar conclusions at pp.413G-414F.

THE FURTHER ISSUE CONSIDERED BY MR JUSTICE MAURICE KAY

54 Mr Justice Maurice Kay also addressed a further issue: whether tissue typing requires a licence under the 1990 Act.

55 As explained in the Judgment of Lord Phillips of Worth Matravers MR at paragraph 20, this issue does not go to the heart of the case. That is because the Authority accepts that the creation in vitro of an embryo, the extraction of cells by biopsy, and the implantation of the embryo all require a licence and so can only be lawful if they are within the scope of treatment services under paragraph 1 of Schedule 2 to the 1990 Act.

56 But the Authority does maintain that the use of embryonic material for tissue typing does not of itself require a licence. Section 3(1) requires a licence for specified activities: action taken to:

"(a) bring about the creation of an embryo, or
(b) keep or use an embryo".

It does not require a licence for the use of material derived from the embryo. cf section 3A(1) in relation to germ cells.

57 Indeed, there are very good reasons why Parliament regulated the creation, keeping or use of an embryo, but not the use of an embryonic cell. The extraction of embryonic cells amounts to the manipulation of a live embryo with the potential to develop into a person, and is a procedure that risks harming that embryo. Similarly, placing an embryo into a woman raises similar concerns. Also keeping an embryo needs to be licensed because it has the potential to become a human being. By contrast, the testing of an embryonic cell which has already been extracted from an embryo does not raise any such problem. It is material which has no capacity itself to develop into a human being.

58 Lord Justice Mance decided this matter in favour of the Authority at paragraphs 110–111.

CONCLUSION

59 PGD and tissue typing, as well as many other developing scientific processes concerned with fertilisation and embryology, raise complex and sensitive ethical issues. Parliament decided (save where express prohibitions were imposed) to entrust those issues to the Authority by giving it power to license the screening of embryos before implantation to identify genetic and chromosome characteristics in order for a choice to be made whether to proceed with implantation.

60 Your Lordships' House is invited to dismiss this appeal for the following

REASONS

(1) The 1990 Act, construed by reference to its language and purposes, confers power on the Authority to license PGD and tissue typing.

(2) The Court of Appeal correctly dismissed this application for judicial review.

GOOD PRACTICE SUGGESTION

- Key dates[15]

  If you are not putting in a formal chronology make sure that you refer in the body of the skeleton to the relevant key dates. Again, be highly discriminating about what it is necessary to refer to.

- Citation[16]

  The amount and extent of citation of authorities depends on the intellectual density of your argument, particularly where issues of law are more extensive than factual issues. Be reasonably sparing in citing any. Only refer to key parts. Do not disrupt the flow of text. Most judges will look at the authorities themselves, and prefer to do so. Therefore use dicta within your skeleton only if you have a particularly riveting passage, and then just the bit that works. A good rule of thumb is to cite at length only when to do so makes the point better than you can. In a really difficult question you can set out the whole of the relevant passage but it must be very much on point to retain the judge's interest.

  Even where fairly extensive legal argument may be required try to use your best authority or one where your position is most persuasively put in order to make your propositions of law seem self-evidently right. There is nothing worse than a collection of bits of citation.

---

[15] See also Example A.

[16] See also Examples D and K.

It may be a useful discipline for juniors to have authority for everything they propose, but such an approach matures over time. As an advocate the more senior or experienced or respected you become, the easier it will be both to decide what to omit by way of supporting authority, and what the court will accept from you without citation.

EXAMPLE O

Judicial Committee of the Privy Council - Petition for leave to appeal - Skeleton argument of the Respondents by Jonathan Sumption QC in March, 2004 - 9pp.

Ithaca (Custodians) Limited and Another v Perry Corporation and Others concerned whether, as a result of a sale by the Respondent of shares in a public company and equity swaps entered into the same day by certain banks for a quantity of that company's shares corresponding to the number sold, the Respondent had a disclosable interest in the shares within the meaning of s5(1) Securities Amendment Act 1988. The New Zealand Court of Appeal had held there was no such disclosable interest.

The skeleton opens with a summary of the Respondent's assertions. The manner is direct, even bold. The language used is business like but not legal, and occasionally idiomatic. The Board is informed quickly and with minimal effort what the issue is. There is no extraneous information by way of a history of the proceedings.

The law is mainly relegated to footnotes. The argument is a narrative - it is lucid, cogent and contains minimal citation. Strong reliance is placed upon principle to forestall the petition for leave being granted.

Leave to appeal was refused.

SKELETON ARGUMENT OF THE RESPONDENTS

THE PRESENT APPLICATIONS

1. This is not an appeal which Your Lordships should entertain, for four reasons:

    (1) There is no appeal as of right, because it does not involve a claim or question respecting property worth more than NZ$5,000.
    (2) There is no point of general or public importance.
    (3) Successive appeals on issues of fact arising out of the statutory regulation of the securities markets ought to be discouraged.
    (4) This particular appeal would have no real prospect of success.

2. The Respondents also submit:

    (5) that there is in any event no justification for the interim relief that the Petitioners seek, which would prevent Perry Corp

disposing of its own property without achieving any legitimate objective of the Claimants. Background

BACKGROUND

3. The Securities Amendment Act 1988 (as it was then called) requires disclosure of any 'relevant interest' in 5% or more of the voting securities of a public company. A 'relevant interest' includes an 'agreement, arrangement or understanding' under which a person has the 'power to acquire' a security: Section 5(1)(f)(iii).[1]

4. Where there is reason to believe that a relevant interest has not been disclosed, application may be made to the Court under Section 31 for appropriate orders. The application may be made by the Securities Commission, or by holders of the company's securities {among others). The present proceedings were not brought by the Securities Commission. They were brought by the Petitioners, on the basis that they were shareholders in Rubicon and had a personal claim for damages.[2]

5. In spite of the considerable volume of oral and documentary evidence put before the courts below, the real issue between the parties has always been comparatively narrow:

    (1) On 31 May 2001, Perry Corp sold shares in Rubicon to two highly reputable investment banks, UBS and Deutsche Bank, retaining some shares, but less than 5%. It has never been suggested that this transaction was a sham, or that it was anything other than an outright sale.

    (2) On the same date, Perry Corp entered into equity swaps with each bank for a quantity of Rubicon shares corresponding to the number sold. An equity swap is a derivative instrument, by which the parties agree to make net payments to each other depending upon the returns yielded by a specified security (or index) over a specified period.[1] The effect of these transctions was that the banks agreed to pay to Perry Corp the amount by which the actual return exceeded a specified ('fixed') return based on LIBOR, and Perry Corp agreed to pay to the banks the amount by which it fell short of that return. This was a purely financial instrument, settled by the payment of cash differences. It conferred an economic benefit (or detriment) equivalent to that of actually

---

[1] The relevant provisions of the Act are appended to the Judgment of Potter J. at p. 28Off.

[2] Under Section 34 of the Act the Court has a discretionary power to award compensation to a person who has suffered loss by entering in transactions, in circumstances where the Defendant has failed to disclose a relevant shareholding.

[1] By 'return' is meant the combined financial effect of dividend receipts and changes in the market price of the security: see Potter J., paras. 46-7.

holding the relevant number of shares. But the Petitioners accepted at both stages below that it did not in itself create any disclosable interest in shares, because it conferred no power over any shares. Indeed, the banks were not contractually required to hold any shares.[2] There is a statutory rule to that effect. If New Zealand is to go out on a limb, by adopting as a matter of common law some different approach to an established financial instrument, then it would have to do so for locally compelling reasons. Questions of policy of this sort are very much matters for the courts of New Zealand. Yet the Trial Judge did not adopt this course, and the Court of Appeal expressly refused to do so.[1]

(3) It has always been common ground that although under no contractual obligation to do so, in practice a bank entering into an equity swap of this kind will usually, in its own interest, want to hedge its potential exposure. Where the transaction relates to a relatively illiquid security such as Rubicon stock, it will probably choose to hedge by holding the corresponding quantity of that stock. If it does this, it will probably wish to dispose of the shares when the swap comes to an end. In that case, they will be available for purchase by the counterparty (or, in theory, any one else).

(4) The issue in the courts below was simply whether there was to be inferred from the circumstances in which the swap was agreed an arrangement or understanding collateral to its terms that the banks would hold corresponding quantities of Rubicon shares and would sell them back to Perry Corp when the swap transaction came to an end.[3] This was a pure question of fact. It has always been common ground that if such an arrangement or understanding existed, Perry Corp had a disclosable interest in Rubicon. If not, not.

6. The matter was resolved below as follows:

(1) The Trial Judge inferred that there must have been such a collateral arrangement or understanding, although she said that she was unable to determine its exact terms, nor how or by whom it was arrived at.[1] Her reason was essentially that the existence of

---

[2] The Petitioners' position is summarised by the Court of Appeal, at paras. 5 and 54. Both courts below accepted this analysis: see Potter J. at paras. 59-64; and Court of Appeal, at para. 57.

[1] See Court of Appeal, at paras. 76-7.

[3] There was an alternative argument, somewhat tentatively advanced for the Petitioners, based on Section 5(2) of the Act, to the effect that the banks were 'accustomed to act' on the directions of Perry Corp. There was never any evidence to support this argument, which was ignored by the Judge and rejected by the Court of Appeal: see Court of Appeal, at paras. 193- 201. It does not feature in the Petition, and may no longer be relevant.

[1] Potter J., atpara. 219.

such an agreement or understanding was the most likely explanation for (i) the apparent confidence of Rubicon, and to some extent of the banks and Perry Corp as well, that the shares would be available for repurchase at the term of the swap, and (ii) Perry Corp and Rubicon continuing to behave as if the former were a large shareholder. Rubicon was not, of course, party to the alleged collateral agreement or understanding.

(2) Since the Trial Judge's conclusion turned on inferences from the primary facts, the Court of Appeal was entitled to examine the merits of those inferences for themselves. They rejected the Trial Judge's conclusion for reasons which appear from their long and careful analysis of the evidence. The main points were these. The behaviour of Perry Corp and Rubicon was equally consistent with the former's possession of a substantial economic interest in the performance of Rubicon's shares by virtue of the swap, and with its continuing status as the registered holder of a stake which varied over the relevant period up to a level just under 5%. The shares sold to the banks were in practice 'almost certain' (in the case of UBS) and 'highly likely' (in the case of Deutsche Bank) to be retained for hedging purposes and available for repurchase at term, whether or not the alleged collateral arrangement or understanding existed.[2] So the facts from which the Trial Judge inferred that there was an arrangement or understanding were equally consistent with the opposite inference.[3] The Court of Appeal also pointed out that the Trial Judge had quite unjustifiably ignored the important evidence given by Mr. Cohen of Deutsche Bank and and Mr. Gray of UBS. They had no axe to grind, and their evidence was quite inconsistent with there having been any such collateral agreement as the Petitioners alleged.[1]

(3) In the Court of Appeal, the Petitioners ran an alternative argument, which they had previously disavowed, that although a swap transaction for cash settlement did not in itself confer a power over shares, nevertheless if it was 'inevitable' that the shares would in practice be available for repurchase at the term of the swap, that was enough to establish (apparently as a matter

---

[2] Court of Appeal, paras. 62-66.

[3] See, in particular, Court of Appeal, at para. 132.

[1] Court of Appeal, paras. 164-82. Mr. Cohen and Mr. Gray both gave evidence that their banks had not, and on principle never would, enter into a collateral agreement with a swap counterparty relating to its internal risk-hedging processes. Deutsche Bank and UBS followed the ordinary banking practice of separating the swap dealing function from the function of holding and dealing in physical securities. Thus at Deutsche Bank, Mr. Cohen knew nothing about any deal with Perry Corp about the repurchase of Rubicon stock. He would have had to know of such an arrangement or understanding if it had existed, since he was responsible for custody of and dealings in securities held by the bank for hedging purposes and would have regarded himself as being at liberty to deal with them by way of, for example, stock-lending. In fact, when Perry Corp sought to repurchase the shares at the termination of the swap the bank officials involved did not assume that the shares were available but had to enquire of Mr. Cohen whether they were.

of fact) the existence of a relevant arrangement or understanding. This was said to follow even if there was no overt exchange at all between Perry Corp and the banks.[2] This argument received short shrift in the Court of Appeal.[3]

7. It should be noted that there is no longer any claim by the Petitioners to damages. The Judge found that they had suffered none, because 'GPG was not a victim of market price distortion to which Section 34 is directed.' The price which they paid for their shares was unaffected, and they would have done nothing different if they had known what the Judge regarded as the full facts.[4] The Petitioners did not appeal these findings to the Court of Appeal and they are therefore common ground before Your Lordships.

POINT (1): APPEAL AS OF RIGHT

8. The ground on which leave is sought as of right is that the appeal 'involves, directly or indirectly, some claim or question to or respecting property or some civil right amounting to or of the value of five thousand New Zealand dollars or upwards': see Rule 2(a) of the Order in Council.

9. It has been settled law for many years that Rule 2(a) means that the Petitioner himself must, directly or indirectly, have an interest at stake worth NZ$5,000, to which the claim, question or civil right relates. The judgment appealed from must be considered 'as it affects the interests of the party who is prejudiced by it, and who seeks to relieve himself from it by appeal': *Macfarlane v. Lechdre* (1862) 15 Moo. P.C. 181, 187 [15 ER 462, 465]; *Allan v. Pratt* (1888) 13 App. Cas. 780, 781-2; *Meghji Lkhamshi & Brothers v. Furniture Workshop* [1954] AC 80, 87-8; *Fletcher v. Income Tax Commissioner* [1972] AC 414, 419. The fact that the Petitioner may have an important and valuable business interest in the outcome makes no difference unless that interest is itself the subject-matter of the proposed appeal: *Royal Hong Kong Jockey Club v. Miers* [1983] 1 WLR 1049, 1053-4.

10. In the present case:

   (1) There is a question, and arguably a claim (to relief), but there is no civil right.

   (2) The question or claim to relief relates to shares which belonged at the relevant time to the banks but over which Perry Corp is said to have had a power of disposal. They are worth more than

---

[2] See Court of Appeal, at para. 54.
[3] Court of Appeal, para. 78.
[4] Potter J., at paras. 246-59, esp. paras. 250, 254, 256.

NZ$5,000, but no pecuniary interest of the Petitioners relating to those shares turns on the outcome of the appeal.

(3) The Petitioners have their own shares, which they say will be worth more if Perry Corp's holding is forfeited. But there is no question or claim at all relating to the Petitioners' shares.

(4) These points may be tested by supposing that the Securities Commission had brought the proceedings. They could not have claimed to have an interest at stake worth NZ$5,000. Once the Petitioners' claim to damages fell by the wayside, their position could be no different. The only relief claimed now is relief of an essentially public law nature.

11. There is no reason for the Board to shrink from applying these well-established principles. It can always give discretionary leave in a case which really ought to be heard.

POINT (2): NO GENERAL OR PUBLIC IMPORTANCE

12. There is no issue of law.

13. The highest that the Petitioners can put their case is that there is a factual situation which may recur. But the only fact alleged in this case is the existence of a collateral arrangement or understanding between Perry Corp and these two banks that they would be able to buy back the shares at the term of the swap. That question depends on the facts of this case. Your Lordships' findings about it are most unlikely to have any bearing on other cases in which similar allegations are made, on their own facts. It is accepted that the purpose of the statute is to inform the market, and that that is an important public purpose. So far as the Petitioners' affidavits seek to make this point, it is not disputed. But it does not follow that the application of the statute to these facts has any implications for other cases.

14. The only finding of Your Lordships which might have wider ramifications would be a finding that there was a disclosable interest merely by virtue of the fact that the stock was illiquid, so that the bank would be very likely to hold it as a hedge and sell it to the counterparty if the latter wanted to buy. This was the Petitioners' alternative case in the Court of Appeal. However, the Petitioners always accepted, as they were bound to, (i) that it was necessary to prove a consensus to the effect that the shares would be available for repurchase by the counterparty at term, and (ii) that this was not inherent in the mere agreement to settle cash differences.[1] Once these points are accepted, the alternative case adds nothing to the main one. Whether there was a consensus going beyond the agreement to settle cash differences can

---

[1] The need for consensus was accepted by the petitioners at the trial, as the Judge recorded: Judgment, para. 43. It is clear from her analysis of the authorities at paras. 31-44 that she also accepted it. So did the Court of Appeal, at paras. 68-75, esp. para. 73.

only depend on the facts of the particular case. A commercial likelihood, however great, is manifestly not the same as a consensus.

15. It is right to add that whatever arguments the Petitioners may wish to try out on Your Lordships, the Court of Appeal has gone out of its way to explain that its own decision was specific to the facts of this case. It cannot therefore he suggested that consequences of any general or public importance will follow from a decision to dismiss the Petition and leave matters where they presently stand.

POINT (3): UNDESIRABILITY OF SUCCESSIVE APPEALS

16. In principle, it is submitted that this is the kind of case in which a further appeal is particularly undesirable. Perry Corp purchased the Rubicon shares from the banks nearly two years ago, in a transaction which was prima facie lawful. The continuance of the dispute leaves it uncertain who is entitled to exercise practical control or substantial influence over the affairs of a public company. The proper regulation of the securities markets requires prompt and final decisions, particularly where the forfeiture of substantial shareholdings may be involved. This is so, not just in the interest of Perry Corp as a user of the New Zealand securities markets, but in that of Rubicon and the investing public at large. The original trial and the appeal to the Court of Appeal were both expedited for these reasons. A second tier of appeal by way of rehearing of the same arguments on the same facts, in circumstances such as these, would be contrary to good regulation and to the public interest.

POINT (4): LACK OF MERIT

17. The proposed appeal has, frankly, no realistic prospect of success. It depends on the Petitioners being able to persuade Your Lordships on the substantive hearing of an appeal, that a unanimous decision of a full court of the Court of Appeal was wrong. They would have to discharge that burden in circumstances where (i) it is not suggested that there was any direct evidence of an agreement, arrangement or understanding, (ii) the principal parties to the alleged collusion have denied it, (iii) the undisputed facts were that the shares sold to the banks were likely in practice to be available for repurchase whether there was an agreement to that effect or not. The Respondents can do no better than refer to the reasoning of the Court of Appeal.[1]

18. Most developed securities markets have some form of obligation to disclose substantial holdings of a company's voting stock. Equity swaps for cash settlement are routine transactions in all such

---

[1] See, in particular, Court of Appeal, paras. 79-192.

markets.[2] Yet in none of them are such transactions treated as giving rise to an interest in or power over shares held by the bank counterparty to hedge its position, except for Hong Kong, where there is a statutory rule to that effect. If New Zealand is to go out on a limb, by adopting as a matter of common law some different approach to an established financial instrument, then it would have to do so for locally compelling reasons. Questions of policy of this sort are very much matters for the courts of New Zealand. Yet the Trial Judge did not adopt this course, and the Court of Appeal expressly refused to do so.[1]

POINT (4): NO CASE FOR INTERIM RELIEF

19. The Petitioners have failed to establish that they suffered any recoverable loss, and now accept that. They are therefore in reality prosecuting these proceedings by way of enforcement of public law, in circumstances where they cannot assert any right, entitlement or interest of their own which falls to be protected by an interim order. Their case is simply that Perry Corp should be prevented from selling the shares which they bought back from the banks at the termination of the swap, so that the penal power of forfeiture will still be available if the appeal is allowed.

20. An interim order restraining the disposal by Perry Corp of its shares would deprive them of the ability to exercise a proprietary right, which it is not disputed that they have. That is a serious infringement of their rights which would be liable to cause them substantial losses, whereas the refusal of interim relief would cause no loss to the Petitioners.

21. The Petitioners say that they would benefit by the forfeiture of Perry Corp's shares because the proportion of Rubicon's equity represented by the Petitioners' holding would increase. It does not require much commercial cynicism to perceive that the Petitioners' real purposes are (i) to exercise an increased degree of practical control by virtue of their own holding, and (ii) to have something to trade in a settlement. These are collateral purposes which form no part of the public interest underlying the power of forfeiture.

---

[1] See Potter J. al para. 63, and Court of Appeal, at para. 77. Hong Kong appears to be the only market which has sought to extend disclosure obligations to purely economic interests derived from derivatives transactions.

[2] See Court of Appeal, at paras. 76-7.

GOOD PRACTICE SUGGESTION

- Structure of argument[17]
  When forming your arguments on paper start from the end, your desired conclusion, and shape your argument so as to arrive there.

  Like the use of language, or the development of a style of writing, the way in which advocates structure their arguments is too eclectic to draw any general conclusions. The factors which influence how an argument is prepared are variable and may depend on the type of proceeding and place in it at which the parties have arrived, which party is being represented, the tribunal before whom the advocate will appear, the level of court, how specialised is the area of practice, and even the time available. What has been possible for senior practitioners to provide is guidance, in the form of worthwhile tips concerning their various approaches to preparing argument:

- You must deal with every issue that is live. If it is peripheral say so.

- When preparing argument clear your mind and focus on the logical detail. It is a useful exercise in self-discipline to establish the logical order to the argument or its ordered progression. This can be done in a number of ways, but all are based on progressive development where points are taken consecutively, thus

  Merits > solutions > law > facts

  or if a legal framework dictates

  duty > breach > causation > damage

  Consecutive steps may be taken by using the chronology, the key to building arguments, or otherwise by headings. If you deal with issues chronologically do so point by point as they arise, rather than advancing your best point first.

---

[17] See also Examples F and J.

CHAPTER 10

CONCLUSION: 15 KEY POINTS TO WRITING A SUCCESSFUL SKELETON

Here is a simple truth. Preparing a skeleton argument is not a chore to be put up with. It is not a mechanical process devoid of thought and proper attention. It is not a waste of time simply because argument will have to be prepared again for the hearing itself. It is an opportunity to sway the mind of the tribunal in favour of the client and against that of an opponent before the advocate opens his mouth.

It is an extraordinary opportunity, and one not to be thrown away. Counsel can grab the Judge's attention; can earn his gratitude for showing him the way into the case; can capture his interest; and can create a momentum with written argument that makes his case appear right and obvious and irresistible. If an advocate applies himself properly to the task, he can get more than half way to winning before he arrives at court.

This is what the most successful advocates have learned and understand. It means they have a reasonable chance – nearly one in two – of succeeding on appeal without being called upon to argue their case orally. It means that a trial Judge will lean in their favour, either consciously or subconsciously, from the outset of the proceedings. It gives counsel who are skilled in expressing themselves in writing an edge in interim applications. And they do it by the skilful preparation of, and application of thought to, their skeletons.

There are key points to be found in all successful skeleton arguments, irrespective of their intended use or the style of the writer. Here are 15 of the most effective:

1. Engage the Judge by giving him a way into the case.
2. Persuade him you have an overview that makes sense.
3. Make him feel confident that you have given considerable thought to the document, that he can use it and come back to it.
4. Ensure that it is completely accurate and reliable as to the facts.
5. Make it as short as the subject matter permits.
6. Always start with what the hearing is for.

7. Describe briefly in the first paragraph what the dispute is about, and roughly what your client says.
8. Say something reasonably interesting about the case within the first two paragraphs.
9. Tell a good, easy-to-follow story using uncontentious facts or propositions in such a way as to make your client's case appear irresistible.
10. Try and keep the language low key.
11. Get to the heart of the matter very quickly.
12. Take every live point and tell the Judge everything he needs to know, but no more.
13. Do not bore the reader.
14. Try to give the impression there is no sensible view to reach other than your own.
15. Your overall perceived intention should be to 'help' rather than persuade, so that Judge forgets you are trying to win the case. Be seen more as a judicial assistant than a partisan figure.

PART 4
WRITTEN ADVOCACY
OUTSIDE THE COURTS

CHAPTER 11

INTER-PARTES CORRESPONDENCE: THE 'DEAR JUDGE' LETTER

Less than ten percent of all claims or disputes result in proceedings being issued. And less than two per cent of issued claims go to trial. So, in over ninety eight per cent of claims, either liability is conceded and the case settles, or the claim is withdrawn. Invariably the defendant or the claimant, respectively, is persuaded of the merits or demerits of the claim in the course of *inter-partes* correspondence. This provides a tremendous opportunity to develop and practice written advocacy skills: every litigation solicitor should have a firm grasp of the tactics of adversarial writing, and the use of language to persuade. English is particularly well suited to be a language of debate, with its diversity of meaning, nuances, subtleties and tone, and the quaintness of professional jargon.

Practitioners rarely have time to really polish and hone their correspondence, but a well-phrased and well-timed letter can have a devastating effect on the confidence of the other side. It may also have a significant impact on the judicial reader who will come upon it months, or perhaps even years after it has been written, and who will evaluate its importance in the context of the dispute as a whole. That evaluation may have a significant bearing on the outcome of the claim, either substantively or on the question of costs. As a consequence every letter that you write to the other side should be composed with one eye on how it will read to a judge.

This can be done on two levels: at its highest you can send a positive, subliminal message to the judge. Whatever you may be writing to your opponent you are actually saying, 'Dear Judge, look how I am bending over backwards to explain to the other side the merits of my client's case as clearly as possible; look how correct his case is; and look how reasonable he is being in pursuit of his claim' Or conversely you could say, 'Dear Judge, look what the other side are doing: obfuscating a case which is devoid of merit; making us deal with unmeritorious points, and generally acting unreasonably in driving up costs.' This may well impact on the trial judge's view of the merits. It may help him in his quest to do substantive justice. And it may make him less inclined to favour a party of whose conduct he disapproves. At a lower level you are flagging up issues for consideration later when costs come to be considered.

The moral is simple. Write your letter. Make it as forceful or vituperative as you like, but never send it without asking yourself, 'What is the Court going to make of this when the time comes?' It is not a mechanical exercise and may provide very concrete benefits to your client.

Once this activity was conducted only by the astute litigator. Now it should be a feature of universal litigation practice in view of CPR Part 44: the Court is concerned with conduct, with proportionality, and with the parties being seen to act reasonably towards one another and to the Court.

When writing adversarial correspondence these simple tips should be of assistance:-

- *Courtesy* Observe the usual professional courtesies, particularly in titles, mode of address and references to the respective clients and their witnesses. Judges are easily irritated by a failure to do so.
- *Do not use emotive language.* Be business-like. Litigation is not a drama. Overly emotive language may well offend the opposite party and diminish the chance of settlement.
- *Adverbs* Do not argue by adverb: 'clearly', 'obviously', 'undeniably', 'patently', 'undoubtedly,' or use them in a different form e.g. 'it is plain that.' This is precisely the same point as the guidance offered for skeleton arguments.[1] Base your assertions on the facts, with substantive argument by reference to the evidence.
- *Do not assert your opinion.* If you have that of counsel, or of an expert, so be it. Otherwise, confine yourself to the facts, or the law. Let these speak.
- *Argue rationally and logically.* If what you assert does not make sense, or offends common sense or natural justice, it is unlikely to persuade.
- *Be costs conscious always.* This should condition your whole approach to litigation practice.
- *Avoid trench warfare.* Your client has enough on his plate with his own dispute. He does not need the costs and aggravation of you opening up a second front by complaining that the opposing party's lawyers have not complied with this or that particular direction, unless it is vital to his case. You will create an entirely secondary dispute, the costs of which will make the claim that much harder to settle.
- *Always, always, always check grammar and spelling.* Not only are mistakes an irritant and unprofessional, they serve as a great distraction to the reader. Poor spelling may not matter to our present educators, but to your opponent and certainly to a judge it will demean your firm, and your competence will be questioned.

---

[1] See p.38.

CHAPTER 12

PRE-ACTION PROTOCOL LETTERS OF CLAIM AND REPLY

In Chapter 10 of his final report (*Access to Justice* 1996), Lord Woolf said that what was needed was a system which would enable parties to a dispute to embark on meaningful negotiations as soon as the possibility of litigation was identified and to ensure that as early as possible they had the relevant information to define their claim and make realistic offers to settle. Pre-action protocols, he said, "are intended to build on and increase the benefits of early but well informed settlements which genuinely satisfy both parties to disputes".[1]

One of the principal themes of the Civil Procedure Rules 1998 (CPR) was to introduce a "cards on the table" approach, enforced by a penalty costs regime. This had been developing in litigation procedure in the 1990s, especially with the introduction of exchange of witness statements and experts' reports. The courts now expect co-operation between the parties and their legal representatives from an early stage, in disclosing their case in outline in letters of claim and response, and by exchanging information, including key documents.[2]

The structure and timetable for the pre-action provision of information are now contained in the various protocols that inform practitioners of what their case outline should consist. Just because templates are offered the possibility of effective written advocacy is not shut out – rather the contrary. The astute practitioner will enhance the information he is required to provide by making his case persuasive from the very outset. If he is acting for a claimant he will wish to overwhelm. If he acts for a defendant his reply will try to disappoint the claimant, at least to the extent of deflating his expectation. The earlier this is done, the greater the cost saving in the long run.

---

[1] *White Book* Vol 2. C1A-001.
[2] C1A-002.

And it is entirely proper to do this, since it accords with the policy of the CPR:

- to focus the attention of litigants on the desirability of resolving disputes without litigation;
- to enable them to obtain information they reasonably need in order to enter an appropriate settlement;
- to make an appropriate offer (of a kind which can have costs consequences if litigation ensues);
- if pre-action settlement is not achievable, to lay the ground for expeditious conduct of proceedings;
- to define and narrow the issues in dispute before proceedings are issued so that the case can be allocated to a track, a timetable set for the disclosure of evidence and the trial at an early case management stage.

Even where protocols do not currently apply it is still good practice for the claimant to send a detailed letter of claim to the prospective defendant and to wait a reasonable period for the defendant to respond before issuing proceedings. This is entirely consistent with the expectation of the Court. CPR r.1.1 (2) and paragraphs 4.1–4.7.

Make it clear that the approach to all disputes in future should be:

- The claimant to write a reasonably detailed and self-contained letter of claim, enclosing copies of essential documents and asking for those in the defendant's possession.
- The claimant to set a reasonable timetable in the letter for the defendant to admit or deny liability, (one month is suggested for many claims).
- The defendant to acknowledge the letter within 21 days and reply within the suggested timescale if possible or as a minimum explain steps that are being taken to look into the matter and when a full reply is likely to be possible.
- The defendant's reply should accept the claim and make proposals for settlement, or if disputing the claim explain why and enclose essential documents.
- Both parties should reply to the other's reasonable requests for further information.
- Both parties should show a willingness to consider a settlement, including mediation or other form of ADR.
- The specimen letters of claim and templates for letter of claim and response in the personal injury, clinical disputes and judicial review protocols could be adapted for other types of disputes.

Failing to send a letter of claim at all is unreasonable conduct, which will invariably attract a sanction.[3]

At the time of writing, pre-action protocols are in force for personal injuries, clinical negligence, construction and engineering disputes, defamation, professional negligence, judicial review, industrial diseases and housing disrepair claims. The personal injury protocol is primarily designed for those road traffic, tripping and slipping and accident at work cases which include an element of personal injury with a value of less than £15,000 that are likely to be allocated to the fast track. However, the "cards on the table" approach advocated by the protocol is equally appropriate to some higher value claims, particularly in respect of letters before action, exchanging information and documents and agreeing experts.

Each of the protocols provides for early notification. The claimant's solicitor may wish to put the defendant and/or his insurer on notice of a claim as soon as they know it is likely to be made, but before they are able to send a detailed letter of claim, particularly for instance, when the defendant has no or limited knowledge of the incident giving rise to the claim or where the claimant is incurring significant expenditure as a result, for example, of the accident which he hopes the defendant might pay for, in whole or in part. The personal injury, clinical negligence and judicial review protocols provide specimen letters of claim at Annex A to C2–005 of the *White Book*.

C2–007 deals with the status of letters of claim and response. These are not intended to have the same status as a statement of case in proceedings since matters may come to light as a result of investigation after the letter of claim has been sent, or after the defendant has responded, particularly if disclosure of documents takes place outside the recommended three-month period. These circumstances could mean that the "pleaded" case of one or both parties is presented slightly differently than in the letter of claim and response. It would not be consistent with the spirit of the protocol for a party to "take a point" on this in the proceedings, provided that there was no obvious intention by the party who changed their position to mislead the other party.

Under the protocol letter of claim for personal injury the claimant has to set out a clear summary of the facts on which the claim is based together with an indication of the nature of any injuries suffered and of any financial loss incurred. In cases of road traffic accidents, the letter should provide the name and address of the hospital where treatment has been obtained and the claimant's hospital reference number. The letter should ask for details of the insurer and that a copy should be sent by the proposed defendant to the

---

[3] *Phoenix Finance v. Federation International L' Automobile* [2002] EWHC 1028 (Ch); *Taylor v. D Coach Hire* (2000) CL November 3; *Northfield v. DSM (Southern) Ltd* [2000] C.L.Y. 461; *Linton v. Williams Haulage Ltd* [2001] C.L.Y. 516

insurer where appropriate. Sufficient information should be given in order to enable the defendant's insurer/solicitor to commence investigations and at least put a broad valuation on the "risk". If the defendant denies liability, he should enclose with the letter of reply, documents in his possession which are material to the issues between the parties, and which would be likely to be ordered to be disclosed by the court, either on an application for pre-action disclosure, or on disclosure during proceedings.[4] Where the defendant admits primary liability, but alleges contributory negligence by the claimant, the defendant should give reasons supporting those allegations. Where the defendant admits liability in whole or in part, before proceedings are issued, any medical report obtained by agreement under this protocol should be disclosed to the other party. The claimant should delay issuing proceedings for 21 days from disclosure of the report, to enable the parties to consider whether the claim is capable of settlement.

The C2–016 Annex A Letter of Claim set out below (and modified for use in clinical negligence and judicial review claims) is fairly skeletal, and therefore provides considerable scope for enhancement by the solicitor who wants to persuade insurers from the outset that there is little prospect of contesting liability or raising contributory negligence.

Dear Sirs

Re: Claimant's full name
    Claimant's full address
    Claimant's Clock or Works Number
    Claimant's Employer (name and address)

We are instructed by the above named to claim damages in connection with an accident at work/road traffic accident/tripping accident on day of (year) at (place of accident which must be sufficiently detailed to establish location).

Please confirm the identity of your insurers. Please note that the insurers will need to see this letter as soon as possible and it may affect your insurance cover and/or the conduct of any subsequent legal proceedings if you do not send this letter to them.

The circumstances of the accident are:
(brief outline)

The reason why we are alleging fault is:
(simple explanation, e.g. defective machine, broken ground)

---

[4] Para 3-10, Personal Injury Pre-action Protocol.

A description of our clients' injuries is as follows:
(brief outline)

(In cases of road traffic accidents)
Our client (state hospital reference number) received treatment for the injuries at (name and address of hospital).

He is employed as (occupation) and has had the following time off work (dates of absence). His approximate weekly income is (insert if known).

If you are our client's employers, please provide us with the usual earnings details which will enable us to calculate his financial loss.

We are obtaining a police report and will let you have a copy of the same upon your undertaking to meet half the fee.

We have also sent a letter of claim to (name and address) and a copy of that letter is attached. We understand their insurers are (name, address and claims number if known).

At this stage of our enquiries we would expect the documents contained in parts (insert appropriate parts of standard disclosure list) to be relevant to this action.

A copy of this letter is attached for you to send to your insurers. Finally we expect an acknowledgment of this letter within 21 days by yourselves or your insurers.

Yours faithfully

The clinical negligence letter of claim should, in more complex cases, include a chronology of the relevant events particularly if the patient has been treated by a number of different healthcare providers, and refer to any relevant documents, including health records. Sufficient information must be given to enable the healthcare provider defendant to commence investigations and to put an initial valuation on the claim. By Part C3–023 Annex C the template for the clinical negligence letter of claim lists its essential contents as:

1. Client's name, address, date of birth, etc.;
2. Dates of allegedly negligent treatment;
3. Events giving rise to the claim;
4. Allegation of negligence and causal link with injuries;
5. The Client's injuries, condition and future prognosis;
6. Request for clinical records (if not previously provided);
7. The likely value of the claim.

Optional information which may be provided includes what investigations have been carried out, suggestions for obtaining expert evidence, suggestions for meetings, negotiations, discussion or mediation and an offer to settle made without supporting evidence.

The Construction and Engineering Protocol applies to all construction and engineering disputes and must be read in conjunction with CPR Part 60 (Technology and Construction Court claims). It includes professional negligence disputes against building professionals. A feature of the pre-action correspondence is that the claimant is required to include the remedy sought and details of how it has been calculated. The letter of claim must state the principal contractual terms and statutory provisions relied on and the nature of the relief claimed: if damages are claimed, a breakdown showing how the damages have been quantified; if a sum is claimed pursuant to a contract, how it has been calculated; and if an extension of time is claimed, the period claimed.

The Defamation Protocol should be read with CPR Part 53 (Defamation Claims). The letter of claim should identify specifically the publication, words, inaccuracies or unsupportable comments to which the claimant objects, together with any special facts with regard to the interpretation or meaning of the words or in relation to the damage caused. Where possible, a copy or transcript of the words complained of should be enclosed. The defendant is required to respond to the letter of claim as soon as possible, preferably within 14 days and must either admit liability and offer a remedy, or deny the claim and give reasons.

The Professional Negligence Pre-action Protocol[5] requires that the letters of claim and response should be detailed and "open", i.e. not without prejudice; the letter of claim should include a chronology and enclose key documents, should particularise the allegations of negligence and explain how they have caused the loss, which should be calculated (and supporting documents should be enclosed) and should identify any experts appointed. The defendant may send a separate letter of settlement on a without prejudice basis with the letter of response.

The letter of claim should state:

(a) The identity of any other parties involved in the dispute or a related dispute.
(b) A clear chronological summary (including key dates) of the facts on which the claim is based. Key documents should be identified, copied and enclosed.

---

[5] C7A–001; see also Guidance Note C3.1.

(c) The allegations against the professional. What has he done wrong? What has he failed to do?

(d) An explanation of how the alleged error has caused the loss claimed.

(e) An estimate of the financial loss suffered by the claimant and how it is calculated. Supporting documents should be identified, copied and enclosed. If details of the financial loss cannot be supplied, the claimant should explain why and should state when he will be in a position to provide the details. This information should be sent to the professional as soon as reasonably possible. If the claimant is seeking some form of non-financial redress, this should be made clear.

(f) Confirmation whether or not an expert has been appointed. If so, providing the identity and discipline of the expert, together with the date upon which the expert was appointed.

(g) A request that a copy of the letter of claim be forwarded immediately to the professional's insurers, if any.

The letters of response and settlement can be contained within a single letter. It should contain a reasoned answer to the claimant's allegations:

(a) if the claim is admitted the professional should say so in clear terms;

(b) if only part of the claim is admitted the professional should make clear which parts of the claim are admitted and which are denied;

(c) if the claim is denied in whole or in part, the letter of response should include specific comments on the allegations against the professional and, if the claimant's version of events is disputed, the professional should provide his version of events;

(d) if the professional is unable to admit or deny the claim, the professional should identify any further information which is required;

(e) if the professional disputes the estimate of the claimant's financial loss, the letter of response should set out the professional's estimate. If an estimate cannot be provided, the professional should explain why and should state when he will be in a position to provide an estimate. This information should be sent to the claimant as soon as reasonably possible;

(f) where additional documents are relied upon, copies should be provided.

A separate letter of settlement will normally be a without prejudice letter and should be sent if the professional intends to make proposals for early settlement. It should set out the professional's views to date on the claim identifying those issues which the professional believes are likely to remain in dispute and those that are not and make a settlement proposal or identify any further information that is required before the professional can formulate proposals.

The Judicial Review Pre-action Protocol letter before claim should contain the date and details of the decision, act or omission being challenged and a clear summary of the facts on which the claim is based. It should also contain the details of any relevant information that the claimant is seeking and an explanation of why this is considered relevant. C8–002 Annex A provides a standard template.

The Housing Disrepair protocol[6] requires an early notification letter to be sent to the landlord giving:

(i)   the tenant's name, the address of the property, tenant's address if different, tenant's telephone number and when access is available;
(ii) details of the defects, including any defects outstanding, in the form of a schedule, if appropriate;
(iii) details of any notification previously given to the landlord of the need for repair or information as to why the tenant believes that the landlord has knowledge of the need for repair;
(iv) the identity of a proposed expert and proposed letter of instruction;
(v)   the tenant's disclosure of such relevant documents as are readily available.

This is to be followed by a letter of claim which should provide any information not already given together with the effect of the defects on the tenant and details of any special damages.

Templates for letters in the hands of experienced advocates should be like bare clay to a sculptor, ready to absorb his creativity. In producing this correspondence you have a choice. You can make it an information giving exercise, or, by applying your mind, you may turn what is a requirement into an important opportunity to create an instrument of persuasion.

---

[6]   C10A–001.

CHAPTER 13
PART 36 OFFERS

The formal regime for offers to settle claims, whether or not upon the basis of payments being made into court, is set out in CPR Part 36. The form and content of Part 36 offers are set out in CPR Part 36.5. Such an offer:

(1) must be in writing;
(2) may relate to the whole claim or to part of it or to any issue that arises in it; and
(3) must

    (a) state whether it relates to the whole of the claim or to part of it or to an issue that arises in it and if so to which part or issue;
    (b) state whether it takes into account any counterclaim; and
    (c) if it is expressed not to be inclusive of interest, give the details relating to interest set out in rule 36.22(2).

The offer must be clear, and must comply with the provisions of r.36.5(3) to be effective. If the offer is insufficiently clear the recipient can apply for clarification under r.36.9

Rule 36.10 enables the Court to take into account an offer to settle made by any party before the commencement of proceedings.

Both of these provisions create scope for effective written advocacy by the practitioner who is tactically astute, irrespective of which side he represents. The trick is to measure to a nicety the minimum amount that the claimant is likely to accept in satisfaction of his claim. From the claimant's point of view it is what he will settle for to avoid the risk and costs consequences of proceeding further; for the defendant, it is that sum which will adequately pressurise the claimant to walk away or otherwise risk a Pyrrhic victory.

Where advocacy comes in is to persuade the other side that the sum offered is, on the one hand (i.e. acting for the claimant), the right amount to pay, and on the other (acting for the defendant), the best amount achievable with the minimum of risk and inconvenience. To be successful at doing so the practitioner who devises and settles a Part 36 offer must have certain qualities. He should:

- be confident in, and realistic about, his own case;
- be able to hold his nerve;
- be able to assess and explain the risk in the litigation, and to convey that risk to other side; and
- be analytical and unemotional.

When you convey your Part 36 offer to the other side to make it effective:

(a) Use language that is flat, fact based and business like.
(b) Convince your opponent that the offer will not change.
(c) Justify the figure offered by reference to either (i) the perceived litigation risk or (ii) some factual or legal impairment that you think will damage or undermine the other side's case or (iii) some particular fact in your own case.
(d) Wherever possible offer the figure as a reasoned mathematical calculation.
(e) Do not just provide a figure with no explanation or justification.
(f) Always break down the claim into its component parts to attribute value, or lack of it.
(g) Do not criticise the claimant or defendant on a personal level, or his lawyers.
(h) Take into account interest and deal with it – both as to liability and quantum.
(i) Prepare to be questioned about your assessment of risk.
(j) Do not try to bluff or exaggerate – if you have a weak case grasp the nettle – nuisance value is also a useful negotiating tool.
(k) Deal with the adverse costs consequences of a refusal in real terms i.e. with reasonably accurate costs projections being given.

Remember that you have two aims that must be balanced. First, you wish to cause your opponent to despair about his case, or an aspect of it. Second, you must identify the minimum amount of money on the table which will enable your client either to accept a payment with good grace, or to buy off the other side as cheaply as possible, and in either case you must be able to persuade him that this is the right sum.

CHAPTER 14
WORKED EXAMPLES

I am grateful to those firms of solicitors and their lay clients who have granted permission for me to reproduce, in anonymised form, letters before action and replies, drawn from real claims. They are detailed, fact orientated, unemotional and businesslike. Both claims and defences are particularised, and in three cases authority supports the material contentions.

They are not produced here as models or precedents, but to demonstrate the adversarial nature of correspondence. All seek to persuade the recipient that their client's position is both correct and reasonable and, as important if not more so, (a) to dissuade the other side from taking further steps towards or within the litigation and (b) to recognise the adverse costs implications of doing so. The detail makes these examples lengthy. But the facts are used either to justify threatening proceedings or to stop a potential claim in its tracks. Such advocacy within correspondence is a key part of negotiation, and, should it subsequently have to make an award of costs, an important feature of the Court's consideration under CPR Part 44 of the parties' behaviour.

As in Part 3, 'Good Practice Suggestions' are provided at the end of each example, for use by experienced practitioners as much as a checklist of what they ordinarily do as an encouragement to develop an effective adversarial style of writing.

EXAMPLE P

Letter of claim combined with claimant's pre-action Part 36 offer under the Professional Negligence Pre-Action Protocol and CPR Parts 3.1(4) and 5, and 44.3(5)(a). This was a claim brought against solicitors for breach of retainer arising from the sale of a property by the claimant, in which it was advised wrongly that it could, without risk, rescind a contract of sale with a purchaser and retain the deposit, and then exchange contracts for sale with a second purchaser.

The detailed history of the complaint is set out. Core documents are sent in a bundle attaching to the letter, thus providing pre-action disclosure at the earliest opportunity. A list of *dramatis personae* is included. Liability and causation are addressed separately and in depth with a view to snuffing out the possibility of a defence. As much detail of the heads of damage available is provided, together with supporting documents, to lay the ground for an early Part 36 offer, the quantum of which can be justified on the claimant's case.

The language used is non-emotive, fact-drive and therefore rather understated.

The claim settled before the issue of proceedings.

Dear Sirs

ABC Limited trading as Fleet Street Homes
Re: 1 Kings Road, London, W27

We refer to our letter of 5 April, 2004.

We act for the above-named company which has instructed us to bring a claim for damages for breach of professional retainer against your firm. This letter is written in accordance with the Professional Negligence Pre-Action Protocol and CPR Parts 3.1(4) and 5, and 44.3(5)(a). We respectfully suggest that you pass it without delay to your professional indemnity insurers.

We further invite you to note our client's offer of settlement in connection with this matter. To that end this letter should also be treated as an offer made in accordance with CPR Part 36.10(1).

In order to assist your early investigation of our client's claim we append herewith a paginated bundle of documents to which reference is made thus '[1]' in the body of this letter. For your ease of reference we have also numbered the substantive paragraphs of this letter.

Background

1. In early May 2002 your firm was instructed to examine information concerning a property at auction and on 13th or 14th May 2002 after the auction your firm by Mr Z was instructed by Mr B, the managing director of our client, who is also an architect in private professional practice, to convey the purchase by our client of property at 1 Kings Road, London, W27 which was acquired at the FPD Savills' auction on 13 May, 2002. The purchase price was provided by Mr and Mrs B and a group of private investors, with the balance by way of bridging

finance. Mr Z was also instructed to convey the mortgage. By a letter dated 19 May 2002 [1-2] Mr Z was given instructions about the investment arrangements. By a letter dated 27 May 2002 [3-4] Mr Z advised our client that a trust fund should be created into which the various investors place monies for the company to purchase property and carry out development. He also prepared an outline document and timetable [5-8] entitled 'Notes Regarding Legal Documentation for Fleet Street Purchase and Development of 1 Kings Road, London W.27.' It will be seen from this that Mr Z advised the settling of a trust deed and a second legal charge which would be registered against the property to protect the interests of the investors.

2. We are instructed that Mr Z was made aware that this project was intended by the company and its investors to be the first of a series of property development ventures specialising in 'backland' or 'small brownfield' sites using bridging finance.

3. The declaration of trust was settled by Mr Z and executed [9-15] on 16 September 2002. Although he settled a second charge we are instructed that it was never registered; fortunately we have been unable to ascertain any loss flowing from such failure.

4. In December, 2002 a buyer, OP Properties Ltd afterwards COD Properties Limited, was found for the property and on 20 December the sale was agreed in the sum of £500,000. We are instructed that the seller agreed to sell to OP Properties as apparently it did not require finance and could complete quickly. We append a copy of Mr Z's attendance note record [16] of that date.

5. On or about 8 January 2003 your firm by Mr Z was retained by our client to conduct the conveyance of the sale and redeem the mortgage on the property. We append a copy of the estate agent's letter of 7 January and memorandum [17,18] and three letters dated 9 January 2003 from Mr Z to our client [19], the mortgagee [20] and the agent [21], and his letter dated 13 January 2003 [22] to the buyer's solicitor. We regret that we have been unable to find any client care letter passing from Mr Z to our client in respect of this instruction in compliance with Practice Rule 15 (13.02.7 of the Guide to Professional Conduct of Solicitors, 8th Edition) and the OSS Client Care Guide for Solicitors. If one exists no doubt you will forward it to us in due course.

6. Our client's claim derives from the negligent conduct by Mr Z of this piece of conveyancing, and in particular the advice, or lack of it, provided by him to our client in May, 2003 which, we are instructed, has caused our client recoverable loss. To that end we consider it may be of assistance to you in your investigation to set out the dramatis personae involved in the subject matter of our client's complaint:

Dramatis Personae

BEE	Mortgagee's solicitors
Fleet Street Homes	Trading name of seller
B,	Seller's director
Z,	Seller's conveyancer
COD Properties Ltd	Buyer
HD	Seller's agent
Hoxtons	Seller's estate agents
L Mortgage Corporation Ltd	Mortgagee
KH	Third party buyer
KD	Buyer's conveyancer
KS	Buyer's conveyancing solicitors
ABC Ltd	Seller
MG	Seller's counsel
PA	Buyer's conveyancing assistant
OP Properties Ltd	Buyer's former name
RHY	Third party buyer's solicitors
RI	Seller's litigator
Ss	Buyer's litigation solicitors

The Claim

7. On 10 March, 2003 contracts for the sale of the property were ex-changed in accordance with Law Society Formula B with completion on 22 April, 2003 (Mr Z's attendance note of 7 March [23] and letter of 11 March [24] refers). However, notwithstanding the fact that the seller was ready willing and able to complete on that date, the buyer was not. We are instructed that Mr B of our client sought specific advice from Mr Z by telephone as to what the seller's options were, and that Mr Z rang him back after he himself had sought advice from a col-league, to say that the seller should either wait and see what transpired or serve a notice to complete under the terms of the contract. Having explained to Mr B what such a notice was, Mr Z was instructed to serve one upon COD Properties' solicitors, KS.

8. We should make the point at this stage that in our view, and that of counsel, the attendance records kept by Mr Z are entirely unsatisfac-tory in respect of this transaction. The attendance notes are incomplete, and in any event appear to be simply lists of telephone messages. This is best illustrated from the fact that over the period 22, 23, 24 April, 2003 Mr Z's lists of messages [25, 26, 27] does not record the fact that the buyer had failed to complete, or any conversation prior to 24 April which states that Mr B was so informed. Since a Notice to Complete under condition 6.8 of the Standard Commercial Property Conditions of Sale (1st Edition) was served on 23 April [28] this strongly suggests that the telephone conversations between Mr B and Mr Z outlined

above went unrecorded. Certainly it appears that any advice provided to Mr B was not reduced to writing and sent by letter which is a feature of Mr Z's conduct throughout.

9. On 28 April, 2003 your firm recorded a telephone message note [29] from AP say that the buyer was not ready to complete because it was awaiting a report from its bank's surveyor. On 1 May the List of Messages [30] shows that Mr K telephoned to say that the buyer's mortgagees had down-valued the site and confirmed that the buyer needed finance. On 6 May the List of Messages [31] indicates that Mr B instructed Mr Z that unless the buyer completed by Friday 9th May, 2003 the property would be put back on the market.

10. We are instructed that Mr Z was so instructed as a result of advice which Mr B sought from Mr Z, namely what was the position of the seller if the buyer failed to comply with the notice to complete. Mr Z advised Mr B that if COD Properties did not complete *the seller could rescind the contract at any time* and forfeit the buyer's deposit. We understand that this advice was repeated orally by Mr Z on either three or four occasions between 6 May and 23 May 2003. Although it was not reduced to writing by Mr Z support for the assertion that this is the advice which was given is to be found in paragraph 30 of the witness statement prepared for Mr B by Mr R of your firm in the ensuing litigation, both in its draft form prepared 29th October 2003 [32-40] and in its final form signed under a statement of truth dated 21 November, 2003 [41-49]. We flag up at this stage that the advice given was not qualified in any way.

11. On 8 May the buyer sought, and on 9 May the seller agreed that there would be an extension of time for the expiry of the notice to complete until 4.00 p.m. on Friday, 16 May, 2003 upon payment of a further sum of £10,000 by way of deposit (the letter of 9 May, 2003 from KS refers [50].) In fact this sum was not sent.

12. We are instructed that Mr B sought specific advice from Mr Z should the buyer fail to complete by close of business on 16 May. Mr Z explained that the seller could bring an action for specific performance but an action against a company with limited funds would result in a judgment being fruitless. Mr B asked Mr Z to explain the meaning of rescission, a word with which he was not familiar, and was informed that it was the cancelling of the contract for the failure of the other side to meet its obligations; and that the seller could keep the deposit and sue for damages. Mr B informed Mr Z that the seller's expenses on the sale were between £30,000 and £35,000 and asked whether he was sure that the entire deposit of £50,000 could be kept, since if that were so the seller would not sue for any additional damages. Mr B was aware that during the day on 16 May a revised completion statement was sent to KS, and that an agreement had been reached on estate agents' fees by him directly with Mr H.

13. We are instructed that Mr B gave no instructions to Mr Z between 16 May and 20 May, 2003. This would appear to be born out by the absence of any listed telephone records or any notes in writing that we have seen.

14. On Monday 19 May the seller placed the property back on the market at the same price as previously agreed with COD Properties. Mr B telephoned a number of agents on 19 and Tuesday 20 May and the seller received offers to purchase almost immediately. On 21 May the seller held a confirmed offer to purchase from a Mr KH for £500,000.

15. It transpires from Mr Z's List of Messages dated 20 and 21 May, 2003 [51, 52] that Mr Z was continuing to make arrangements with Mr K for the completion of the sale to COD Properties. To that end Mr Z indicated to Mr K on 20 May [51] what monies he expected to receive from KS and informed Mr B that completion could take place on 21 May.

16. At 13.40 on 21 May KS sent a fax [53] to your firm indicating that it had transferred £528,750.88 to be held to order with a view to completing the transaction. At or about 2.00 p.m. Mr B orally instructed Mr Z to rescind the contract with COD Properties, who thereupon left a message to that effect with KS [52] and sent by fax timed at 14.17 that day a letter of rescission [54] and arranged for the return of the monies which were in any event £83.22 short of one day's interest. Later that day Mr B advised Mr Z [52] that the seller wished to exchange contracts with Mr KH within 24 hours and complete with him within two weeks, and that terms would be agreed the following day. The attempt to return the monies to KS was too late for the transaction to be effected on 21 May. We are instructed that Mr B was aware that the COD monies had not yet been returned overnight and sought an assurance from Mr Z that the seller could properly rescind. Mr Z informed him that since insufficient monies had been provided by KS the position on rescission was unaffected.

17. On 22 May, 2003 KS faxed a letter to your firm [55] denying that the seller was entitled either to rescind the contract with COD Properties or to forfeit the deposit. By a faxed reply sent 09.35 on 23 May [56] your firm took issue with the factual basis upon which the letter from KS was advanced and asserted *"The completion notice expired over a week ago and accordingly our client was entitled to rescind the contract at any time"*. On the same day Messrs Ss, litigation solicitors for COD, wrote a letter before action to your firm [57-58] threatening an action for specific performance unless by 9.30 a.m. on 27 May you confirmed that the seller would complete at the earliest possible date after funds had been retrieved.

18. On 23 May, 2003 Mr Z had three conversations with Mr B, as appears by his List of Messages for that day [59]. We are advised that Mr Z reiterated to Mr B that there had been no completion and that the seller was entitled to rescind. We are advised that Mr B, in reliance upon that

advice instructed Mr Z to exchange contracts with Mr KH's solicitors, which he did on that date, with completion to take place on 20 June, 2003. At the time of writing this letter we have not received from your firm our client's conveyancing file relating to the sale to Mr KH despite our original request.

19. On 2 June 2003 Ss wrote to your firm [60] indicating that counsel was currently settling proceedings for issue against the seller and that they had registered a caution against dealings against the property which they would lift against an undertaking by the seller not to dispose of any interest prior to the determination of their client's claim. It will be our client's contention that no prior warning of the possibility of this happening was given by Mr Z to Mr B, who had anticipated that funds from Mr KH might be used by the company to fight the anticipated litigation.

Ensuing Litigation

20. On 4 June, 2003 COD Properties issued proceedings in the High Court against ABC seeking specific performance, or the return of the deposit and damages.

21. On 9 June your firm's files were transferred from the conveyancing department to the litigation department. Mr Z prepared a memorandum [61-62] for RI who on 11 June delivered papers and sought the advice of MG of counsel. By paragraph 7 of the Instructions to Counsel [63-68] your firm wrote "*The Defendant ... now finds itself acutely embarrassed by the proceedings and, potentially exposed to a claim for breach of contract from the third party. There are also possible professional implications for Instructing Solicitors...*"

22. Your firm, together with MG of counsel, very properly indicated to Mr B the existence of a conflict of interest. Indeed it appears that on 19 June, [69] RI was concerned that your firm were negligent in permitting ABC to exchange contracts with Mr KH. Entirely without prejudice to such conflict your firm were retained in the conduct of the litigation and on 18 June Mr B signed a client care letter, which he had been sent by yourselves.

23. Between 20 June and 25 November, 2003 your firm and counsel advised our client that the COD action could be defended successfully on the basis that there had been no action on the part of Mr Z after the expiry of the notice to complete on 16 May, 2003 which could be construed by the court as an unequivocal promise or representation not to rescind the contract. This advice was reduced to writing in a letter dated 24 November, 2003 [70-73]

24. On 24 November Messrs. Ss served on your firm draft Amended Particulars of Claim [74-89] and three supplementary witness statements [90-103] all of which went to the effect of the conduct of Mr Z on 20 May, 2003, and which it was now said could be properly

construed as an unequivocal promise or representation not to rescind the contract. We are instructed that Mr B had not previously been made aware of the List of Messages of 20 May [51] or the significance of its contents. In view of the paucity of the record Mr Z was unable to gainsay the new contention of the claimant, and on 25 November in a pre-settlement meeting Mr G advised Mr B that the company's position was no longer tenable.

25. On 25 November the parties agreed a settlement by way of Tomlin Order [104-107] sealed 10th December, under the terms of which our client was to repay the sum of £45,000 inclusive of interest with no order as to costs, whereupon the claimant would release its caution against the property. We have no complaint about the terms of the compromise which, on any objective view, were beneficial to the company.

26. On 19 December, 2003 the sale of the property to Mr KH completed.

Breaches of Retainer

27. Our client has had the benefit of the advice of senior professional negligence counsel who takes the view, which we share, that the conduct by Mr Z of your firm's retainer of the sale of the property departed from that standard of care to be expected of a reasonably competent and careful conveyancer in the circumstances. It is our client's contention that on more than one occasion between 22 April and 23 May 2003, when advising Mr B of the legal effect of the failure by COD Properties to complete the purchase of the property in compliance either with the provisions of the Standard Commercial Property Conditions contained in the contract, or the Notice to Complete of 23 April, 2003 as extended, Mr Z failed:-

   (i) to qualify his statement that the seller could rescind at any time;
   (ii) to advise Mr B of the effect in law on the contract and or notice to complete of the doctrines of affirmation, waiver of time limits and estoppel;
   (iii) to have regard to the line of authority on implied extensions of notices to complete, namely *Webb v Hughes* (1870) LR 10 Eq 281; *Luck v White* (1973) 26 P&CR 89; and *Buckland v Farmer & Moody* [1978] 3 All ER 929 which required reasonable notice to be given to a defaulting buyer that the seller would rescind;
   (iv) to have regard to his conduct in continuing to deal with Messrs KS after 16 May 2003, namely whether such conduct might affirm the contract, or waive the time limit contained in the extended Notice to Complete, or give rise to an estoppel, or otherwise impair the ability of the seller to rescind and or to seek express instructions about such conduct in the light of full and adequate advice;

   (v) to consider and advise the seller adequately upon the legal effect and or consequences of the letter from KS dated 22 May 2003 [55] or the letter before action from Messrs Ss dated 23 May 2003 [57-58] and seek express instructions from the seller only in the light of that advice having been given and received;

  (vi) in view of the foregoing, to warn the seller against exchanging contracts with Mr KH and or explain adequately the legal consequences of doing so;

 (vii) to advise that COD Properties Ltd could register a caution against dealings against the property and so prevent or suspend the sale to Mr KH.

28. The foregoing breaches are not intended to be exhaustive and it may well be that a closer inspection of the documents we have received, together with a perusal of those we have yet to receive from your firm, will uncover more causes of action or particulars thereof.

Causation

29. We are instructed by our client that had Mr B been properly and adequately advised by your firm it would not have exchanged contracts with Mr KH, but would have completed the sale to COD Properties Ltd on 21 May, 2003 utilising the monies available of £528,750.88 subject to an undertaking being given for, or the early receipt of, the missing interest of £83.22.

30. It follows that had that been the case (i) the litigation which ensued would not have come about; (ii) our client would have had the use of the sale proceeds on 21 May, 2003 rather than 19 December; and (iii) our client would also have discharged the encumbrances and its obligations in respect of the property seven months before it could do so.

Heads of Recoverable Loss

31. Our client's claim is based on the consequences which flowed from your firm's failure properly to advise. Some of the heads of claim represent losses which continue, or which continue to attract interest for the loss of use of money. That being the case this calculation is to be regarded as confined to the date of this letter, and you will understand that if proceedings are issued the sum claimed will be greater.

  (i) *Litigation costs*

Our client incurred fees and disbursements in respect of litigation, which would have proven unnecessary to expend:

(a) Fees and disbursements charged by your firm and taken from the proceeds of sale: £19,802.25 [108-110].

(b) Litigation costs of Mr KH: £2,784.75 [109-111].

(ii) Costs associated with retaining the Property until 19 December 2003 rather than completing 21 May 2003

(c) Additional insurance premium: £50.35[112].

(d) Additional Community Charge Business Rates: £966.00 [113].

(e) Emergency repairs to dangerous wall, September 2003: £520.00 [114].

Extended bridging finance beyond June 2003. It was within Mr Z's knowledge that our client's existing facility was only for 12 months from 7th June 2002.

(f) Facility and exit fees: £10,300.00 [115-116] .

(g) Additional interest on bridging finance: £19,467.00 [117-124]

(iii) Costs associated with Mr KH's purchase, which would not have occurred

(h) Conveyancing costs of KH purchase: £2,570.00 [109] (N.B. The aborted conveyancing costs of the COD transaction have not been claimed, as these fall outside the ambit of the negligence).

(i) Additional interest incurred by Mr KH from 23 May to 19 December 2003: £16,746.58 [111]

(iv) *Loss of profit*

32. We refer to paragraph 2 of this letter. Had the property been sold on 21 May 2003 our client would have discharged its borrowing of £206,000 and had available around £300,000 (to include bank balances, interest and additional funds) to inject into a new project. Our client's primary case is that it would have been able to do so quite easily in May or June, 2003. Mr B is able to produce a portfolio of development opportunities in which he was interested at the time and he had two employees who were engaged in looking for the appropriate deals. On 22 April, 2003 Mr B alerted Mr Z to the next potential project, a tenanted property in Vauxhall costing £300 -£350,000 [125-126].

33. The transaction involving the property, the subject matter of these proceedings, was to have generated a profit of some £90,000 had completion been effected in accordance with the contract. Our client anticipates that it could reasonably have generated £100,000 profit on

the next development opportunity over the course of the twelve months between late May / early June 2003 and June, 2004. Therefore should this matter be litigated we are instructed to advance a claim in respect of loss of profit of £66,000 which our client believes to be both reasonable and conservative.

Interest as damages

34. Our client has been deprived of the benefit of the use of the monies which it should have received on 21 May, 2003 namely £528,834.10. After deducting the bridging finance of £206,000 which would have been paid on the redemption of the mortgage subtracting your fees, the bridging finance exit fees, VAT and adding the deposit and VAT on agent's fees, it has lost the use of £281,182.17 for seven months less two days. At 8% per annum simple we calculate the value of that loss to be £13,126.97.

35. Should our client not be able to prove to the court its case on loss of profit, its secondary position will be to advance in the alternative the claim for interest at £13,126.97 to 19 December 2003 and thereafter continuing at the rate of £61.62 daily.

Interest as interest.

36. Our client contends that each of the sums referred to at paragraph 31(a)-(i) above should not have been incurred, and that having been incurred our client has lost the benefit of the use of that money which, together amounts to £73,206.93. Although these sums attract interest each from the date which they were discharged, for the purpose of this letter only our client will advance its claim for interest on that sum at 8% per annum from 1 January, 2004 to the date of this letter, namely £1,813.12 and continuing at the rate of £16.04 daily.

Mitigation and Credit

37. Our client will give credit for the sum of £5,000 plus interest of £366.66 retained from the COD deposit, which was forfeited on 21 May 2003, and which did not pass back under the terms of the Tomlin Order. That apart it is difficult to see how our client could reasonably have mitigated any of the foregoing heads of damage particularly in view of the contents of paragraph 23 above.

Settlement

38. Both counsel and this firm have advised our client that as presently instructed your firm does not appear to have any proper defence to this claim. However it is not the wish of our client to pursue the matter to

litigation if there is any reasonable prospect of settlement, although you should please be assured that proceedings will be prosecuted if necessary. To that end we have been instructed that the issue of proceedings on behalf of our client is to be regarded as a last resort, and we are happy to meet with your insurers and or yourselves, once you have had a chance to investigate this claim, to attempt to reach a satisfactory compromise without incurring unnecessary expense. Our client is prepared to take a pragmatic view and to offer a discount against his recoverable losses in order to secure an early payment and avoid the costs of preparing this matter for proceedings to be issued and thereafter pursued.

39. We have advised our client that its primary claim is conservatively worth something in excess of £145,000.00. We believe of that sum some £90,000 is beyond argument, subject to proof of quantum. We are prepared to attribute a 55% litigation risk to the balance of £55,000, in your favour. We have therefore advised our client, and it has instructed us to say that **for the purposes of CPR Part 36(10)1 we will accept the sum of £120,000 in full and final settlement of its claim herein, inclusive of interest, but exclusive of our client's costs which it requires you to pay, to be assessed if not agreed.**

40. In view of the requirements of the timetable contained in the Professional Negligence Pre-Action Protocol this offer will remain open for 3 calendar months from the date of this letter. This offer is therefore worth an additional saving in interest of a minimum of £2,400 a fact that we shall bring to the attention of the court if required at the appropriate time.

We look forward to the favour of your early reply.

Yours faithfully

GOOD PRACTICE SUGGESTIONS

- Do not worry about length, particularly if the facts are detailed or the matter is complex.
- Stand back and ask yourself, 'Does this work? How would I feel as the recipient of this letter? If possible ask his opinion of a colleague who has no knowledge of the matter.
- Keep in mind adversarial writing is intended to persuade – in this example to overwhelm by detail – but it is not combative for its own sake. Never make an idle threat since to do so is both self defeating and likely to be a breach of professional conduct. Use the facts.

EXAMPLE Q

Post-issue letter of claim suggesting moratorium for investigations under the Professional Negligence Pre-Action Protocol. This was a claim brought against Surveyor Planning Consultants for breach of retainer arising from the proposed development of a property by the claimant, in which the size of the proposed development was misstated on the drawings, leading to building works being made the subject of a stop order when it became apparent to the local authority that the building was disproportionate to the site and planning permission was withdrawn.

Proceedings were issued to protect the claimant's position on limitation. The detailed history of the complaint is set out. Core documents are sent in a bundle attaching to the letter, thus providing pre-action disclosure. The claimant was unable to determine the full extent of his financial loss and unable to make a pre-action part 36 offer.

The recipient accepted an offer of moratorium in order to conduct its own investigation.

Dear Sirs

Our Client: **A**
Re: **1 High Road, Easton, London W15 XL5**

Letter of Claim pursuant to the Professional Negligence Pre-Action Protocol

Further to our previous correspondence we act for Mr A and wish to draw to your attention the following detailed claim which we are instructed to bring against you. You will recollect that on 16th September, 2004 we effected service upon you of a Claim Form in claim no. 0CL0000 issued out of the Central London County Court. This was undertaken to preserve Mr A's claim within the primary limitation period.

We are content to suspend the further operation of proceedings to enable you to undertake such further investigation under the Professional Negligence Pre-Action Protocol as you may feel necessary to be able properly to respond to this claim. Should you not wish us to suspend the operation of time we shall serve upon you Particulars of Claim which are in the process of being settled by counsel. We should also indicate at the outset that, notwithstanding the strength of Mr A's position, for the sake of avoiding unnecessary costs he will be prepared to entertain either a negotiated or mediated settlement at your early convenience.

We include for your perusal and consideration by way of early disclosure a bundle of relevant documents, marked [*] in the text of this letter.

The facts

1. At all material times Mr A was the owner of property at 1 High Road, London W.15 and land neighbouring it which he wished to develop by constructing a new four-bedroom/eight room house on what was a corner plot adjacent to Station Road.

2. On 31st May 1998 Z Property Services ('Z') were retained by Mr A [*] and appointed to prepare initial drawings and carry out initial planning research with Easton Borough Council Planning Services ('LA') (the relevant Local Planning Authority) in respect of the site, namely part of the garden of No. 1 High Road. The site survey and drawings were in fact prepared by XYZ Design and Detailing Services who were engaged to do so by LA. Consequent upon the preparation of drawings Z were instructed by Mr A [*] towards the end of July, 1998, to apply for planning permission in accordance with them.

3. On 5th August 1998 Z sought planning permission [*] from Easton for a development of a four-bed roomed detached house. The application described the house as having a floor space of 190m2 on a site of 345m2 and was accompanied by drawing no.98/00/2A [*]. On 7th January 1999 permission was granted [*] in terms of the application.

4. W Limited were appointed as contractors and AAD Limited as supervising architects. Work commenced in the summer of 1999 and the house was constructed to plate level in accordance with the approved designs. The site boundaries were defined and went unaltered.

5. In or about January 2000 Easton apparently received complaints from nearby residents concerning the position of the house on the plot and caused a building inspector to attend the site. Subsequent site visits concluded that the original site area had been incorrectly surveyed and the site was substantially smaller (329m2) than noted in the planning application, although the house was being built to the dimensions originally approved.

6. Accordingly on 28th March 2000 Easton served a stop notice on Mr A [*] requiring the development to cease. In order to deal with this Z met with Easton at the end of April, 2000 and by a letter dated 15th May [*] advised Mr A as to the ways in which the problem might be resolved. In accordance with such advice he first made a revised planning application for permission to Easton for a house considerably reduced in size (floor space 177m2). This scheme was approved on 3rd August, 2000. Mr A then sought to amend this permission to cover the house as built. A further application was duly made by Z on 18th December 2000 for a larger house (floor space 184m2) on the same site. This application was refused on 8th March 2001, and Easton served an enforcement notice for the demolition of the partially as-built house [*].

7. Mr A appealed the enforcement notice, thereby making a deemed application for the as-built house, and the refusal of his December

application, and sought a Certificate of Law Development. On 14th May 2002 in determining the appeal the Inspector decided that a Certificate of Lawful Development be refused but that the deemed planning permission for the as-built house be allowed subject to conditions; the Inspector also awarded Mr A his costs of the appeal. In June, 2002 Mr A transferred his interest in the property to his son.

The Claim

8. Counsel has advised that no reasonably competent and careful planning consultant in the position of Z would have prepared and submitted a planning application to Easton based on a site size of 345m2, and that Z was accordingly negligent and in breach of the implied term giving rise to a duty of care in its retainer by Mr A. But for such negligence and breach of retainer Mr A would, on the balance of probability, have obtained appropriate planning consent for a building scheme which would have proceeded to completion uninterrupted by a stop notice, and he would have completed the development of the property during the course of 2000. As it was Mr A had to incur additional financing costs, insure, secure and otherwise deal with an incomplete and inactive building site, obtain additional professional advice and make further planning applications.

Heads of damage

9.1 Mr A was financing the costs of the development from bank borrowings. He seeks (i) the cost of arranging additional finance [*]; and (ii) the additional interest payments on the account (Lloyds TSB 123456) from April, 2000 to May 2002 inclusive, namely 26 months [*]

9.2 Mr A incurred the cost of an additional site survey on 23rd August 2001 at a cost of £822.50 [*].

9.2 Mr A paid additional property insurance premiums for 2001 and 2002 [£1645] [*] which he would not have incurred if he had completed and sold the property in 2000.

9.3 Mr A was obliged to secure and maintain the site between 28th March 2000 and May, 2002 by the use of hired block work and fencing at a cost of [£1,050] [*]

9.4 In making the revised planning applications and conducting the planning appeals Mr A expended legal costs and disbursements in the sum of £21,667 plus VAT; the amount not recovered from Easton amounted to £6,286 plus VAT. [*]

9.5 In addition Mr A seeks interest on all such sums from 1st June 2002 until payment at the judgment rate of 8%.

10. The following are not to be taken as an exhaustive list, although it is not anticipated that any further major claims arise. It is hoped that the appended documents are sufficient to provide you at this early

stage, with sufficient information by which Mr A expects to substantiate his claim against Z in respect of both liability and quantum.

We therefore await your early acknowledgement of receipt of this letter and its enclosures and invite you, in the first instance, to indicate whether you wish to suspend the operation of time for the purpose of taking advantage of the three month window available under the Professional Negligence Pre-Action Protocol. Failing that indication we will be obliged to instruct Counsel to finalise Particulars of Claim to be served upon you in due course which we would wish to avoid if there was a reasonable prospect of early settlement in this matter.

Yours faithfully,

GOOD PRACTICE SUGGESTIONS

- Be consistent with your cards-on-the-table approach. If you are missing information but pressed for time, for example owing to the approach of limitation, provide as much as you can while you protect your client's position.
- If you have a difficulty tell the other side what it is, but tell them also how you intend to meet it. It is not a weakness but an opportunity: remember, 'Dear Judge, look how reasonable I am being. I want to cash in my brownie points as costs in the future...'

EXAMPLE R

Letter in reply to a Pre-action Protocol claim of solicitor's negligence. No Part 36 offer is made and no settlement proposals are offered. The letter is designed to be a complete answer to the claim and sets out a detailed analysis of the issues of liability, causation, contributory negligence, failure to mitigate and quantum of damage with strong support from legal authority. The language is polite but firm and business-like.

Again, the key to success is in the detail, which is intended to overwhelm the claimant's solicitor and force the claimant to look again at the strength of the case, certainly to see whether it is cost effective to proceed any further.

No proceedings were issued.

Dear Sirs,

AB
1 Zoo Road, St. Johns Wood, London N.W.8.

We write further to our letters of 28 June, 31 July and 5 September 2002.

Having considered our original files, examined the material which you have kindly supplied and consulted experienced specialist Counsel we are now in a position to deal substantively with your letter of 26 June 2002 in which you raised a detailed claim against this firm in accordance with the professional negligence pre-action protocol.

As you rightly say, this firm was retained by your client to convey the purchase by her on 1st September 1997 of a long lease of a flat at 1 Zoo Road, St John's Wood. London N.W.8 for £73,500. To the knowledge of your client the property was then tenanted by a Mr Z who had entered into occupation in October 1995 and signed a standard form document entitled Residential Assured Shorthold Tenancy Agreement and a statutory notice under s.20 Housing Act 1988, both dated 10th October 1995, for a tenancy commencing on 13th October 1995. Mr Z held over on a monthly basis after the expiry of his fixed term. So far as this firm was instructed the property was being purchased as an investment by your client and was not intended for occupation by her.

In February 2001 Mrs B instructed this firm upon the sale of the property with vacant possession to a buyer who was prepared to pay £150,000. In March 2001 it became apparent that there might be difficulties in securing vacant possession because of the status of Mr Z and JS of counsel was instructed to advise upon the position and settle the appropriate Housing Act notice to quit for service upon Mr Z. Counsel advised that certain defects appeared upon the face of the Assured Shorthold Tenancy Agreement and section 20 Notice which raised the possibility that Mr Z was not an assured shorthold tenant but an assured tenant, in respect of whom Mrs B would require an appropriate Housing Act case in order to obtain a possession order. On 8th May 2001 the buyer rescinded the contract as he was entitled to do under its terms.

We have considered with our Counsel the matters raised by the Advice dated 21st March 2001. The principal difficulty is that the section 20 notice appears to have been unsigned by either the landlord or landlord's agent, however it may well be that the copy actually served on Mr Z was signed, since his signature indicating its receipt appears on the Claimant's retained copy. Notwithstanding that, the conclusion to which Counsel has come is that, applying *Mannai v Eagle Star*[1], *York and Ross v Casey*[2] and the conjoined appeals in *Ravenseft Properties Ltd v Hall; Chubb v White; Freeman v Kasseer*[3] it is sufficiently arguable that the section 20 notice was valid and the status of Mr Z is that he was and is an assured shorthold tenant. We will advance that contention notwithstanding the factual analysis of Ms X, the Casework Support Officer of Shelter Legal Services in her letter to you of 11th October 2001, by which she considered it inappropriate for your client to proceed against Mr Z by way of accelerated possession proceedings.

We refer to the numbered paragraphs in your letter. We agree the outline of facts contained in paragraphs 1-8. However, we do not accept that the omissions set out in paragraph 8 amount of themselves to any act of negligence nor, in the circumstances are they a breach of retainer since a reasonably careful and competent conveyancer would not have sent a copy of the tenancy agreement to his client prior to exchange of contracts, nor would he reasonably have "highlighted the position under s.20 of the 1988 Act" to his lay client if he was himself satisfied that Mr Z was an assured shorthold tenant.

As to your analysis at paragraph 9 we do not accept that the advice of Mr T was incorrect. We are advised that as a matter of construction, in view of the insertion by the parties of a clause 6.2 and subsequently their signatures, they would be taken by the Court implicitly to have agreed clause 6.1.

It seems to us that the highest at which you can put your client's case is that Mr T failed to advise that the position of Mr Z was less certain than he believed. We reiterate our view that this failure was not a departure from the reasonable conduct by this firm of its retainer, and accordingly we are not in a position to make any admission of liability.

However, even were it the case that Mr T departed from the requisite standard of care, we take issue with the causation of each aspect of the claim for damages you have raised on behalf of your client. You contend on her behalf that had she been properly advised of the potential difficulty in removing Mr Z, Mrs B either would not have purchased the property or would have attempted to negotiate a substantial reduction in the purchase price. You claim on her behalf to recover (this being a non-exhaustive list) a) the difference in value between the property "as it is now" and the value that it would have if Mr Z was either not in occupation or capable of being evicted; b) all of the legal costs she has occurred in attempting to evict Mr Z since the beginning of 2001 and c) damages for distress and inconvenience. With respect, we suggest that each of these claims is misconceived in law.

---

[1] [1997] 1 EGLR 57
[2] (1999) 31 HLR 209
[3] [2001] EWCA Civ 2034

It appears to us that that even if, which is not accepted, Mr T was in breach of duty to your client, if Mr Z is an assured shorthold tenant, the only loss caused to Mrs B which falls within the scope of the duty owed[4] is the additional cost of removing him occasioned by the difficulty in clarifying the position.

If, on the other hand, Mr Z is in law an assured tenant, either because our analysis is wrong or on the basis of your client's serving upon him a notice under section 8 Housing Act 1988 as amended, the discontinuance of her possession proceedings, or by other concession made by you (as to which we refer below in connection with the failure of your client to mitigate her position and or contributory negligence), the loss falling within the scope of the duty owed by this firm will extend to your client having an assured tenant in occupation rather than an assured shorthold tenant. The law would, we suggest, limit the loss occasioned by the breach of duty complained of to the following:

(i) If Mr Z is in law an assured tenant rather than an assured shorthold tenant then the normal measure of damage representing the true loss to a claimant is the difference in the value of the property[5] she was purchasing having regard to that fact, at the date of purchase.[6] This follows the established principle that unless there is an exceptional distinguishing feature a claimant will be awarded such damages at the date of the breach as will put her back into the position she would have been but for the breach. Since Mrs B contends that she would not have permitted contracts to be exchanged on her own case the relevant date is 29th August 1997.

(ii) If you contend that she would not have purchased at all, in our view she must prove what else she would have done with the purchase price, and give credit for both the rental income and the value of the property at trial. On that basis any provable loss has been extinguished by the substantial increase in the value of the property even in occupation by an assured tenant.

(iii) If, as is more likely, your client would have negotiated a better price the maximum measure of her loss is the difference in value on that date between the property as purchased with a perceived assured shorthold tenant and the property with an assured tenant in occupation, since that is what the law apprehends she might have negotiated. We have obtained an expert valuation report and have been advised that this figure is unlikely to exceed 10% of the market value, namely £7,350. This together with interest, we submit, is the maximum value of your

---

[4] As to which see *South Australia Asset Management Ltd v York Montague* [1997] AC 191 on the scope of the duty argument.

[5] see *Ford v White* [1965] 1 WLR 885; *Hayes v Dodd* [1990] 2 All ER 815; *Watts v Morrow* [1991] 1 WLR 1421

[6] see *Wapshott v Davies Donovan & Co* [1996] PNLR 361

client's claim subject to our defence on liability, causation, contributory negligence and failure to mitigate. Taking such matters into account we suggest that the true value of your client's claim is either nothing or very little.

(iv) The costs claimed by your client are not recoverable in law for a number of reasons:

    (a) The flat was being purchased with a tenant in situe. By virtue of section 1 Protection from Eviction Act 1977 Mr Z as a residential occupier could only be removed by the grant and execution of a possession order, whether he was an assured or assured shorthold tenant or even a squatter. Thus legal costs would be incurred in removing him in any event, and that being so this head of loss falls outside the scope of the breach of duty complained of.

    (b) The costs occasioned by an application under Case 8 were in any event outside the scope of the breach of duty complained of since this firm did not warrant that Mr Z would pay his rent, and the possession proceedings were brought against him on that basis.

    (c) The valuation exercise which distinguishes between the discount from the market value to be applied to an assured tenant and that to be applied to an assured shorthold tenant must be taken to factor in the additional cost of removing the assured tenant. Thus this element of the claim is already absorbed into the diminution in value.

    (d) The costs which your client seeks are in respect of possession proceedings which failed. If the proceedings failed such costs cannot be visited against this firm since it is self-evident that such an attempt at mitigating the Claimant's position, if that is how it could be deemed, should not be regarded as reasonable.

(v) In the absence of physical distress and inconvenience flowing from the breach, the law does not extend so to make recompense for distress not affecting health.[7] Mrs B purchased the property as an investment from which to derive a rental income. Even if she was inconvenienced after May 2001 when her sale fell through against any award of damage she would have to give credit for the rent stream after that date, and possibly the increase in the capital value of the property. This would extinguish the maximum value of her claim.

Counsel has also considered in cases such as this the more traditional measure of damage in dealing with "defective title" claims is the cost of remedying the defect. In this case that would be the cost of removing Mr Z. This measure is mutually exclusive to the diminution in value measure: if

---

[7] *Hayes v Dodd* [1990] 2 All ER 815; *Watts v Morrow* [1991] 1 WLR 1421; *Johnson v. Gore-Wood* [2001] 2 WLR 72; *Channon v Lindley Johnstone* [2002] PNLR 884.

Mr Z were removed there would be no residual, consequential or separate damage recoverable in law. However, in considering this approach, we are led inexorably to the conduct of your firm as a *novus actus* in abandoning the contention that Mr Z was in law an assured shorthold tenant.

It is our view, and we have been so advised, that the principal cause of your client's present situation is the failure of your firm, having sought to mitigate the position, to argue that Mr Z was in law an assured shorthold tenant, which it remains our view he was. In conceding by paragraph 3 of the Particulars of Claim for Possession dated 15th November 2001 that Mr Z was an assured tenant (with a statement of truth signed by a member of your firm) and then discontinuing the proceedings, you have presented Mr Z with the opportunity of running issue estoppel on his status and attracting an unassailable *Henderson v Henderson* abuse of process defence to any further attempt to remove him on Schedule 2 Housing Act 1988 grounds.

We believe that this goes to both causation and substantial contributory negligence, however were we wrong in that regard it is undoubtedly a significant failure to mitigate. In that regard your client should be looking for her principal loss not to this firm but to your own.

It follows from the foregoing that we believe we have a complete answer to the matters that you have raised and we have no proposals to offer. We invite a careful analysis of the contents of this letter and those authorities which we have cited in support of our position which we hope will persuade your client that there is nothing to achieve by continuing to prosecute this claim.

Yours faithfully

GOOD PRACTICE SUGGESTIONS

- Meet letters of claim with a detailed rebuttal. Some claims, if inadequately formulated, are balloon-like, floated to see what response will be given. These should be burst, together with the claimant's expectation, by the reply giving a careful analysis of duty, causation and quantum: don't automatically reach just for a denial of breach, which is the typical gut reaction of the defendant.
- Always be polite and business-like, no matter how preposterous the claim or the form in which it is advanced.
- Be sympathetic where possible. If there is no legal liability, an apology costs nothing and may be all that the claimant (though not necessarily his lawyer) seeks.

EXAMPLE S

Extract of a letter in reply to a threat of injunction in commercial proceedings. The claim concerned a dispute between a franchisor and its regional licensees. The correspondence was outside the pre-action protocol regime but illustrates the use of argument and persuasion to ward off precipitate court action.

The language is formal and legalistic, but the writer succinctly undermines his opponent's position by referring to the parties different positions under the contract in question, and showing how this is likely to impact on the remedies available to the Court.

The threatened injunction was not proceeded with. The parties negotiated an overall settlement.

"… It has become perfectly apparent to our client that by the conduct of Mr C, amply illustrated above, your clients have evinced an intention no longer to be bound by the terms of their respective Agreements.

Accordingly our client intends to accept your clients' repudiatory breaches and to terminate immediately the Agreements under clauses 24.1.2, 24.1.3 and 24.1.4 thereof. By way of courtesy we append for your information copies of the termination notices we have today served upon the registered offices of Z (Scotland) Ltd, Z (Northern Ireland) Ltd and upon Mr C as principal under both Agreements.

We have given careful thought to your threat of injunction proceedings. It appears to us that commercial relations between our respective clients have broken down completely, on our instructions by Mr C's disruptive behaviour, which does not attract the support of either his co-regional licensees or, more importantly, the franchisees themselves. Our client holds both the intellectual property rights (as defined) and the know-how and goodwill in the franchise: see clauses 4.1, 4.3, 4.5, 4.7, 4.12 of the Regional Licence Agreement and the definition and clauses 10.1, 10.3, 10.4 and 10.5 of the Standard Franchise Agreement. On that basis even if, which we deny, your clients may claim to have an action in damages against our client, which we would in any event defend and set-off, it would not be appropriate for the Court to grant an injunction to force our client either to continue its licence to yours, or to have our client engage in business with yours when no business confidence remains.

Our client, on the other hand, has a legitimate commercial interest in the protection of both its intellectual property and its entire franchise network, by injunction if necessary. We remind your clients' of their post-termination obligations set out in clause 25.1 of the Agreements and the sub-clauses set out thereunder. In particular your client is proscribed from making or receiving telephone calls in connection with the franchise (clause 25.1.2). To that end your clients should henceforth make no attempt to contact the franchisees. Our client will shortly direct what its requirements are in effecting the transfer of business telephone line subscriptions. Your clients will deliver up to ours all copies in their possession of the operating manual. Your clients will change their corporate name to cease to use the word "Z....s" which forms part of our client's intellectual property rights.

In accordance with clauses 25.1.10, 26.1 and 26.1.1 of the Agreements our client requires Mr C as director of Z (Scotland) Ltd, Z (Northern Ireland) Ltd, and as principal, to execute an assignment of each of the Standard Franchise Agreements in favour of our client in a form to be settled and supplied by us within the next seven days.

We feel sure, having absorbed the contents of this lengthy letter and taken instructions, it will be apparent that your clients' best interest will be served by complying with their obligations and so avoiding litigation which would certainly follow should they decline to do so. We, like you, consider that commercial disputes are best resolved in the market place and not by having resort to the Courts. Financial claims apart, the issues between our clients boil down to whether it is appropriate in the circumstances for your clients to continue to act as our client's regional licensees. We consider it most unlikely that a Court would agree that they should against our client's wishes. Whilst we hope that it will be entirely unnecessary for the Court to examine this question, your clients should be aware of the resolve of our client. Accordingly would you confirm by return whether your clients will be complying with their post-termination covenants, and, as necessary, whether you have instructions to accept service of proceedings.

Yours faithfully"

GOOD PRACTICE SUGGESTIONS

- Be quick to deal accurately with any misapprehensions of the law by the other side. Taking the wind out of the opposing lawyer's sails is the most effective way to stop a claim. At the very least it will make him re-think his position, and may damage the confidence in him of his lay client.
- The same technique should be adopted with mistakes of fact. Disclose at the earliest opportunity any core document that will demonstrate objectively that the claimant's view of a fact is either wrong, or, if not, at least any court will think it wrong.

EXAMPLE T

Part 36 offer. County Court, claim and counterclaim for trespass and nuisance. The claim concerned an interference with neighbouring property by excessive drainage from higher land to lower.

The offer is the subject of considerable detail and deals with each cause of action separately.

Without Prejudice

Part 36 Offer

Dear sirs,
Re: X v Z

We write further to your letters of 6 April 2001.

This letter constitutes a part 36 offer and will remain open for acceptance for 21 days from the date it is made. After that period of 21 days the Defendant may only accept it if the parties agree the liability for costs or if the court gives permission.

As you are aware there are a number of issues between the parties and by this letter the Claimant puts forward his proposal for the settlement of each of them. In order to reduce the number of issues between the parties in the litigation the Claimant's offers in respect of the various issues identified below are independent of each other. That is to say the Defendant may accept all or any of the offers in respect of the various issues and the acceptance of any offer will be without prejudice to the rights and claims of the parties in any remaining issues.

The Outlet Pipes

Our client's proposals regarding the pipes located at points A, B and C on the plan annexed to the Defendant's Defence and Counterclaim ("the Plan") are as follows:

(1) the Claimant will grant the Defendant and his successors in title an easement to discharge water into the pond via a pipe located at points A, B and C on the Plan provided that:

  (a) the pipes shall not have a greater diameter than the pipes presently installed;
  (b) the burden of the easement shall not be increased.

(2) it shall be a condition of the said easement that the Defendant and his successors in title install and regularly maintain a silt trap on the pipe located at point C on the Plan;

(3) the Defendant will acknowledge that there are no pipes discharging water from his land into the pond other than those located at points A, B and C on the Plan and that he has no right of drainage into the pond other than under the easement to be granted;

(4) this proposal is made without prejudice to and does not compromise the Claimant's claim that the installation of the pipe at point C on the Plan has caused damage to the Claimant's land and the pond in particular which must be made good;

(5) The parties shall return their own costs on this issue.

Damages for Trespass

Our client's proposals in relation to his claim for damages for trespass are as follows:

(1) the Defendant shall pay the claimant the sum of £100 in respect of the acts of trespass referred to in paragraphs 2 and 4 of the Claimant's Particulars of Claim;

(2) the Defendant shall undertake not to enter the Claimant's land without permission provided that the Defendant may when reasonably necessary enter the Claimant's land to repair and maintain the outlet pipes at points A, B and C on the Plan;

(3) this proposal is made without prejudice to and does not compromise the Claimant's additional claim that the acts of trespass committed by the Defendant have caused damage to the Claimant's land which must be compensated or made good

(4) The Defendant shall pay half of the Claimant's costs on this issue.

Damage to Claimant's Land – Silting of Pond

As a result of the Defendant's works a considerable amount of silt has entered the pond which must be removed. As well as forming part of the Claimant's claim for damages an order that the Defendant remedy this damage is included at paragraph 3 of the prayer. Our client has obtained a quotation for the removal of the silt for £14,800 plus VAT (a copy of which is served with our second letter sent today). Our client's proposals in relation to the removal of the silt which has entered the pond as a result of the Defendant's conduct are that:

(1) the Defendant pay £4,000 towards the costs of de-silting the pond;

(2) The Defendant shall pay half of the Claimant's costs on this issue.

Damage to the Claimant's Land – the Sill

Our client's proposals in relation to the damage to the sill at the northern end of the pond are as follows:

(1) your client will pay for the necessary work to re-instate the sill to its condition prior to December 2000 in accordance with the specification served;

(2) the work will be contracted by submitting a specification to tender to no less than three contractors having no connection with either party and the Claimant shall accept the lowest tender

(3) The Defendant shall pay the Claimant's costs on this issue.

The Boundary

There has already been correspondence regarding the terms on which the parties are prepared to settled this issue. Our client's proposals regarding the location of the boundary between the Old Hall and New Farm are as follows:

(1) the parties agree that the boundary runs along the top of the bank of the pond at its present location;

(2) the parties will hold a site meeting for the purpose of agreeing the top of the bank and therefore where the boundary runs;

(3) in the event the parties are unable to agree on the location of the top of the bank at the site meeting the parties are to jointly instruct a surveyor at their joint expense (to be nominated by the President of the Institute of Chartered Surveyors in the event the parties are unable to agree upon whom to instruct) to decide where the top of the bank is and the joint surveyor's decision will be binding on both parties;

(4) There be no order as to costs on this issue.

We look forward to hearing from you in due course etc.

GOOD PRACTICE SUGGESTIONS

- It is essential to build up a case that is going to justify your negotiating position. You may have to defend yourself to a costs judge months or even years later.
- Your offer should be reasoned. You should be able to break it down if asked.
- Never bluff. The risk of being found out, and your house of cards falling down with adverse costs consequences, is too great.

CHAPTER 15
CONCLUSION

Written advocacy is no less important than skilled oratory for being in writing. On the contrary, its relative permanence as a medium enables you to craft and perfect it, and in particular to identify and revise those flaws that may slip out under the pressure of scrutinised speech.

If you practice in contentious business your approach to the composition of persuasive writing in dealing with an opponent should be no different whether it is in correspondence or the preparation of written submissions for the court. Nor should it matter at what stage the case has reached. Be firm; be polite; be justified in your assertions of fact and law; and be seen to be reasonable. Measure your position to a nicety and always ask yourself how best you are serving your client's case by what you are doing. Write with one eye on the judge at your shoulder, and you should protect your client's position on costs even if you cannot persuade the other side of the merits of your case.

SELECT BIBLIOGRAPHY

BOOKS

Aldisert, Judge Ruggero J. *Winning on Appeal: Better Briefs and Oral Argument* (1999)

Garner, Bryn A. *Legal Writing in Plain English: A Text With Exercises* (Chicago 2001)

Garner, Bryn A. *The Winning Brief: 100 Tips for Persuasive Briefing in Trial and Appellate Courts* 2nd Edn. OUP 2004

Goodman, Andrew *How Judges Decide Cases: Reading, Writing and Analysing Judgments* xpl 2005

Hooper QC, Toby ed. *Inner Temple Advocacy Handbook* 7th edn 2004-5

Orwell George *Politics and the English Language* Four Collected Essays (New York 1968)

Rutledge, Wiley B. *Advocacy and the King's English* in *The Appellate Brief* (1942)

Wydick, Richard C. *Plain English For Lawyers* (1998 4th edn)

Wiener, Frederick Bernays *Briefing and Arguing Federal Appeals* (2001 Lawbook Exchange, N.Jersey)

Bentele, Ursula & Cary, Eve *Appellate Advocacy: Principles and Practice* 3rd edn 1998

Blake, Gary and Bly, Robert W. *The Elements of Technical Writing* (1993)

The Chicago Manual of Style (Chicago 1982)

The Economist Pocket Style Book 1986.

ARTICLES

Hamilton, Hon. Clyde H. *Effective Appellate Brief Writing* (1999) 50 SCL Review 581

Hunt, The Hon. Mr Justice James *The Anatomy Lesson* Counsel Feb 2002 18

McElhaney, James W. *Writing to the Ear* Dec 1995 ABAJ 71

Michel, Hon. Paul R. *Effective Appellate Advocacy* Litigation Summer 1998 19

Pannill, William *Appeals: The Classic Guide* Litigation (Winter 1999) vol 25. no 2 p6.

Porto, Brian L *The Art of Appellate Brief Writing* 2003 29 Vermont Bar Journal and Law Digest 30

Appellate Advocacy: Some Reflections from the Bench (1993) 61 Ford L. Rev 829.

LECTURES

Davis, John W. *The Argument of an Appeal* (address to the Association of
the Bar of the City of New York 22.10.1940) 26 ABAJ 895

Lightman, The Hon. Mr Justice *'Advocacy – A Dying Art?'* (address to the
Chancery Bar Association Conference, 26th January 2004)

INDEX

ALSO OF INTEREST FROM XPL

How Judges Decide Cases

Andrew Goodman, Barrister, 1 Chancery Lane

This unique book offers a practical guide to deconstructing judgments for the purpose of fair criticism and appeal. It shows how judgments are written and examines the style and language of judges expressing judicial opinion. The work is founded upon independent research in the form of interviews conducted with judges at every level from deputy district judge to Lords of Appeal in ordinary, and the practical application of existing academic material more usually devoted to the structure and analysis of wider prose writing. It is illustrated by reference to reported judgments, both well-known and obscure, of the past 100 years. It will assist experienced practitioners, newly appointed recorders and tribunal chairman, and vocational students alike.

Contents include:

- The nature of judgment
- How to read a judgment
- The use of language in judicial opinion
- Argument and legal logic
- Fair criticism
- Writing judgments
- How judges decide
- The appellate judgment
- Problems with law reporting
- Judicial style

ISBN 1 85811 331 8

Civil Evidence for Practitioners

Dr Joseph Jacob, London School of Economics, Previous Editions Professor Peter Hibbert

The third edition comes at a time when three key developments have placed evidence ever firmly at the heart of successful litigation: the CPR and case management mean ever more emphasis on avoiding waste of costs – in turn meaning that practitioners must focus clearly on the evidence that is necessary for the case and no more, as well as its weight The advent of conditional fee agreements means accurate assessment of the risks inherent in bringing a case becomes of paramount importance to the financial success of the lawyer. *Civil Evidence for Practitioners* is unique among works of evidence - it is practical, readable and authoritative.

ISBN 1 85811 314 8

To order:

xpl publishing, 99 hatfield road, st albans, AL1 4EG
tel 0870 143 2569 fax 0845 456 6385
web: www.xplpublishing.com

Printed in the United Kingdom
by Lightning Source UK Ltd.
109302UKS00002B/49-126